To DEACON RON SMITH:

I HOPE YOU ENJOY THIS GIFT FROM HILDA TOMPKINS. MAY THIS BOOK BE A BLESSING TO YOU.

Danny Freeman

Published by Darda Press. Cover design by BudgetBookDesign.com

All scripture quotations are from the King James version of the Holy Bible.

This book is sold with the understanding that the author and the publisher are not engaged in rendering legal, accounting, or financial advice, and they assume no legal responsibility for the completeness or accuracy of the contents of the book.

୬ଛ୬ଛ

Certified Copy – First Edition
First Printing – December 2003

Book Number __*489*__ of 1000   Verified By *D. Freeman*

୬ଛ୬ଛ

Cataloging-In-Publication Data

Freeman, Danny

> Building wealth through spiritual health / Danny Freeman. -- 1st ed. --
> Winston-Salem, NC : Darda Press, 2004, c2003.

> p. ; cm.

> Includes bibliographical references and index.
> ISBN: 0-9744974-0-1

1.†Finance, Personal. 2.†Finance, Personal--Religious aspects. 3.†Wealth--Religious aspects. 4.†Wealth--Biblical teaching. 5.†Spiritual life. I.†Title.

HG179 .F74 2004
332.024--dc22   0403

Building Wealth through Spiritual Health

Danny Freeman

DARDA PRESS

In loving memory of Mom

Table of Contents

Acknowledgements i
Disclosures ii
Preface iii

Part I – Wealth Building

1 True Wealth Building 3
2 Spiritual Disobedience and Its Results 18
3 Spiritual Obedience and Its Rewards 36
4 The Role of Financial Wealth in Your Life 40

Part II – Nut & Bolts, Tips & Tools

5   The Financial Plan 57
6   Debt Management 74
7   Investing 100
8   Smart Ways to Save for College 137
9   Securing a Worry-Free Retirement 148
10 The Real Deal on Real Estate 172

Part III – Pathways to Success

11 Have You Worked Your Garden? 205
12 The WOW Factor! 209
13 Managing the Wealth-Building Process 236
14 Final Thoughts 252

❦❦❦

Bible Outline 262
Bibliography 285
Index 286

Acknowledgements

It took me over three years to finish this project. Even though I am the author, I must say that I could not have gotten it done without the support of many others. So, let me give credit where credit is due:

- To God, through Whom I realize, more than ever, that I can truly make a difference. Thanks for all of the late night conversations!
- To my wife, Debora, who has been a constant source of love, support, and direction. Thank you.
- To my children, Erica, Alexandra, and Christopher. I love you and I'm proud of you. In between getting on my nerves, you make me laugh.
- To my parents, Ozell Freeman, Sr. and the late Lucille Freeman, Proverbs 22:6 states that you should "Train up a child in the way he should go: and when he is old, he will not depart from it." I am what I am because of the love, training, and support you have given me.
- To my brothers, Tyrone and Ozell, Jr. You are great brothers and good friends. Thanks for all of your support and good advice.
- To my clients, I thank you for your life stories, your questions, your criticisms, and your advice. You were my inspiration for this book.
- To Gregory Barnes, a client and my friend. If you had not given me that article on Scripture and personal finance back in 1995, none of this would have happened. Thanks.

There are many more people whom I would like to acknowledge, but space will not allow me to do so. If our paths have crossed, then you have touched my life, and I thank you.

Disclosures

The information provided here is intended to help you understand general investment concepts and does not constitute any tax, investment or legal advice. Consult your financial, tax or legal advisor regarding your own unique situation, or your company's benefits representative for rules specific to your retirement plan.

All investment examples are hypothetical and are provided for illustrative purposes only. They are not intended to indicate the performance of any specific investment mentioned. In general, most investments, especially stocks and mutual funds, do not offer constant rates of return.

Other than some bank investments such as savings accounts and CDs, most investments are not guaranteed or protected from decline. The growth of your investment will be based on actual rates of return provided by the investment you choose. Past performance is not a guarantee of future results.

Continuous or periodic investment plans do not assure a profit and do not protect against loss in declining markets. Additionally, such plans involve continuous investment in securities regardless of fluctuating price levels of such securities. Investors should consider their financial ability to continue any purchases through periods of low price levels.

Indices are unmanaged and are not available as investment vehicles. It is not possible to invest in an index. You can invest in a fund or other security that seeks to replicate an index, but you can't invest directly in an index.

All trademarks and registered trademarks are the property of their respective owners.

An attempt was made to make this book as gender neutral as possible. Although one gender may have been specifically mentioned, the other could have been as suitable.

Preface

There are many excellent books about finance and investments, but many of them have little or no information about the Word of God and how it should be used to direct your financial decisions. There are also many books on the Scriptures and finances. However, many of them have great scriptural references, but lack specific information regarding financial planning and investment strategies. I have written this book to bridge the gap between the two.

Building Wealth through Spiritual Health is part Bible study and part financial guidebook. As a Bible study, this book provides scriptural lessons in true wealth building. The Bible is very interpretive and, when studying it, you must look at the context in which a verse is being presented, and you must also understand the meaning of the words and names within that verse. Doing so allows you to discover the true meaning and power of God's Word. The Scriptures in this book are from the King James Version of the Holy Bible. Although I will provide an explanation and interpretation of the Scriptures presented, you may want to study the same verses by using one of the modern language Bibles. Some of these versions may help provide additional understanding.

As a financial guidebook, I will discuss many concepts and terms that may affect you throughout your life, and explain in a way that virtually anyone can understand. It has been my experience that it is difficult to make good financial decisions unless you understand the basics. You don't have to be an expert, but you should understand the basics. If you can learn the basics and mix in a healthy dose of common sense, you should be able to achieve your goals.

Successfully achieving your goals will provide you with options. The more options you have, the more enjoyable life can be. In most cases, the quality of life you experience boils down to the quality of decisions you make. Access to good information will help you to make good decisions.

I believe that you will find that there is a lot of good information in this book. It draws on my many years of experience as a consultant, banker, and financial advisor. Some things will follow widely held views of proper financial planning, and there will be some points of view that are not so mainstream. It is not designed to be the only financial guidebook you will ever need, but to be more of a stepping stone to encourage you to learn more.

This book is divided into three parts:

Part One – Wealth Building

Part Two – Nuts and Bolts, Tips and Tools

Part Three – Pathways to Success

Although each part stands on its own, I believe you will get more out of the book if you read each section in order. The first section defines and discusses what true wealth building is all about. The next section explains the nuts and bolts of financial management, investing, and financial planning. Finally, section three will show you how to use what you've learned in the previous two sections to develop a meaningful action plan.

I had never really thought about the concept of Scripture and finances until 1995. It was then that a client gave me a copy of an article that addressed the subject. Through the years, I developed an interest in it that ultimately turned into a passion. Until then, I had thought of myself as being a pretty smart guy. I had a management degree from the University of Georgia and an MBA in Finance from Wake Forest University. I thought I had myself together. My career was going well. However, a series of personal ups and downs soon showed me that I wasn't as together as I thought. In a search for answers, I began to study Scripture.

Through my study, I learned many things that opened my eyes. Before, when I heard someone quote Scripture with regard to money and finance, I believed what they said was true. I had no real reason to doubt them. What I soon found out was that some of these folks were leaving things out, and that made me angry. However, I was not angry with them. I was angry with myself. Why? Because all I had to do to become enlightened was to read the Word for myself. These words changed me and gave me a new perspective on life and on managing money, not only for myself, but for my clients as well.

This is the primary reason why I think you will find this book relevant. I have lived some of the financial struggles that are addressed in this book, and I have helped many of my clients deal with the same. I am a front-line soldier. The words in this book can be your battle plan.

That, my friends, is the real beauty of Scripture. It is truly a blueprint for doing things the right way. Whether it is your finances, or any other part of your life, Scripture can provide many answers. It can provide wisdom, knowledge, comfort, and hope, as revealed in Romans 15:4:

> For whatsoever things were written aforetime were written for our learning, that we through patience and comfort of the Scriptures might have hope.

*"If you don't know where you're going,
any road will take you there."*

Part I

Wealth Building

Chapter 1
True Wealth Building

Wealth Defined

What is wealth? Wealth is defined as an abundance of valuable material possessions or resources. Money, in addition to being a medium of exchange, is defined as being a store of wealth. It is no wonder that many people think of the accumulation of financial assets and the many things that it can buy when they think about wealth. But is that what wealth is really about?

How often have we heard someone refer to another person as "having a wealth of knowledge"? Or, how frequently have we heard the old saying, "if you have your health, you have every-thing"? How about this one: "That person has a heart of gold." Surely a person with a heart made of gold would be worth a lot of money. Then it really gets confusing because we are frequently told that the best things in life are free!

When I sit down with people and talk to them about what they want out of life, they usually start listing things like a bigger home, a good education for their children, or early retirement. But, when they talk about what makes life satisfying, most people mention such things as love from their family and friends, good health, and being able to help others. Interestingly, financial wealth is not required to achieve any of these.

Whenever I meet someone who feels that they have achieved many of the things previously listed for having a satisfying life, they simply describe their achievements as being "blessed." Financial wealth only serves as a tool to help you experience or enhance the things in life that really matter. It should never be the end goal.

What does it really mean to be blessed? The Bible gives us the answers in the fifth chapter of the Book of Matthew. Jesus had been teaching, preaching, and healing the sick throughout the land. Word of His wonders was spreading like wildfire, and a great multitude of people began to follow Him. In Matthew 5:1–12 it is commonly believed that at this point, it is not only the twelve disciples that He is about to address, but everyone in the multitude that desired to learn from Him. Verses 1 through 12 read as follows:

1   And seeing the multitudes, He went up into a mountain: and when he was set, his disciples came unto him:
2   And he opened his mouth, and taught them, saying,
3   Blessed are the poor in spirit: for theirs is the kingdom of heaven.
4   Blessed are they that mourn: for they shall be comforted.
5   Blessed are the meek: for they shall inherit the earth.
6   Blessed are they which do hunger and thirst after righteousness: for they shall be filled.
7   Blessed are the merciful: for they shall obtain mercy.
8   Blessed are the pure in heart: for they shall see God.
9   Blessed are the peacemakers: for they shall be called the children of God.
10   Blessed are they which are persecuted for righteousness' sake: for theirs is the kingdom of heaven.
11   Blessed are ye, when men shall revile you, and persecute you, and shall say all manner of evil against you falsely, for my sake.
12   Rejoice, and be exceeding glad: for great is your reward in heaven: for so persecuted they the prophets which were before you.

Verses 3–12 are often referred to as the Beatitudes. Let's discuss each one of the blessings in more detail:

Blessed are the poor in spirit: for theirs is the kingdom of heaven. Everything you have or could ever want is dependent upon God's grace and mercy. By humbling yourself before Him, you essentially become a poor soul, begging at the gates of Heaven. It is this state of being "poor in spirit" that should make you hunger for the Word of God. Just as the hunger of a starving man can only be satisfied with the taste of food, your starving spirit can only be satisfied with the Word of God. Continue to satisfy your spiritual hunger with the Word of God, and the Kingdom of Heaven will belong to you.

Blessed are they that mourn: for they shall be comforted. This is mourning for your own sins, your shortcomings, and the sins and shortcomings of the world. You mourn because, in spite of all that God has done for you, you still seem to fall short of His expectations from time to time. It is this mourning that helps you to develop humility and compassion. It is this mourning for which you will be comforted.

Where will you find comfort? From Him who is the Comforter. You will be comforted by the Holy Spirit. You will be comforted by the Word of God. As a true believer, God's love and comfort frees you from the worries of the world. This intimate relationship with God is your blessing.

Blessed are the meek: for they shall inherit the earth. When someone is referred to as being meek, we often consider him or her to be weak. But meekness is actually a sign of strength. Jesus could speak on this with authority because He was the perfect example of strength through meekness. As Jesus' ministry began to grow, He increasingly incurred the scorn, ridicule, harassment, and jealousy of the religious establishment. In fact, it is believed that He was in the area where the Sermon on the Mount was delivered because He was trying to temporarily get away from all of the headaches and hassles.

Although He was relentlessly chastised, He continued to show patience and kindness to those who mistook His meekness for weakness. His willingness to submit Himself to the adversities of the world was actually a submission to the will of God. Therefore, meekness can be considered a gift from God because it helps you to endure. Jesus showed us that it could be used as an advantage.

The beauty of meekness is that others are ultimately drawn to it. They want to know how, in spite of everything that you've been through, you continue to remain calm. This blessing of meekness will often give you the opportunity to tell others of God's grace, mercy, comfort, and protection. It becomes a testimony of how having God in your life is a source of strength. It is this blessing that will allow you to inherit the earth.

When you inherit something, it usually means that there has been a transfer or sharing of ownership. It is written in Psalm 24:1 that "the earth is the Lord's, and the fullness thereof." When do the meek receive the inheritance? When they enter the Kingdom of Heaven to begin eternal life as promised by God. At that point all that God has, also belongs to you.

Blessed are they which do hunger and thirst after righteousness: for they shall be filled. When you thirst and hunger after righteousness, instead of worldly pleasures and material possessions, this is an enlightened pursuit of the righteousness of God. This is a righteousness that comes from the Gospel and the Holy Spirit. Because you genuinely seek it, you will be filled with this righteousness of God and all of its benefits, which are joy, peace, spiritual completeness, and contentment.

Blessed are the merciful: for they shall obtain mercy. This blessing addresses what forms the basis of your compassion for others. God has told us to love mercy. Not just receiving God's mercy, but showing mercy toward others: the poor, the afflicted, the unfortunate, and the needy. To be merciful will not only give you access to God's mercy here on earth, but more so in Heaven.

Blessed are the pure in heart: for they shall see God. Many have the outward appearance of a pure heart by their actions or words. Unfortunately, we sometimes discover that their motivations were anything but pure. It is difficult to know with certainty what is in the heart of our fellow man. Our hearts are stained by sin, and it is not within our power to permanently remove that stain. Only through the righteousness of Jesus Christ can our hearts be made pure. God knows and sees all. Those that are pure in heart are blessed and shall see God.

In this mortal life, we are only able to see God through the eyes of faith. This type of sight is achieved through spiritual vision. When we reach Heaven, we shall see Him face to face.

Blessed are the peacemakers: for they shall be called the children of God. God is the Author of peace (1 Corinthians 14:33).

In our quest to live as He would have us live, we should seek peace, not only for ourselves, but for others as well. In these times, you will have many opportunities to promote peace: in your home, your neighborhood, your church, your job, your city, your country, or virtually anywhere in the world.

Blessed are they which are persecuted for righteousness' sake: for theirs is the kingdom of heaven. Diamonds are formed when carbon is crystallized under immense heat and pressure, deep in the earth's crust. If the carbon is heated too much, it will vaporize. If it cools too quickly, it becomes graphite. Diamonds are precious stones because of this rare combination of heating, cooling, and pressure. Christians who seek righteousness are diamonds in the rough.

The world will place massive pressure on you to conform to its ways. When you walk in the path of righteousness, this pressure will only increase. Why? Because your dedication to a life of righteousness serves to illuminate the ways of the ungodly. Things may get a little hot for you sometimes. Don't worry, because they will eventually cool off. Everything will work out in the end, and you will be rewarded.

⸎⸎⸎

What is wealth? My definition of wealth is enjoying all that God's blessings afford us through our faithfulness to His Word and commandments. When you are blessed, you feel fortunate. You feel that you have more than you need. When you have more than you need, you are wealthy. The more blessings you have, the wealthier you are. Jesus is telling us in His Sermon on the Mount how to build true wealth. The Beatitudes are a form of spiritual mountain climbing. It is this form of exercise that gives us a healthy spirit. With a healthy spirit, we can discover our true reward when we get to Heaven.

Why Bother?

You may be saying, "If this is true, then what's the point in learning about financial planning and investment strategies?" The reason you need to know these things is because we now live in a world that is dependent upon money. It takes cold, hard cash to make things happen in this world. If you want to feed the hungry, it takes money. If you want to help the poor, it takes money. God uses us as channels to help ourselves and to help others. When you've been blessed financially, you need to know and understand good financial concepts and investment strategies so that you can take what God has given you and make it into more. Doing so will allow Him to use you to better help yourself while having a greater capacity to help others. This learning is part of your task in being a good steward.

There are certain laws that God has put in place to govern our existence on this earth. For example, we all eventually learn and understand the law of gravity. When we jump into the air, the force of gravity pulls us back down to earth. That's why we know we shouldn't jump off tall buildings. Doing so would cause us great injury or harm. We also understand the laws of physics, where an object of less density cannot go through an object of greater density. That's why we don't try to run through brick walls. Doing so would cause us great injury or harm.

Just as God created the laws of gravity and physics, He also created the laws of finance. Unfortunately, some of us act like the laws of finance are from another universe. One of the basic laws of finance is that you should not spend more than you earn. Many of us know that doing so can cause great injury or harm to our personal finances. But some of us violate this basic law of finance almost every day. Just as we understand the laws of gravity and physics, we should take the time to learn and understand the laws of finance. They represent the natural way that God means for things to occur.

God is a God of nature, meaning He often interacts with us through the occurrence of natural as well as supernatural events. Some may call it luck or fate, but it is really the Hand of God. There are far too many Christians who think that when they are having problems, particularly financial problems, God is going to just magically make them disappear. While He certainly has the power to do that, He rarely does so because it would make faith too easy. If we haven't handled our personal finances as we should, we must ultimately be prepared to suffer the consequences. As we work through our financial problems, there are always lessons to be learned because it is one of the many ways that God speaks to us.

Financial crises can teach you many things. First and foremost, they can teach you humility. There is nothing like having a car repossessed, or a house foreclosed on to knock you down a few rungs on the social ladder. Financial crises can be very embarrassing as well. Perhaps that is why we fight so hard to avoid them. Humility allows us to have a closer relationship with God.

The duration of a financial crisis can teach you patience. It teaches you how to wait on God. Maybe the result is not what you wanted, but in many cases it is just what you needed. Tough financial times can teach you that you can make it with much less than you previously thought. It teaches you to be thankful to God for what He has already given you. A financial crisis can be an opportunity to separate yourself from the things that get in the way of serving God.

The best lessons learned are usually the ones that are the hardest. Educating yourself about sound financial concepts will help you put those lessons learned to the best use.

We Love Our Stuff

Although many of us think of ourselves as good people and living as God would have us live, it is our affinity for material things that tends to get us in trouble. In the Book of Acts (Acts of the Apostles), chapters 4 and 5, Peter and John had been speaking to a multitude of people, much to the dismay of the Sadducees. The Sadducees were a materialistic Jewish sect that did not believe in the oral Law of Moses, only the written Law. They also did not believe in heaven, angels, or spirits. To no surprise, they did not believe Jesus to be the Messiah, and they conspired to have Him arrested. Although they threatened Peter and John to make them stop preaching, it was to no avail. Peter and John were perceived to be uneducated and ordinary. In spite of this, the people were still amazed at their ability to preach the Word, and recognized them as being companions of Jesus. Later, as they more boldly proclaimed the Word of God, a wonderful thing happened:

> *Acts 4:32–35*
> 32 And the multitude of them that believed were of one heart and of one soul: neither said any *of them* that ought of the things which he possessed was his own; but they had all things common.
> 33 And with great power gave the apostles witness of the resurrection of the Lord Jesus: and great grace was upon them all.
> 34 Neither was there any among them that lacked: for as many as were possessors of lands or houses sold them, and brought the prices of the things that were sold,
> 35 And laid *them* down at the apostles' feet: and distribution was made unto every man according as he had need.

As usual, there was a bad banana in the bunch. In fact, there were two and their names were Ananias and his wife, Sapphira. Ananias and Sapphira were obviously moved, as were others, to sell their possessions for the common good of the group. But after conferring with each other, they decided to hold back some of the proceeds just in case this group sharing thing didn't work out as they thought it would. So, unlike everyone else, Ananias laid the partial proceeds from the sale of the land at the apostles' feet. But, Peter knew that Ananias was holding back and he confronted him. How did Peter know? Remember, the Holy Spirit was among them all. The Holy Spirit is God, and the Holy Spirit is a discerner of the truth. Peter asked Ananias, "Why has Satan filled your heart to lie to the Holy Spirit and to keep back part of the proceeds of the land?...You did not lie to us but to God!" (Acts 5:3–4). After Ananias heard those words, he dropped dead. When everyone in the gathering heard about what had happened, they became very afraid.

Now sometime later, Sapphira came in and she had not heard

what had happened. Giving her a chance to own up to what she had done, Peter confronted her and asked whether the land was sold for the price indicated by Ananias. Sapphira, trying to make sure she had her story straight, said, "Yes, that was the price." Again, Peter chastised Sapphira and said to her "How is it that you and Ananias have agreed to put the Spirit of the Lord to the test? Look, the same men who buried your husband are at the door, and they will carry you out too." Immediately she fell down at his feet and died (Acts 5:7–10).

Ananias and Sapphira met their untimely demise because they were not complete in their faith. They failed to realize that everything they thought they owned already belonged to God. Somehow, they felt they needed to hold on to some of the proceeds. Maybe they had their eye on a new camel. But for some reason, what they thought their wealth could buy was worth more to them than what God said He would provide. It was this inability to separate themselves from financial wealth that ultimately cost them their true reward.

Our personal wealth means more to some of us than we are sometimes willing to admit. We treat people right. We try to live by God's commandments, but we love our "stuff." Consider another story in the Book of Matthew, Chapter 19, verses 16–24:

16 Then someone came to him and said, "Teacher, what good deed must I do to have eternal life?"

17 And he said to him, "Why do you ask me about what is good? There is only one who is good. If you wish to enter into life, keep the commandments."

18 He said to him, "Which ones?" And Jesus said, "You shall not murder; You shall not commit adultery; You shall not steal; You shall not bear false witness;

19 Honor your father and mother; also, You shall love your neighbor as yourself."

20 The young man said to him, "I have kept all these; what do I still lack?"

21 Jesus said to him, "If you wish to be perfect, go, sell your possessions, and give the money to the poor, and

you will have treasure in heaven; then come, follow me."

22 When the young man heard this word, he went away grieving, for he had many possessions.

23 Then Jesus said to his disciples, "Truly I tell you, it will be hard for a rich person to enter the kingdom of heaven.

24 Again I tell you, it is easier for a camel to go through the eye of a needle than for someone who is rich to enter the kingdom of God."

How many of us would have a difficult time selling all of our possessions to gain our heavenly treasure? Would we hold a portion back, like Ananias and Sapphira? Or, would we simply grieve as we sold our possessions and begrudgingly handed them over? Remember, you have control over anything that you can walk away from. What you cannot walk away from has control over you.

The problem with wealth when defined purely in financial terms is that it can become a form of worship. With financial wealth comes power. When you are not spiritually healthy, you run the risk of putting your trust in the power of that kind of wealth. If you allow financial wealth to occupy a place of prominence in your life, you open the door for Satan to use it as a device that may lead you to make sinful choices.

If you have been financially blessed in your life, it would be silly for me to suggest that you should want to give it up. There aren't many people who would want to go from a state of financial prosperity to one of poverty. However, if the circumstances of life lead you to a situation where your financial resources may lessen or even completely disappear, then you must be willing to accept that as part of God's will, or a result of your own disobedience.

Be Thankful

As humans, what do we really need to survive? When you think about it, the list is fairly short:

- Food
- Air
- Shelter
- Water
- Clothing
- Love

Some of us will struggle every day just to have our basic needs met. Others will never worry about meeting their basic needs at any point in their lives. Life is so short and so precious. Although there may be other things that trouble you in your life, you should be thankful for every day that air fills your lungs because the next day is not promised to anyone.

Unfortunately, many of us take the basic needs of life for granted. We *expect* to have those needs met. When that happens, we begin to confuse wants with needs. We think that we "need" a new car. We think that we "need" a bigger house. We think that we "need" new clothing, although we have unworn clothing in the closet with the tags still attached. In many cases, these are all wants, not needs.

Confusing your wants with your needs can lead you to make poor choices. It can cause you to spend your money on something that you really can't afford. It can lead to jealousy and covetousness, or what we used to call "trying to keep up with the Joneses."

I don't believe that there is anything fundamentally wrong with wanting more than what you already have. The key is to learn how to wait on God to bless you for it. Many years ago, I would often talk of the things that I wanted to achieve and acquire in life. There would be times when I would become frustrated because I was not achieving or acquiring those things as quickly as I thought I should. However, it took me a while to realize that three things must occur for those things to happen. First, it must be part of God's will for me. Next, I must be complete in my faith and obedience to God. Finally, I must do whatever is physically and mentally required of me to make it happen. If I never achieve or receive the things that I want in life, and I am satisfied that the three things listed above did occur, then I will not be disappointed. Why? Because God has told me that He will take care of my needs. Also, I know that my true reward is not on this earth, but in Heaven.

Consider what Paul wrote in Philippians 4:11–12:

11 Not that I speak in respect of want: for I have learned,
in whatsoever state I am, therewith to be content.

12 I know both how to be abased, and I know how to
abound: every where and in all things I am instructed
both to be full and to be hungry, both to abound and to
suffer need.

13 I can do all things through Christ which strengtheneth
me.

In these Scriptures, the Apostle Paul is telling the Philippians
how he has learned to accept whatever his state of being is at that
time. This letter was written when Paul was in prison. In verse 12,
he tells them he has had hard times before, but he has also had times
when he prospered. He knows what it is like to have had a seven-
course meal, and he knows what it is like to be starving and in need.
Nevertheless, in verse 13 he proclaims he knows how to handle
himself because he can do all things, not just some, but all things
through Christ. His faith and trust in God gives him the power to
prosper as well as the strength to endure bad times. Paul was just
plain thankful.

We should learn to be like Paul and be thankful for what we
have. This concept is further addressed by the Apostle Paul in 1
Timothy 6:6–8:

6 But godliness with contentment is great gain.

7 For we brought nothing into *this* world, *and it is* certain
we can carry nothing out.

8 And having food and raiment let us be therewith content.

If you can live life on this earth as God would have you to do and,
be content with your current state of being, you will have acquired
the greatest treasure of all. Verse 7 reminds us that we came here
with nothing, and we leave the same way because we all know that
when you die, you can't take it with you. Finally, Paul tells us that if
we have food and clothing, we have all that we need, so we should be

satisfied.

I have found that once you shake yourself of the need to acquire things because of worldly influences, then it won't matter whether you have a penny in your pocket or a million dollars. You will praise God just the same because you are simply happy for whatever He has blessed you with. Any feelings of necessity over and above the basics of life may be a sign of spiritual sickness.

Confidence in God

The key to building any type of wealth is confidence in God. You must be steadfast in your belief that God will provide you with things that you need and bless you with things that you want. All you have to do is ask and believe. We find guidance on this in James 1:5–7:

> 5 If any of you lack wisdom, let him ask of God, that giveth to all *men* liberally, and upbraideth not; and it shall be given him.
> 6 But let him ask in faith, nothing wavering. For he that wavereth is like a wave of the sea driven with the wind and tossed.
> 7 For let not that man think that he shall receive any thing of the Lord.

To build wealth, you need wisdom. If you feel that you lack wisdom, ask God for it and He will give it to you. He won't even scold you for asking. All you have to do is ask for wisdom, and He will give it to you, and give it generously. However, there is a catch: You must ask in faith and never waver in your faith. It is this unwavering faith that keeps you steady, giving you confidence. You believe that God is going to give you the wisdom to make good financial decisions. If your faith is not strong, you run the risk of making poor financial decisions because you are not sure what to do. This state of uncertainty is like a wave being tossed at sea by the wind. This is what James is talking about in verse 6. Then he makes it very clear in verse 7 that if you are not firm in your faith, there is one thing you can be sure of: You shall not receive anything of the Lord!

There are some people who believe that all you have to do is ask God for something, believe it, and poof! It's yours. I have often heard these same folks use the phrase "name it and claim it." Just name what you want, claim it in Jesus' name, and it's yours. As justification for this point of view, they will often quote the part of a verse of Scripture that says, "ye have not, because you ask not." These words are part of verse 2 in the fourth chapter of James. For a complete understanding of what the words really mean, let's look at James 4:1–3:

1 From whence *come* wars and fightings among you? *come* they not hence, *even* of your lusts that war in your members?
2 Ye lust, and have not: ye kill, and desire to have, and cannot obtain: ye fight and war, yet ye have not, because ye ask not.
3 Ye ask, and receive not, because ye ask amiss, that ye may consume *it* upon your lusts.

In verse 1, James asks why we have wars. Why do we fight among ourselves? Isn't it because of our lusts or desires? Sure, we will give reasons or excuses as to why such actions are justified. But it often just boils down to the fact that someone wants something that belongs to someone else. In verse 2, he challenges us to consider the real reason why we do not have the things that we desire. There are things that you would love to have, but it seems that you can never make it happen. Others kill for the things they want, but still don't get them. The real reason you do not have is because you haven't asked God for it.

Now some of you may say that you pray to God and ask Him for things all the time, but with no results. If this is the case, then verse 3 may provide an answer as to why. You ask and don't receive because you ask for the wrong reasons. You ask God for things because of selfish desires. You ask God for things because of jealousy.

It is these types of petitions to which God turns a deaf ear.

How can we be sure that God will hear us when we ask Him for things? The answer is in 1 John 5:14–15:

> 14 And this is the confidence that we have in him, that, if
> we ask any thing according to his will, he heareth us:
> 15 And if we know that he hear us, whatsoever we ask, we
> know that we have the petitions that we desired of him.

There is only one thing that you can depend on in this world, and that is the will of God. If you ask for anything according to His will, you can be confident that He will hear you.

Confidence is based on trust. When you trust someone or something, you know that you can depend on it. Additionally, Psalms 118:8 tells us where we should place our trust:

> It is better to trust in the LORD than to put confidence in
> man.

How ironic is it that on every piece of currency in the United States, you can find four words that should remind you where your real trust should be placed. What are those words? In God We Trust! When you trust in God, He becomes your confidence. Consider the following from Proverbs 3:26:

> For the LORD shall be thy confidence, and shall keep thy
> foot from being taken.

When God is your confidence, He will keep you from being ensnared in the traps of sin. Learn to be confident in God and you will be successful in building both spiritual and financial wealth.

Chapter 2
Spiritual Disobedience and Its Results

When we are not healthy spiritually, we disobey God. When we disobey God, bad things happen to us. God's Word directs us through laws and principles. God's laws are absolute and are usually presented to us in the form of commandments. Failure to live by a commandment usually results in punishment. God's principles are His instructions to us on how to do things. There may be other ways to do it, but God's way is the best way.

From Riches to Rags

When people discuss God and financial prosperity, they most often mention Solomon. Solomon was the last-born son of David and Bath-Sheba. As David approached death, he selected Solomon to assume the throne as King of Israel.

As Solomon began his rule, God was with him (2 Chronicles 1:1). He directed Solomon's ways and began to bless him with prosperity. In 2 Chronicles, Solomon goes to Gibeon to prepare a massive sacrifice of 1000 burnt offerings. God was very pleased and appeared to Solomon later that night, as told in 2 Chronicles 1:7–12:

7 In that night did God appear unto Solomon, and said unto him, Ask what I shall give thee.

8 And Solomon said unto God, Thou hast shewed great mercy unto David my father, and hast made me to reign in his stead.

9 Now, O LORD God, let thy promise unto David my father be established: for thou hast made me king over a people like the dust of the earth in multitude.

10 Give me now wisdom and knowledge, that I may go out and come in before this people: for who can judge this thy people, *that is so* great?

18

11 And God said to Solomon, Because this was in thine
heart, and thou hast not asked riches, wealth, or honour,
nor the life of thine enemies, neither yet hast asked long
life; but hast asked wisdom and knowledge for thyself,
that thou mayest judge my people, over whom I have
made thee king:

12 Wisdom and knowledge *is* granted unto thee; and I will
give thee riches, and wealth, and honour, such as none
of the kings have had that *have been* before thee, neither
shall there any after thee have the like.

As mentioned earlier, God was very pleased with the offering
that Solomon had made. Upon appearing to Solomon, God asked
him to name anything he wanted, and He would give it to him.
Solomon was still a relatively young man. He could have asked for
the mother of all retirement packages, bought a nice riverside palace,
and watched the grass grow on the banks of the Euphrates while he
waited for the mailman to bring him his retirement check every
month.

But Solomon did not use this as an opportunity to selfishly take
care of himself. In verse 9, Solomon is very aware of the fact that God
has made him king over a large number of people. Knowing what it
will take to rule the Israelites and do a good job, Solomon asked God
to give him wisdom and knowledge (verse 10). In verse 11, God is
very pleased that Solomon did not selfishly ask for riches, wealth,
honor, etc. In verse 12, He not only grants Solomon's request for
wisdom and knowledge, He also grants him riches, wealth, and
honor to a degree that no king had known before him, and no king
after him shall ever know.

You would think that anyone who got a personal visit from God
would be obedient to Him for the rest of his life. But noooooooo, not
Solomon! Sure, he started off good. But eventually, he ended up on a
slow slide to disobedience that cost him his great kingdom. How did
this happen? Solomon's ego got out of control, and in this case, ego
stands for **Ease God Out**!

With all that God had blessed him with, Solomon began to

think too much of himself. He led a very luxurious life, but to extremes. He married heathen women, and eventually had 1,000 wives and concubines. Through mandatory labor and excessive taxation, he oppressed his own people. Sadly, he turned his back on God and sanctioned idolatry. Solomon's wealth allowed him to experience life to the fullest. He had it all. But his wisdom began to fade, leading him to make sinful choices.

Solomon's disobedience resulted in him being a tormented soul. In all of Solomon's writings, there is little mention of the science and business knowledge that allowed him to be a leader in commerce and the creation of financial wealth. Instead, many of his writings boil down to these themes:

- Vanity is a source of trouble and gets in the way of your relationship with God.
- Financial wealth means nothing.
- Hold on to wisdom, for it will guide you and protect you.
- Love, obey, and serve God.

As Solomon reflected on his life, he wrote about what was most important. He wrote about the lessons he learned from being disobedient.

Why Don't We Listen?

As I have read and studied the Bible, I am amazed at the number of stories that show spiritual disobedience. God, either directly or indirectly, told people that He would provide for them, deliver them, or protect them. All they had to do was obey. In many cases, God issued rather simple instructions. Amazingly, they still wouldn't listen. Why? The answer may be found in Proverbs 1:7, where Solomon offers the following words:

The fear of the LORD is the beginning of knowledge: but fools despise wisdom and instruction.

Since all knowledge and wisdom comes from God, and God is perfect, there is only one reason why we do not follow His principles and instruction, and that is a lack of faith. Maybe some of you have had this conversation with God:

"Lord, I know You said that I should wait on your blessings, but the department store is having a 30% off sale this weekend. Is there any way that You can kind of speed things up? Besides, think of how much You'll save on the blessing!"

When we are about to go against God's principles, we try to rationalize things as much as possible. But, the fact of the matter is that we do not really believe that when we receive God's blessing, it will be at the very best time to receive it. In fact, when we act on our own to try to get the things we want, we are telling God that we think our way is the best way.

God is our Father and we are His children. Our reluctance to wait on God's blessings is typical behavior that some of us exhibited as children. Do you remember when you were younger and you wanted to get a cookie out of the cookie jar, and your parents said no? It didn't matter that you might have already eaten and enjoyed a few cookies. Maybe dinner would soon be served and your parents didn't want you to ruin your appetite. All that you could think about was that you wanted a cookie and you wanted it now! Did you fall down and throw a tantrum? Maybe you would sneak and get a cookie anyway. If your parents were anything like mine, you got a whippin' if you got caught with another cookie (and you usually got caught!). Many of us have not changed from those days. We see something that we want and we want it now. But sometimes, God says no. How does He do this? When you see the beautiful bracelet for $499 that you absolutely must have and you only have $49 in the bank, that's God saying no. When you want to buy that new car that you would look so good in and you can't even afford to get the oil changed in the car you're driving, that's God saying no. Now just because God says no, doesn't mean He is saying never.

God will provide for your needs, and He will sometimes bless

21

you with what you want. What you must realize is that His plan is a perfect plan. Therefore, things happen on God's schedule and not yours. In 2 Peter 3:8, we read the following verse:

> But, beloved, be not ignorant of this one thing, that one day is with the Lord as a thousand years, and a thousand years as one day.

Sometimes, when we ask God for His help, we tend to look for an immediate response. When help doesn't come as expected, we become tempted to take matters into our own hands.

Are You Frog Stew?

I have been told that if you want to make frog stew, you can't just throw a live frog into a pot of boiling water because he will jump right out. To successfully make a pot of frog stew, you must fill the pot with water that is at room temperature. As you add your other ingredients, slowly turn up the heat in the pot. The frog adjusts to the temperature change and continues to float and swim happily in the pot.

Doesn't the frog know what's about to happen? Can't he see he's part of the menu? Won't he try to save himself? Well, at some point, he probably will try to get out of the pot. Sadly, it will be too late. You see, as you were turning up the heat in the pot, the frog didn't realize that the increased heat was causing nerve and tissue damage, causing his vital organs to fail. The frog soon knows he is in trouble. He just can't do anything about it.

Satan works the same way. If we immediately felt the pain of our disobedience to God, we would stop right away. We live in a world that is slowly desensitizing us to what is outrageous and sinful. From a financial perspective, we are constantly being thrown into that pot at room temperature. Satan adds ingredients to the pot:

- Here is a pre-approved credit card, just what you needed to go shopping.

- Go ahead and buy that car. Sure, it'll stretch your budget, but you deserve it.
- Spend your savings now. You'll put it back later
- No need to save. You could be dead tomorrow!

All of the ingredients listed above may make your life comfortable, temporarily. However, Satan is steadily turning up the heat. If you're not careful, you may find yourself in a situation (i.e., the pot) that may be difficult to get out of. Like the frog, you become desperate and confused. You may become paralyzed with stress, fear, and uncertainty. Satan desires to have you on his menu. It is at this point that you become most susceptible to being devoured by sin.

Temptation

When Jesus taught the disciples the Lord's Prayer, I can see why He wanted us to recite it often. Zoom in on that one line that says "...and lead us not into temptation...." It is temptation that really causes us problems in building wealth.

The economic system of the United States of America is based on capitalism. A capitalistic system revolves around the idea of individuals or businesses buying and selling things. Marketing plays a much larger role in our daily lives than many of us realize. The reason you do not have to pay for broadcast television and radio is because it is advertiser supported. TV and radio stations charge companies to air their commercials. Commercials are opportunities for businesses to convince you to buy or use their products and services. Because of this, we are constantly bombarded with messages and images that tell us to spend, spend, spend. For the spiritually weak, this poses a problem on multiple fronts.

Some Christians get into financial trouble because they cannot distinguish between what they want and what they need. This speaks to the very core of our relationship with God. God has told us that He will take care of all our needs. He will sometimes bless us to get the things that we want. However, we must learn to wait on the Lord, and that is where things get sticky.

Technology and innovation also put a lot of pressure on today's Christian. Hardly a day goes by without the trumpeting of a new product or service that is bigger, better, and faster. If you don't have the money to pay for it today, that's okay because there are easy credit terms that allow you to go ahead and get it now.

Get it now! That seems to be the motto of our society today. When the temptation of what we want gets to be too much, we sometimes give in and try to get it anyway. A good friend of mine once told me that getting the stuff you want is easy. It's the paying for it that is hard. Learning to be content with what you have goes a long way in helping you develop the patience needed to wait on God.

Why Are We Allowed to Face Temptation?

There are two reasons why we are allowed to face temptation. First, we are allowed to face temptation so that we can be given the opportunity to prove ourselves to God. Second, we are allowed to face temptation so that we can develop a sense of what our own personal boundaries are. It is a type of stress test.

The purpose of a stress test is to see how much something can bear before it breaks. The thing that is being tested, in this case, is your faith. As you go through life, you will be tempted on many occasions to disobey God. This is nothing more than Satan trying to break your faith. Sometimes you will be successful in resisting temptation. Sometimes you will not. Use these experiences to learn what you can and cannot handle.

To minimize the chances that they will suffer a relapse, recovering drug addicts and alcoholics are told to stay away from situations where others are using drugs and alcohol, or may offer it to them. If you know you have a weakness for spending too much when you go shopping, take the appropriate steps to make sure you stay within your budget. If you know there are situations and people that may lead you to make poor decisions, put extra effort into staying away from them.

Backing away from temptation is hard. Satan knows this and, in some cases, he will be relentless in his pursuit to get you to yield.

However, 1 Corinthians 10:13 tells us that not only can you endure, you can escape:

> There hath no temptation taken you but such as is common
> to man: but God is faithful, who will not suffer you to be
> tempted above that ye are able; but will with the temptation
> also make a way to escape, that ye may be able to bear it.

For everything that Satan throws at you, know that God has already provided a way for you to escape. Through faith and obedience, you can survive. You should be confident in knowing that God will not allow you to be tempted with more than you can handle.

Temptation is permitted as a trial of your faith. Consider 1 Peter 1:6–7:

> 6 Wherein ye greatly rejoice, though now for a season, if
>   need be, ye are in heaviness through manifold tempta-
>   tions:
> 7 That the trial of your faith, being much more precious
>   than of gold that perisheth, though it be tried with fire,
>   might be found unto praise and honour and glory at the
>   appearing of Jesus Christ:

In these verses, Peter makes several points. First, in verse 6, he tells us that the pain and suffering we endure in facing temptation won't last long. Next, in verse 7, he tells us that we should appreciate the trial of our faith; for it is worth more than gold. To be "tried with fire" means to be transformed.

For most precious metals to be transformed, they must be heated or "tried by fire." Once they have been subjected to extreme heat, they can be pulled, poured, twisted, hammered, or otherwise handled to be transformed into something more valuable than they were in their original state. For your faith to successfully go through such a process means that it will be something that will offer praise, honor, and glory to God on your behalf on Judgement Day.

In the Book of James, we are also told that enduring temptation provides another benefit: patience. In Chapter 1, verses 2–4, we read the following verses:

> 2 My brethren, count it all joy when ye fall into divers
>   temptations;
> 3 Knowing *this*, that the trying of your faith worketh
>   patience.
> 4 But let patience have *her* perfect work, that ye may be
>   perfect and entire, wanting nothing.

I have often heard people say that they have prayed for God to give them patience. While it is possible for God to give us patience, I believe it is more likely that He will allow us to go through situations where we can learn to be patient. James tells us in verse 2 that we should be glad when different temptations come our way. Why? Because each one is another opportunity for us to develop our patience, and make it stronger. In verse 3, he then tells us that the testing of our faith by temptation puts patience to work. It calls patience into action. Finally, in verse 4, he tells us to let patience do its thing. Let patience do the job that God has designed it to do.

When trying to improve our state of physical fitness, we sometimes employ the services of a personal trainer. The purpose of a personal trainer at the gym is to guide, instruct, assist, push, and encourage. In doing so, she will help you to achieve the goals that you set. Think of patience as your own personal trainer. Patience will guide you down the right path. Patience will instruct you as to the proper course of action to take in resisting temptation. Patience will push and encourage you, telling you that you can make it one more day.

Patience will give you the endurance to make it through the various trials and temptations of life. As James 1:12 tells us, patience will reward us with a more important reward:

> Blessed *is* the man that endureth temptation: for when he is
> tried, he shall receive the crown of life, which the Lord hath
> promised to them that love him.

This crown of life is your true wealth. Don't let temptation rob you of your most valuable asset. Face temptation with confidence, knowing that patience will help guide you through it.

Study the Ways of the Enemy

We spend a lot of time and energy trying to recognize the good in people. However, I think we should spend more time trying to recognize evil when it is coming our way.

When engaged in war, military leaders study the ways of their enemy. They want to know their tactics and strategies, so that they will know the best way to defend themselves. It is no different with the enemy known as Satan. You need to know his tactics and strategies. Satan has three primary modes of attack:

- Master of Deception
- Roaring Lion
- Angel of Light

The Master of Deception

Most of us are familiar with his skill as a master of deception. This was first chronicled in the third chapter of Genesis. In the previous chapter of Genesis, God told Adam and Eve that they could eat of every tree in the Garden of Eden except the tree of the knowledge of good and evil. Everything was just fine and dandy until Satan showed up in the form of a serpent. Genesis 3:1–13:

1 Now the serpent was more subtil than any beast of the field which the LORD God had made. And he said unto the woman, Yea, hath God said, Ye shall not eat of every tree of the garden?
2 And the woman said unto the serpent, We may eat of the fruit of the trees of the garden:
3 But of the fruit of the tree which *is* in the midst of the

garden, God hath said, Ye shall not eat of it, neither shall ye touch it, lest ye die.

4 And the serpent said unto the woman, Ye shall not surely die:

5 For God doth know that in the day ye eat thereof, then your eyes shall be opened, and ye shall be as gods, knowing good and evil.

6 And when the woman saw that the tree *was* good for food, and that it *was* pleasant to the eyes, and a tree to be desired to make *one* wise, she took of the fruit thereof, and did eat, and gave also unto her husband with her; and he did eat.

7 And the eyes of them both were opened, and they knew that they *were* naked; and they sewed fig leaves together, and made themselves aprons.

8 And they heard the voice of the LORD God walking in the garden in the cool of the day: and Adam and his wife hid themselves from the presence of the LORD God amongst the trees of the garden.

9 And the LORD God called unto Adam, and said unto him, Where *art* thou?

10 And he said, I heard thy voice in the garden, and I was afraid, because I *was* naked; and I hid myself.

11 And he said, Who told thee that thou *wast* naked? Hast thou eaten of the tree, whereof I commanded thee that thou shouldest not eat?

12 And the man said, The woman whom thou gavest *to be* with me, she gave me of the tree, and I did eat.

13 And the LORD God said unto the woman, What *is* this *that* thou hast done? And the woman said, The serpent beguiled me, and I did eat.

In this passage, we see that Satan started his attack in a very low-key manner. He asked the question, "Did God tell you not to eat of every tree in the garden?" Eve said that they could eat of any tree, except the one (the tree of the knowledge of good and evil) in the middle of the garden. Then Satan engaged in further deception by telling Eve a big, boldfaced lie. He told Eve that if she ate of the tree of knowledge of good and evil, she would not die. Then Satan told Eve that God told you not to eat of the tree because, if you do, you'll be just like Him.

Then Eve got to thinking. The tree has fruit, which is an essential part of a healthy diet. The tree was pretty to look at, and knowing what is good and what is evil sounds like a good thing. Maybe the serpent knows what he is talking about. This sequence of events is very important to know and study, because it happens to many of us everyday. Satan whispers to us, "Go ahead. You can have it if you want it. Buy it. More is better! Go for it!" Satan wants you to think that the only reason that God doesn't want you to experience the vices and excesses of life is because you might find out that you can have heaven on earth. Don't believe him. It is all a trick, designed to get you to disobey God.

As we all know, Eve ate the fruit. She gave some to Adam, and he ate it too. God confronted them as to whether they ate of the tree He specifically told them not to eat from. At this point, Adam and Eve exhibited behavior that many of us still exhibit today when we disobey God: we blame someone else. In this case, Adam blamed God for his own disobedience. He actually had the nerve to tell God that "the woman *You* gave me handed me some fruit to eat, and I ate it. How was I supposed to know it was the forbidden fruit? None of this would have happened if You hadn't given me that woman!" Then when God confronted Eve, all she could say was, "The devil made me do it!"

The final piece of trickery here is that Satan wants you to blame someone else for your troubles. This helps you to avoid accountability. But the truth is told in the following verses of James 1:13–16:

13 Let no man say when he is tempted, I am tempted of God: for God cannot be tempted with evil, neither tempteth he any man:

14 But every man is tempted, when he is drawn away of his own lust, and enticed.

29

15 Then when lust hath conceived, it bringeth forth sin: and
sin, when it is finished, bringeth forth death.

16 Do not err, my beloved brethren.

It is very important for you to understand that just because you get something that you want, it doesn't mean that it came from God. Satan would have a hard time recruiting people for his team if he couldn't offer them some of the things that they wanted. I have seen people pray for money, houses, cars, husbands, wives, and other objects of desire. When they received these things, they shouted "Thank you Jesus," and told the world how blessed they were. However, they later found out that these things did not bring them the satisfaction they were looking for, and in many cases, led them further away from God.

But, as verse 13 says, God will not tempt you. Therefore, God is not going to bless you with something that you can't handle. When your lust for worldly things gets confused with your needs, Satan is more than willing to send those things your way. The fact that you asked God for these things just makes it easier for Satan to distort the picture.

To determine if a blessing came from God, ask yourself this question:

Is this good *for* me, or is it just good *to* me?

Any blessing that comes from God will be good for you. It will sustain you and make you a better person. Most of God's blessings will be good to you as well. They will make you feel good and bring you joy. But, some of God's blessings don't always feel good to you. You may not like it at the time; it will make you uncomfortable and you may even try to run away from it. Later, you realize that it was something that you needed, and you are thankful. When Satan gives you the things you want, it may be good to you, but it is never good for you. By asking yourself these questions, you can quickly determine what God has blessed you with, and what Satan has sent to make you fall.

Don't be mistaken. When you fall, it is no one's fault but your own. Temptation leads you to make sinful choices. Satan will use many forms of deception to put you in a position to disobey God.

Roaring Lion

Satan's next mode of attack is like that of a roaring lion. It is his most direct form of attack, and perhaps the most vicious. We are warned of this in 1 Peter 5:8:

> Be sober, be vigilant; because your adversary the devil, as a roaring lion, walketh about, seeking whom he may devour.

The lion is considered to be the king of the jungle because he is a powerful hunter. I have often noticed that when a lion attacks its prey, it tries to bite it on the back of its neck, or along the spine. When successful, the lion will use its powerful jaws to break the neck, or sever the spine of its victim. Unable to use its legs to help it escape, the victim is soon devoured by its hunter and other lions in the group.

As humans, the spine is critical to our ability to move and walk upright. It is the supporting structure of the body. Spiritually, our faith is the supporting structure of our soul. Faith is critical to our ability to walk humbly with God. Sin is a sickness that attacks our faith, hoping to sever it and render us vulnerable to the attacks of Satan.

Sometimes Satan says "Forget the tricks, I'm just going to hunt you down." He is hungry for your soul. There will be times when bad things seem to continually come your way. To escape the pain, you will be tempted to make sinful choices. Think clearly and be watchful. Doing so will allow you to escape his waiting jaws of death.

Angel of Light

This mode of attack is Satan's most devastating and destructive. Sadly, it is one that I am seeing more and more of in the world today.

The Apostle Paul warns of this in 2 Corinthians 11:13–15:

13 For such *are* false apostles, deceitful workers, trans-
forming themselves into the apostles of Christ.

14 And no marvel; for Satan himself is transformed into an
angel of light.

15 Therefore *it is* no great thing if his ministers also be
transformed as the ministers of righteousness; whose
end shall be according to their works.

In the verses that precede these warnings (2 Corinthians 11:
1–12), Paul speaks to the Corinthians and asks them why they are
listening to people who are falsely presenting themselves as apostles
of God. Paul acknowledges that these other people are smooth and
fancy talkers, and he is just a regular guy. But he is the one who
preaches of the true Jesus. He is not there to exploit them financially
or corrupt them spiritually, like these false apostles.

As I said before, this "angel of light" attack is becoming more
common every day. Just as in the days of the Corinthians, there are
people today who are posing as men and women of God, but are
nothing more than followers of Satan. They are smooth and fancy
talkers as well, but they twist the Word of God to serve their
deceitful purposes.

One of their primary methods of deceit is to turn you into a spiritual tail-chaser. Here is how it works. One of the cornerstones in the
foundation of your relationship with God is faith. There are
numerous scriptures in the Bible that tell you of the power of faith.
What these "angels of light" want you to believe is that the source of
that power resides in you, not God. All you have to do is believe,
recite positive affirmations of what you want God to do for you, and
it's yours. This is a natural extension of human behavior because we
often want to control the outcomes of events in our lives. Humans
hate uncertainty. If you buy into this line of thinking, you will faithfully go through the rituals, processes, or steps to "speak" into existence the things that you want God to do for you. Unfortunately,
when the desired outcome does not occur, you'll go back to these

"angels of light" and ask, "What went wrong? I did everything you said and nothing happened." Their typical response is, "Your faith wasn't strong enough." Believing that maybe your faith wasn't strong enough, you go back and try the process again. This is spiritual tail-chasing, like a dog spinning in a circle trying to catch his tail. No matter how hard you try, you never get what you're after. This is a form of spiritual and emotional bondage that will keep you from growing as a Christian.

Does Scripture say that your faith can move mountains? Yes, it does (see Matthew 17:20, 21:21). What you must understand is that the moving of that mountain must be of God's will and spiritually good. Just because you want the mountain moved, doesn't mean that it should be moved. The results of a true faith are only manifestations of what God wants for you and others. This is shown in Philippians 2:13:

> For it is God which worketh in you both to will and to do of *his* good pleasure.

Believing through faith that God is going to do something that is not of His will or to His pleasing is nothing more than wasted effort. Nothing positive will result from this type of faith. Unfortunately, this is the type of faith that the "angels of light" want you to have. It is this type of thinking that serves only to corrupt the foundations of your true faith.

As Christians, we tend to listen to our spiritual leaders without question. While I believe that we should listen to our spiritual leaders, we should do so with a discerning ear and a watchful eye. Just because someone speaks the Word of God doesn't necessarily mean that they truly know God.

In the Bible, the word lucre appears six times. Lucre means money or financial gain. In five of the six references, the word lucre is preceded by the word filthy. Here are those five verses:

1 Timothy 3:3
Not given to wine, no striker, not greedy of filthy lucre; but

patient, not a brawler, not covetous;

1 Timothy 3:8
Likewise *must* the deacons *be* grave, not doubletongued, not given to much wine, not greedy of filthy lucre;

Titus 1:7
For a bishop must be blameless, as the steward of God; not selfwilled, not soon angry, not given to wine, no striker, not given to filthy lucre;

Titus 1:11
Whose mouths must be stopped, who subvert whole houses, teaching things which they ought not, for filthy lucre's sake.

1 Peter 5:2
Feed the flock of God which is among you, taking the over-sight *thereof*, not by constraint, but willingly; not for filthy lucre, but of a ready mind;

The Apostle Paul wrote the Books of Timothy and Titus, and the Apostle Peter wrote 1 Peter. As you read the verses listed above, there is a common theme from both writers. They are challenging church leaders, such as bishops, pastors, and deacons, not to go astray or lead other church members astray because of dirty money. The disobedience of these so-called "church leaders" can lead you to disobey God as well. Know that this is just another one of Satan's tactics to ruin your spiritual health.

As usual, Scripture directs us as to how to handle these false teachers. Consider these verses in 2 John 1:9–11:

9 Whosoever transgresseth, and abideth not in the doctrine of Christ, hath not God. He that abideth in the doctrine of Christ, he hath both the Father and the Son.
10 If there come any unto you, and bring not this doctrine, receive him not into *your* house, neither bid him God

speed:

11 For he that biddeth him God speed is partaker of his evil
   deeds.

Anyone who is not abiding in the doctrine of Christ, is not of
God (verse 9). If such a person comes into your presence, do not
listen to them or wish them well (verse 10). Do not let them in your
house. Do not let them in your church. If they are preaching in your
church, do not stay to listen to the sermon. Do not watch them on
TV. Do not buy their books. They are to be avoided. Your mere presence can lead others to think that what they are saying bears
listening to, especially since they see you listening to it. If you offer
them support in any way, or fail to shun or avoid them, you become
a partner in their evil ways (verse 11).

Chapter 3
Spiritual Obedience and Its Rewards

Why should we be obedient to God? Because our obedience to Him shows that we believe His Word to be true. It shows that we believe that He will do what He says He will do. If we are obedient, what do we get in return? Recognize first of all that God owes us nothing. Every day that we exist on this earth is only because of His grace and mercy. But because God is pleased when we genuinely and sincerely live by His word, He offers us several gifts. These gifts are listed in Ecclesiastes 2:26:

> For *God* giveth to a man that *is* good in his sight wisdom,
> and knowledge, and joy: but to the sinner he giveth travail,
> to gather and to heap up, that he may give to *him that is* good
> before God. This also is vanity and vexation of spirit.

Wisdom, knowledge, and joy; these are the building blocks of a spiritually healthy life. What is this wisdom? It is the acknowledgement of God, His providence, His grace, and mercy. It is also the moral and ethical application of knowledge. What is this knowledge? It is the understanding of the workings of the Hand of God in every aspect of our lives, and the world in general. What is this joy? It is the inner peace and satisfaction received from your confidence in Him.

God's Word tells us that obedience is a key factor in building all kinds of wealth. The benefits of obedience are many, as illustrated by the verses in Psalms 112:1–10:

1 Praise ye the LORD. Blessed *is* the man *that* feareth the LORD, *that* delighteth greatly in his commandments.
2 His seed shall be mighty upon earth: the generation of the upright shall be blessed.
3 Wealth and riches *shall be* in his house: and his

36

righteousness endureth for ever.

4 Unto the upright there ariseth light in the darkness: *he is* gracious, and full of compassion, and righteous.

5 A good man sheweth favour, and lendeth: he will guide his affairs with discretion.

6 Surely he shall not be moved for ever: the righteous shall be in everlasting remembrance.

7 He shall not be afraid of evil tidings: his heart is fixed, trusting in the LORD.

8 His heart *is* established, he shall not be afraid, until he see *his desire* upon his enemies.

9 He hath dispersed, he hath given to the poor; his righteousness endureth for ever; his horn shall be exalted with honour.

10 The wicked shall see *it*, and be grieved; he shall gnash with his teeth, and melt away: the desire of the wicked shall perish.

In verse 1, the word "fear" is not used to denote terror, but more appropriately a respect of God. It is this type of fear that is the beginning of wisdom (Psalm 111:10: The fear of the LORD is the beginning of wisdom...). When this fear is combined with a genuine joy (delighteth greatly) to obey God's Word, you have a powerful combination that results with you being blessed. When you are obedient, your children shall be blessed (verse 2).

The wealth and riches that were referenced in verse 3 of this passage are not just financial, but spiritual as well. You have them because your obedience to His word brought you blessings. Your fear of God gave you wisdom and knowledge, which showed you how to take the blessings received from your obedience and turn them into more.

Your obedience further allows you to be blessed, such that when there is trouble in your life, God will send light to brighten your day (verse 4). Because God has shown favor toward you, you are gracious and compassionate toward others (verse 4). Because God has shown favor toward you, you will show favor towards others (verse 5). You take what God has blessed you with, and give liberally to the poor (verse 9). Others will sing your praises and bestow upon you many honors (verse 9), all because of your obedience to God.

When you are obedient, you prosper because God's wisdom allows you to make good decisions with regard to your personal affairs (verse 5). Obedience helps you to develop a good name that will be remembered by many after you're gone (verse 6). You are not afraid of bad things happening to you because you have complete confidence in God (verse 7).

When your enemies seek to destroy you, you can step back and smile, because you know that God is your defender (verse 8). Your enemies will grieve at your state of well being; gritting their teeth in anger because they realize they can do you no harm (verse 10). Disgusted and defeated, they eventually will leave you alone (verse 10).

How wonderful life can be when you are obedient to God's Word. Many people think of money when they hear the word "prosperity." However, the word means more than that. The word prosper is derived from the Hebrew words *tsalach* (tsaw-lakh´) or *tsaleach* (tsaw-lay´-akh). These words mean to advance, make progress, succeed, or be profitable. Don't let the world give you a narrow view of what prosperity really means. Obey Him and watch how He will touch all areas of your life.

It's Not What You Know...

We've all heard the saying "It's not what you know, but who you know." When you know God and you are obedient to His word, you can be confident in knowing that you have the ultimate Friend in High Places on your side.

Consider the following verses in Proverbs 8:32–35:

32 Now therefore hearken unto me, O ye children: for blessed are they that keep my ways.

33 Hear instruction, and be wise, and refuse it not.

34 Blessed is the man that heareth me, watching daily at my

gates, waiting at the posts of my doors.

35 For whoso findeth me findeth life, and shall obtain favour of the LORD.

In verses 32–34, Solomon encourages us to listen to him, just as a father tells his own children to listen. This is important because at the time this was written, Solomon still had a close relationship with God. As such, Solomon considered himself to be a minister of God. Therefore when he spoke, he spoke for God. Because his words at this point in his life were still divinely inspired, they were valuable to those who listened and obeyed. As indicated in verse 35, doing so will allow you to "obtain the favour of the LORD."

Favor can be a great equalizer. It can also be very unfair. In the corporate world, gaining favor from the right upper-level executive can accelerate the advancement of your career. The downside of such favor is that you may end up passing over people who are more qualified or deserving than you. That's the power of favor. God's favor is more powerful, but with one added distinction: It's given only to those who deserve it. To gain God's favor, you must be obedient. If you are obedient, you will be blessed.

How God chooses to bless me for my obedience will be different from how He chooses to bless you for yours. My blessings may be more than yours, or less. He knows what we can handle and will bless each of us accordingly. When others are wondering why so many things in your life seem to be going well, you can tell them with a spiritual confidence that "It's not what you know, it's Who you know!"

Chapter 4
The Role of Financial Wealth
in Your Life

There is a proper place for everything in your life. You have your career, your family, your hobbies, and other interests. Oh yes, and don't forget money. The key is that there must be a balance. You cannot let any of these things gain too much prominence, or it will throw your life out of balance.

I am most dismayed at people I meet who seem to be on this mission to get rich. When you see them, it is almost all they talk about. They measure themselves based on the number and value of things that they accumulate in life. I have said it before and I will say it again, financial wealth should never be a goal in and of itself. It should be a byproduct of your obedience to God.

If you begin to focus too much on how you are going to become a millionaire, financial wealth can become a form of idol worship. The 1980s and 1990s were periods of unprecedented financial wealth creation. However, the new millennium brought us declining stock markets, terrorist attacks, heightened geopolitical conflicts, massive job layoffs, and corporate accounting scandals. There were many who felt that the financial wealth they accumulated in the boom times had solved most of their life's problems. They were confident that their future was bright. When adverse market conditions caused most of their financial wealth to evaporate, they became much more unsure of what the future might bring.

There is an old saying that if you want to see the true nature of a man, observe how he acts when he loses money. I can tell you from first-hand experience that this is true. When investment markets go bad, I am often amazed at how some investors go into a complete state of panic.

While I am very sensitive to anyone's concern about their declining portfolio, such situations are best handled with calm and sound reasoning. But for some, calm or sound reasoning is not an option. Fear and panic are the order of the day. They believe they have to do something, anything, to preserve what they have.

You may be saying to yourself, "What's wrong with that? Isn't that what everyone should do?" Well, yes and no. When faced with investment losses, there are some legitimate things that you should do to protect your wealth. However, there will be times when, no matter what you do, you will suffer losses. In an investment environment like this, making constant changes in your portfolio is a lot like trying to climb a greased pole. There's a lot of motion but not a lot of progress.

One of the best pieces of advice that I ever received from my mother was this: You should never expend a lot of energy worrying about things you have absolutely no control over. Financial markets involve the actions and reactions of humans who by nature are very unpredictable. This fact plays a major role in the short-term unpredictability of the markets. If you are unwilling to accept the outcome of things you cannot control, you are disregarding divine providence.

What is providence? Providence is defined as a manifestation of the care and guardianship that God exercises over his creatures. The world tries to convince us that we control our own destiny. Yes, we have a hand in it, but it is not completely up to us. In biblical times, when people were disobedient, God sometimes allowed or sent droughts and famines. Fortunes were wiped out and hard times were felt by everyone. In today's world, which is dominated by financial markets, I believe He allows or sends recessions, depressions, and stock market crashes. The effect on our lives is much the same.

If you believe in providence, then you know that despite what seems to be impossible conditions, God will take care of you. If you find yourself having a difficult time accepting this, ask yourself these questions:

- Besides money, what else am I afraid of losing? (power, prestige, etc.?).
- Am I afraid of what others will think if they find out I'm not as wealthy as they thought?

41

- Am I afraid of losing control over family, friends, etc.?

Just how important is financial wealth to you? Have you defined yourself by what you have accumulated? Have you defined yourself by what you *want* to accumulate? If so, consider the following parable in Luke 12:15–21:

15 And he said unto them, Take heed, and beware of covet-
     ousness: for a man's life consisteth not in the abundance
     of the things which he possesseth.
16 And he spake a parable unto them, saying, The ground of
     a certain rich man brought forth plentifully:
17 And he thought within himself, saying, What shall I do,
     because I have no room where to bestow my fruits?
18 And he said, This will I do: I will pull down my barns,
     and build greater; and there will I bestow all my fruits
     and my goods.
19 And I will say to my soul, Soul, thou hast much goods
     laid up for many years; take thine ease, eat, drink, *and* be
     merry.
20 But God said unto him, *Thou* fool, this night thy soul
     shall be required of thee: then whose shall those things
     be, which thou hast provided?
21 So *is* he that layeth up treasure for himself, and is not
     rich toward God.

In verse 15, Jesus warns us of the perils associated with covetous-ness. In fact, this is a direct statement against anyone who tries to use Scripture to suggest that God wants you to use what He has blessed you with to buy a bunch of stuff for yourself. A blessed life is not one that is measured by how much stuff you own.

In verses 16–19, Jesus tells the story of a rich man who was living a life of abundance. The man started thinking to himself about how he was running out of room to put all of the things he had acquired. Then it hit him. He would tear down his existing barns and build bigger ones to hold even more possessions. Then he said to himself, "Self, you got a lot stuff stored in these barns. You can be prosperous and happy for a long time!"

I can imagine that this rich man was feeling pretty good about himself. He probably thought he had plenty of time to enjoy all that his wealth would provide. Then, in verse 20, God spoke to him and told him that he had just won the grand prize in the It's Time to Die Sweepstakes. God then said "since you are leaving for good, who is going to enjoy all of your stuff now?" This statement was made to make the man think about what his life was really about. Now separated from the physical world, what does he own now? Can he lay claim to eternal life in Heaven?

The rich man in this parable signifies a type of selfishness that is becoming more prevalent day by day. This man had placed his trust in the things that his wealth could buy. Sadly, his wealth could not buy his salvation. Had he built up a treasury (barn) of faith, good works, and love toward his fellow man, he would have been better off. How many people do you know who have clothes stuffed in just about every closet in the house, many with the tags still attached because they have never been worn? Yet, they continue to shop and buy more clothes. Do you know of a person who hoards their money? These people are often referred to as trying to get all that they can, can all that they get, and then sit on the can. These people are no different from the man in the parable and sadly, will probably face the same fate.

Let me pose the question again. Have you defined yourself by what you have accumulated? Have you defined yourself by what you want to accumulate? Good questions, not-so-easy answers.

Where Do You Lay Your Treasures?

What do you treasure most in this life? Is it your house? Your car? Jewelry? Your investment portfolio? If what you treasure most is of an earthly nature, then I am here to remind you that such treasures are of a temporary nature.

In the Book of Matthew, chapter 6, verses 19–34, Jesus gave us some great insight as to what we should treasure most:

19 Lay not up for yourselves treasures upon earth, where moth and rust doth corrupt, and where thieves break through and steal:

20 But lay up for yourselves treasures in heaven, where neither moth nor rust doth corrupt, and where thieves do not break through nor steal:

21 For where your treasure is, there will your heart be also.

22 The light of the body is the eye: if therefore thine eye be single, thy whole body shall be full of light.

23 But if thine eye be evil, thy whole body shall be full of darkness. If therefore the light that is in thee be darkness, how great is that darkness!

24 No man can serve two masters: for either he will hate the one, and love the other; or else he will hold to the one, and despise the other. Ye cannot serve God and mammon.

25 Therefore I say unto you, Take no thought for your life, what ye shall eat, or what ye shall drink; nor yet for your body, what ye shall put on. Is not the life more than meat, and the body than raiment?

26 Behold the fowls of the air: for they sow not, neither do they reap, nor gather into barns; yet your heavenly Father feedeth them. Are ye not much better than they?

27 Which of you by taking thought can add one cubit unto his stature?

28 And why take ye thought for raiment? Consider the lilies of the field, how they grow; they toil not, neither do they spin:

29 And yet I say unto you, That even Solomon in all his glory was not arrayed like one of these.

30 Wherefore, if God so clothe the grass of the field, which to day is, and to morrow is cast into the oven, shall he not much more clothe you, O ye of little faith?

31 Therefore take no thought, saying, What shall we eat? or, What shall we drink? or, Wherewithal shall we be clothed?

32 (For after all these things do the Gentiles seek:) for your

heavenly Father knoweth that ye have need of all these
things.

33 But seek ye first the kingdom of God, and his righteousness; and all these things shall be added unto you.

34 Take therefore no thought for the morrow: for the
morrow shall take thought for the things of itself.
Sufficient unto the day is the evil thereof.

In verse 19, Jesus tells us not to place too much faith in earthly
treasures because they are temporary. When He uses the phrase
"...where moth and rust doth corrupt," He is using them as meta-
phors. In biblical times, fancy clothing was considered to be part of a
man's personal treasure. However, no matter how fancy and valuable
the clothing was, a moth could still destroy it. His use of the word
"rust" speaks not to the process through which metals are destroyed
through corrosion, but more so to the general process through which
worldly treasures can be corrupted and made unfit for use. In that
same verse, He also warns of another danger of earthly treasures: they
attract thieves! Someone once asked a bank robber why he robbed
banks? He replied, "Because that's where the money is!" You can be
sure that as you accumulate financial wealth, there will be someone,
somewhere, trying to figure out how they can get their hands on it.
But in verse 20, Jesus tells us to store our treasures in Heaven so that
they can be placed under God's care and governance. How do you do
this? By giving liberally to the poor and using your earthly treasures
not only for your enjoyment, but for the betterment of your fellow
man and for the glory of God. It is only at this point that you will
have a treasure that cannot be destroyed by worldly influences.

In verse 21, Jesus gives us a supporting reason for His words in
verse 20: "For where your treasure is, there will your heart be also."
This verse also serves as a warning. If your heart is with earthly treasures, then it will be subject to the same worldly influences and
dangers (moth, rust, and thieves) and end up with the same results
(corruption and destruction). But a heart set on heavenly treasures
will rise above such dangers and gain eternal life.

Finally, in verse 24, He gives us the most important reason as to why we should not get too caught up in the acquisition of worldly treasures: "No man can serve two masters.... Ye cannot serve God and mammon." The ways of the world are in stark contrast to God's ways. Think about it. Could you function in a country that had two governments with two different sets of laws? Adherence to one set of laws could land you in jail because you broke the other set of laws. Mammon is a word that encompasses all worldly definitions of riches, wealth, money, and greed. If your heart is with earthly treasures, you are serving mammon. If you are serving mammon, you cannot serve God. In the end, mammon cannot save you. As it is stated in Matthew 16:26, "For what is a man profited, if he gain the whole world, and lose his own soul?"

As we move on through this passage, verses 25 through 34 can be summed up with this popular phrase: Don't worry, be happy! Because of what Jesus said in verse 19, He tells us in verse 25 not to worry about how we're going to make it. Don't worry about how you will eat or drink. Don't worry about how you will be clothed. These are the basics of life, and He's taken care of all of those things.

In verse 26, He asks us to consider the life of birds. Birds of the wild do not plant seeds or tend the fields. Yet, God provides food for them to sustain themselves and thrive. If He can do this for birds, He certainly can do it for you (...Are ye not much better than they?). This is not to say that you can quit your job tomorrow and sit around waiting for God to feed you. Because you are more than a wild animal, more is expected of you. But for the things that you need to survive as you go about your way to do what God wants you to do, He will provide them for you.

Next, in verse 27, He asks, "Which of you by taking thought can add one cubit unto his stature?" A cubit is a unit of measure that represents about 18 inches, or the length of a forearm. The word stature is usually defined as the natural height of a person. The question can then be restated to ask, "Which of you by just thinking about it can add any length to your height?" The obvious answer is no one. It is impossible, so why try? The real point of this question is to get you to realize that excessive thinking and worrying about things you cannot change is futile.

Verses 28 through 32 repeat some of the same thoughts and concepts presented in the previous verses. In verse 33, He tells us how to dispense with useless worrying: "Seek ye first the kingdom of God." By doing so, you will be taken care of (...all of these things shall be added unto you). Finally, in verse 34, Jesus tells us not to worry about tomorrow, because tomorrow will take care of itself. The troubles of today are enough (Sufficient unto the day is the evil thereof). Why bring the troubles of tomorrow, or the next day, or the next week, into today? Let each day take care of itself. Anxiety leads to worry. Worry leads to fear. Seek God through the Gospel. Don't worry, be happy!

In his excellent article entitled *Contentment: The Antithesis of Prosperity Teaching*, Rick Blinson, founder and director of KneePrints Prayer Ministries offers one of the best explanations I have ever read as to why God wants our treasures to be of a heavenly nature:

> "God's first purpose in our lives is not making us a million-aire, but death of flesh in order to bring life in the Spirit. Only a dead man can be trusted to steward the true riches of God properly. He has nothing to protect, preserve, finance, or defend."

To understand this very powerful statement, let's look at it a little closer. What does the phrase "...death of flesh in order to bring life in the Spirit..." mean? The Apostle Paul tells us in Romans 8:10 that "...if Christ *be* in you, the body *is* dead because of sin; but the Spirit *is* life because of righteousness." To be "dead of flesh" is to recognize the fact that it is man's nature to sin. Therefore, if you are "dead of flesh" and "alive" in the Spirit of God, you will not sin any more, just like a dead man can't get up and walk. Paul further verifies this in Romans 8:13 where he tells us that "For if ye live after the flesh, ye shall die: but if ye through the Spirit do mortify the deeds of the body, ye shall live."

As I mentioned before, many of us "love our stuff!" We love how it makes us feel. We love how others admire it. Our "stuff" defines who we are or what we hope to be. When our "stuff" is in danger, it is only natural that we will often do whatever is necessary to protect, preserve, or defend it. When you are "dead of flesh," earthly treasures no longer mean anything to you. Just like a dead man, you know that you can't take it with you. You no longer have any ownership of them; you have given it all to God for His care and governance. Because of this, God knows that you can focus your attention on His true riches and become a good and faithful steward.

For Richer or Poorer…

Does God want us to be rich? Is poverty a blessing or a curse? These are two questions that can start a very impassioned debate among Christians. Your answer to these questions will say a lot about you and your relationship with God.

There are some people that truly believe that God wants us to be rich. There are several verses that they quote out of the Bible to support their view, but one of the more popular ones is 3 John 1:2, which reads as follows:

> Beloved, I wish above all things that thou mayest prosper
> and be in health, even as thy soul prospereth.

The problem with using this verse as proof that God wants us to be rich is that it assumes that the word "prosper" means to gain financial wealth. As discussed in Chapter 3, the word "prosper" is derived from the Hebrew word *tsalach*, which means to advance, make progress, succeed, or be profitable. A bigger problem arises when you combine that verse with the one that precedes it. Here is 3 John 1:1–2:

1 The elder unto the wellbeloved Gaius, whom I love in the truth.
2 Beloved, I wish above all things that thou mayest prosper and be in health, even as thy soul prospereth.

The real problem with using 3 John 1:2 as proof that God wants us to be rich is that the voice of both verses is that of the Apostle John. In fact, the entire epistle is a letter from John to his dear friend Gaius, a colleague in the ministry. There is nothing in this entire letter that should be interpreted as God revealing through the Apostle John that, above all things, He wants us to be rich.

Another popular verse that some people like to point to as proof that God wants us to be rich is Deuteronomy 8:18:

> But thou shalt remember the LORD thy God: for *it is* he that giveth thee power to get wealth, that he may establish his covenant which he sware unto thy fathers, as *it is* this day.

On the surface, it would appear that since God gives us the power to get wealth, He surely must want us to be rich. However, to truly understand this verse, you must understand the context in which it was written.

Moses wrote the Book of Deuteronomy for the Israelites. In the beginning of the 8th chapter, Moses told them to observe the commandments that he had given them, and be fruitful and multiply as they went into the Promised Land. Then, Moses used several verses to remind them of the many things that God had done for them, and urged them to never forget.

But Moses understood human nature, so he issued some warnings as well. The relevant verses are in Deuteronomy 8:17–20:

17 And thou say in thine heart, My power and the might of *mine* hand hath gotten me this wealth.

18 But thou shalt remember the LORD thy God: for *it is* he that giveth thee power to get wealth, that he may establish his covenant which he sware unto thy fathers, as *it is* this day.

19 And it shall be, if thou do at all forget the LORD thy God, and walk after other gods, and serve them, and worship them, I testify against you this day that ye shall surely perish.

20 As the nations which the LORD destroyeth before your

face, so shall ye perish; because ye would not be obedient
unto the voice of the LORD your God.

We sometimes make the mistake of thinking that any wealth we
obtain is only because we used our brains and we worked hard for it.
What we must always remember is that it is God who gave us the
brains and physical ability to make it happen. In fact, if it weren't for
His simple blessing of air each day, your wealth would be nothing
but a distant memory. The real message of the 18th verse in this
chapter, just as it was with the Israelites, is that we should recognize
that God gives us the power to get wealth so that He can establish
His promise (covenant). His promise to the Israelites was that they
would be justified (saved) by strict adherence to His laws and ordi-
nances, which were written on the stone tablets and further expressed
through Mosaic Law. What is God's promise to us today? Because
Jesus died on the cross, our works, or adherence to the Law can no
longer save us. We are now saved by the grace and mercy of God. A
covenant still exists, but instead of it being written on stone tablets,
it must now be written on our hearts (Hebrews 8:10). Wealth
obtained and not used to establish the new covenant in your own
heart, as well as the hearts of God's children, will lead to your
destruction.

If you think about it, it is silly to believe that God wants us to be
rich in purely financial terms. There are just too many Scriptures
where God warns us of the corrosive nature of financial wealth. In
Chapter 1, we discussed the verse where Jesus said it would be hard
for a rich man to get into Heaven (Matthew 19:23–24). He didn't
say it was impossible, He just said it would be hard. Wealth can't
save you, but God can because all things are possible with Him
(Matthew 19:26).

People who think that God wants them to be rich usually buy
into this line of thinking because they want to believe that their
possession of financial wealth is a validation of God's favor toward
them. They believe that if you're rich, you must be living right
because God wouldn't give you "the power to get wealth" if you
weren't. This is nothing more than one of Satan's old, tired, tricks to

lead you down the wrong path.

If God wants us to be rich, just how rich does He want us to be? Is $1 million the minimum? Maybe it's $5 million. The real truth concerning financial wealth is that it is a relative term that God cares nothing about. What you do with that wealth is what really matters to Him. Are you using it to further His ministry? Or, are you using it for your own selfish desires?

You see, the mere possession of financial wealth is not necessarily a sign of favor from God because Satan can easily reproduce it to lead you astray. As I stated in Chapter 2, just because you get something that you want, doesn't mean that it came from God. Fortunately, one of the things that Satan cannot reproduce is a heart filled with the Spirit of God. When your heart is filled with the Spirit of God, you have a key that gives you access to the treasures of the Kingdom of Heaven. Now, you are truly rich!

Now let's look at the second question. Is poverty a blessing or a curse? In biblical times, there were those who thought that when bad things happened to you, it was because you had sinned against God. Even today, there are some that still feel the same way. However, such thinking ignores the multitude of circumstances that surround poverty.

In some cases, poverty is the result of poor decision making. If you will be obedient to God's word, He will bless you with wisdom and knowledge. Wisdom and knowledge can be used to help you make good decisions that will help lift you out of poverty. There are other situations where your poverty is caused by the poor decisions of others. To solve this problem, you either need to pray for the person or persons that you are dependent upon to make better decisions, or pray for God to reduce your dependence upon them.

Now, there is another situation where you can be living as God would have you to live, but poverty and hard times still come your way. How can this be? You have been a faithful servant. You work hard everyday. Why is it that nothing seems to be going right? For answers, you need to look no further than the story of Job.

Job was a faithful, God-fearing man. He was a man of integrity. According to God, there was no man on earth like him. Job had ten children (seven sons, three daughters). He owned 7,000 sheep, 3,000 camels, 500 oxen, 500 donkeys, and many servants. Job was a rich man. Many people perceived his wealth and good fortune to be a sign of favor from God.

But Satan thought that Job was such a good man only because God had prospered him so much. Satan then made a bet with God: Take away all that You have blessed him with, and Job will surely curse Your name. God agreed to the bet on the one condition that Satan not lay a finger on Job. Soon, Job's life began to change.

His oxen, donkeys, and camels were stolen. His sheep were destroyed by fire. Most of his servants were killed by the fire that killed his sheep, or by the invading forces that stole his animals. Then, a parent's worst nightmare occurred. All ten of his children were killed when the house they were dining in collapsed. What did Job do? He tore up his robe (which was a Hebrew custom under such circumstances), shaved his head, and fell to the ground worshipping God, saying "I came to this world with nothing and I shall leave this world with nothing. The Lord gives and He takes away. May the name of the Lord be praised." Satan lost the bet!

Satan, being the poor loser that he is, came back. He wanted another shot at Job. God was pleased with how Job handled his situation. In spite of all that Job went through, he still maintained his integrity and devotion to God. But Satan told God that "the only reason why Job didn't break was because You wouldn't let me touch him. Let me touch him and he will surely curse your name." God agreed to the bet under the one condition that Satan could touch Job, but he couldn't kill him.

Satan then proceeded to afflict Job with a horrible disease that caused him to have painful sores from the bottom of his feet to the top of his head. Job's wife was of little comfort, as she advised Job to lose his integrity, curse God, and die. Then, three of his friends came to provide comfort and support. Unfortunately, they were of little comfort either because they were convinced that Job must have sinned against God to suffer such calamity. Job, however, maintained his innocence.

Still suffering, Job's patience began to wear thin, and he began to complain to God by asking that question that many of us ask when things are not going well: "Why me, Lord?" Soon, God spoke to Job. God asked Job to consider that since He is the creator and ruler of the universe, wouldn't He have the ability to save Job from his wretched condition? Eventually, Job realized that God's ways are sometimes beyond his understanding and he must learn to trust in His perfect plan. Throughout all of his trials, Job never cursed God. Again, Satan lost the bet!

God healed Job and made him prosperous again. In fact, he became twice as wealthy as he was before. He soon had 14,000 sheep, 6,000 camels, 1000 oxen, and 1000 donkeys. God not only blessed him with children again (seven sons and three daughters), but also with 140 years of life to witness the birth of their children, and their children's children.

Was Job's poverty a blessing or a curse? It was neither. It was simply a process that God used to achieve several objectives that were part of His perfect plan. First, as good as Job was, his relationship with God needed a little work. Job emerged from his trials with a truly unshakeable confidence in God. Next, Job's trials became a testimony to the restorative powers of God. Job's family and friends thought Job was destined to perish. But to God's glory, they witnessed a miracle healing.

This leads me to ask you a few questions. What would you do if all of your financial wealth was taken away? What would you do if all of your family were killed? Would Satan have won the bet if it were you instead of Job? Since you have the benefit of knowing the outcome of Job's story, let me ask you one more question. Are you willing to go through a period of poverty or hard times for your benefit or the benefit of others?

In most wedding ceremonies, the bride and bridegroom usually repeat as part of their wedding vow the phrase "...for better, for worse, for richer, for poorer, in sickness or in health...." Once you accept Jesus as your personal Savior, He promises to have you, to hold you, to love you, to cherish you, for better, for worse, for richer, for poorer, in sickness, or in health. The question is will you be just as faithful to Him? It's easy to praise God and remain faithful to

Him when all is going well. But the true nature of your relationship with God will be revealed when times are hard, you're broke, and your health is failing.

Neither wealth nor poverty is a true indicator of the nature of your relationship with God. The only reliable measure of your relationship with God is what is in your heart.

The Responsibilities of Being Wealthy

If God has blessed you with financial wealth, then you should know that there is a high level of responsibility that goes along with that. In 1 Timothy 6:17–19, the Apostle Paul reminds us of those responsibilities:

17 Charge them that are rich in this world, that they be not highminded, nor trust in uncertain riches, but in the living God, who giveth us richly all things to enjoy;

18 That they do good, that they be rich in good works, ready to distribute, willing to communicate;

19 Laying up in store for themselves a good foundation against the time to come, that they may lay hold on eternal life.

In these verses, Paul issues a challenge to the wealthy. He tells the wealthy not to be too proud or arrogant. He also tells them not to place their trust in the uncertainty of earthly wealth, but to place their trust in God. It is God that blessed you with your wealth and He wants you to enjoy it. Just don't place your trust in it.

With wealth comes power. The wealthy have the power to do much good for themselves, their families, and their fellow man. Sadly, they also have the power to do a lot of harm in the same way. Paul admonishes them to do good, to abound in good works, and to be ready to give when asked, and without hesitation. By doing so, they are building a strong foundation based not on merit, but on the grace of God, by which they may "lay hold on eternal life."

Part II

Nuts & Bolts, Tips & Tools

Chapter 5
The Financial Plan

Why Plan?

I like to think of financial planning as a weighing scale. To be successful, you must balance your desire to achieve a goal with the reality of reaching that goal. Good financial planning can help you gain that balance. There is an old saying that says that "people never plan to fail, they just fail to plan." As catchy as this saying is, I believe that the issue of financial planning goes much deeper.

Why do people fail at financial planning? The reasons are many. The first reason is that it forces them to deal with issues that they may not be ready to deal with. Are you saving enough? Are you spending too much? Who gets the kids if you die? Should you leave everything to your spouse, or should you divide it between your spouse and children? Maybe you should leave it all to the children? Can you really save enough to retire at age 40 or will you have to work to age 70? These are questions that force you to examine yourself and the relationships in your life. Another reason is time. Proper financial planning takes time, and this is true whether you are doing it yourself or paying someone to do it for you. Which leads us to the third reason why people fail at financial planning: cost.

Many people recognize the need for developing a financial plan. They just don't want to pay for it. But don't let the cost of a financial plan stop you from starting. If you are willing to invest some of your time, there are many books and websites that can help answer many of your financial planning questions. Particularly when it comes to the Internet, many financial websites have calculators that will allow you to key in your relevant information and get an answer. How reliable is the answer? As usual, it depends. In general, the more information you are allowed to input, the better your answer will be. In some cases, access to more sophisticated tools can be had for a small fee. Additionally, there are software programs such as Intuit's®

Quicken and Microsoft's® Manage Your Money that have basic financial planning modules that can help you as well.

What if you are willing to pay for a plan? How much should you expect to pay for it? Many financial advisors and planners offer financial plans that range anywhere from no charge to as much as $5,000 or more. One thing for sure, don't assume that the more expensive the plan, the better it will be.

Most financial advisors provide financial plans that are generated by some type of computer software. The advisor gathers all of the relevant information from you, keys it into the software, presses the print button, and out comes the financial plan. In many cases, the plan looks very impressive. There are lots of charts, graphs, and reports, along with some comments and recommendations. No matter how pretty the financial plan, the most important thing is its usefulness. The quality of the plan will depend upon the quality of the information put into it, and more importantly, the quality of the interpretation of the results. Developing the proper financial strategy is the most important part and also the most difficult.

Financial planning is a lot like the game of horseshoes. While it is nice to get a ringer, closeness does count. Your financial plan is something that will evolve over time. Changes in your life will dictate that there will be changes in your plan. It is really useless to try to get a plan that precisely forecasts a certain outcome, because none of us can predict the future. The key is to gather enough information so that you can narrow the range of potential outcomes, and then develop multiple contingency plans (i.e., Plan A, Plan B, etc.) just in case reality falls outside your predetermined range of outcomes

Depending on how in-depth you want your planning to be, here is a partial list of things that should be considered:

- Assessment of your current situation
- Cash Flow (income vs. expenses)
- Net Worth (assets vs. liabilities)
- Insurance Review (Life, Health, & Disability)
- Goal Planning (retirement, education, debt reduction, etc.)

• Estate Planning

The above list is by no means complete. However, it should serve as a guide to help you evaluate the various financial planning options that are available to you. Just remember the words of Solomon in Proverbs 21:5:

> The thoughts of the diligent *tend* only to plenteousness; but
> of every one *that is* hasty only to want.

Diligent thought given to a task before its implementation helps to insure its success, whether the task is spiritual or worldly. Hasty decisions or actions usually lead to results that leave you with less instead of more. Take the time to thoughtfully develop your financial plan.

Strategy

As I stated in the previous section, the most important part of the financial plan is the strategy that you will adopt to implement the plan. The financial products that you will use are fairly common and easily obtained. In fact, when you look at financial products that are in the top 20% of their group, there is not a lot of difference in terms of price or basic features. It is usually the bells and whistles that will lead you to choose one product versus another.

If you are implementing the plan yourself, make sure you do your homework. If you are going to get someone to help you, make sure you get a financial advisor instead of a financial salesperson. Just about anybody can sell you financial products. Also, just because they can sell it to you, doesn't mean that it is the appropriate product to help you achieve your financial goals. A true financial advisor will help you develop a sound strategy first. Selection of the financial products needed to execute the plan is secondary.

Strategy should be discussed in the Recommendations section of the plan. It should detail what is required of you to achieve your financial goals. It should also detail how your investments should be allocated to deliver the rate of return that is necessary for financial success, in accordance to your tolerance for risk. Any financial plan that is not based on a sound strategy is doomed to fail.

Although the selection of financial products is secondary to developing your strategy, it is still important. How do you choose the right product? Based on your financial goals, your strategy should dictate what asset classes you will need to help you achieve your goals. For example, you may have decided that to achieve your retirement goal in accordance to your tolerance for risk, you need to build a moderate growth portfolio. Your asset mix may look like this:

Cash	5%
Fixed Income (Bonds, CDs, etc.)	20%
Equities (Stocks, Stock Mutual Funds)	75%

Now that you have determined the mix of assets for your portfolio, you need to determine what styles you will use. The best way to analyze what style of investment you need in your portfolio is to use the grid system. The grid system is a matrix of nine squares organized into three rows and columns. The columns are labeled for the value, growth, and blend styles of investing. Value investing is a discipline that tries to purchase stocks that are currently selling for less than what they are worth, with the idea that other investors will bid the current price up to its true worth or more, in due time. Growth investing is a discipline that tries to purchase stocks that are growing their revenue and earnings at a faster rate than their industry peers and the market overall. Such stocks pay little or no dividends, instead using the funds to finance further expansion. And of course, blend investing would be a strategy that exhibits characteristics of both growth and value investing.

The three rows are labeled for large, medium, and small capitalization stocks. Market capitalization is usually defined as the current price per share of a stock multiplied by the number of shares outstanding. Although there are differences as to what constitutes small, medium, or large cap stocks, here is an example of how they might be classified:

Small- cap	Up to $1.5 Billion
Mid-cap	$1.5 Billion – $10 Billion
Large-cap	$10 Billion or more

Although there are many stocks or stock mutual funds that may have varying objectives such as growth, growth and income, value, small cap, and many more, they will usually fall into one of those capitalization categories or stretch across several of them. The letter "C" in the style grid indicates which styles may be most appropriate for conservative investors. The letter "M" indicates which styles may be most appropriate for moderate investors. The letter "A" indicates which styles may be most appropriate for aggressive investors. Here is an example of the style grid:

Value	Blend	Growth	
C	C	M	**Large**
C	M	A	**Medium**
M	A	A	**Small**

The main thing you need to know is that the market moves in cycles with regard to which style will perform the best. By utilizing the grid, you can help your portfolio achieve your number one goal in managing your risk: Diversify, diversify, diversify!

Diversification helps to keep your portfolio on track whether the economy is doing well or slowing down. You should pick investments within the grid that best suit your risk tolerance, and then diversify those holdings across different sectors of the economy, such as utilities, energy, financials, industrial cyclicals, consumer durable, consumer staples, services, retail, health care, and technology.

Profits of companies in the basic materials, capital goods, transportation, and consumer cyclicals sectors can be depressed for many years, so investing in them requires a long-term commitment. Technology companies can dominate and deliver solid profits for years, only to have a new company with new technology threaten their very existence. Again, the key is to pick good stocks or mutual funds that will not overweight you in one or more sectors. If you are just getting started, you may want to stick with blue chip stocks. Blue chip stocks are the stocks of large, national companies with a solid record of stable earnings and/or dividend growth and a reputation for high quality management and products. Also, look at the industry leaders. The top two or three companies in the industry didn't get there by mistake. Usually it is because they are the best and they are looking to grow at a solid pace through revenue growth or acquisitions.

Also, do not ignore companies paying dividends. In recent years, most of the growth has been in companies that focus on using net profits for expansion rather than paying dividends. But dividend-paying stocks can be a plus because the dividend can provide an income and that income can provide a cushion during market declines. Still, you should be careful because some stocks with high dividend yields could be very risky. A high dividend payment won't do you any good if your original investment in the stock continues to go down in value. Remember, the higher the return or yield, the higher the probability that the stock has added risks.

You can also use the grid system to evaluate fixed-income investments. Here's what that style grid might look like:

Short Term	Inter-Mediate	Long Term	
C	C	M	High Quality
C	M	A	Medium Quality
M	A	A	Low Quality

The main thing to remember in using this grid is that there are various trade-offs that you must always consider. Long-term fixed-income investments are riskier than short-term ones, but usually offer higher rates of return. High-quality fixed-income investments are safer than lower-quality ones, but their rates of return are usually lower as well. This basically means that you can't have your cake and eat it too. If you want higher yields, it usually means that you are going to have to accept more risk. If safety is of primary importance, then you must be willing to accept lower rates of return.

Managing Planning Risk

Like everything else in this world, you will face several risks while implementing your plan. It takes money to implement a financial plan. For most of us, that means we have to save money from the salary and wages that we earn from our jobs.

Your ability to earn money in this world is usually dependent upon three things:

1. You must be alive
2. You should be able bodied
3. You should be healthy

For items 2 and 3, there are various levels at which one can operate and still earn a good living. However, for item 1, there is one indisputable fact: If you are not alive, you can't make a living! Now, some of you may take issue with that statement because you would be quick to point out that there are many people, particularly deceased entertainers, that continue to earn money after they have passed away. For example, take Elvis Presley. Even though a long time has passed since his death, his records continue to earn millions of dollars each year. However, despite many Elvis sightings, I don't think that he is here to personally collect on his earnings.

The point of all of this is that your ability to earn a living is probably the most important asset that you and your family have. The best way to protect it is through insurance. To protect your life, you need life insurance. To protect against disability, you need disability insurance. To protect against failing health, you need health insurance and long-term care insurance. Insurance helps you to manage the after effects of any of these risks coming to bear. Remember that insurance is a risk management tool first, and a possible investment second. The primary reason you purchase insurance is to deal with the risks previously described. Any investment features that it may have are secondary.

There are two primary types of life insurance. The first is called term insurance. Term insurance is insurance where the insurance company promises to pay a certain amount of money (the death benefit) to whomever you have named as beneficiary if you die during the term for which the policy is in effect. Premiums for this type of insurance can increase each year (annual-renewable) or can be fixed for a set period of time (level-premium), then increase. Term insurance does not build up any type of cash value. This is why it is often referred to as pure insurance.

The other primary type of insurance is called whole life insurance. Whole life insurance has two parts to it. One part is for pure insurance and the other part is for a reserve (cash value). Every premium payment that you make is divided between the two parts. As you get older, the portion of your premium that pays for insurance increases while the portion of your premium that goes into the reserve decreases. Your premiums are usually fixed for the life of the policy. The reserve portion (cash value) increases with time. Should you die, the amount received by your beneficiary is a combination of the face value of the policy and the net cash value.

There are other types of life insurance, such as universal life and variable life. Both can build cash value like a whole life policy. However, the growth of the cash value will be based on the performance of the underlying investments (stock and bond mutual funds, etc.). These types of life insurance contracts have added risks. If you are not paying a high enough premium, and the investment performance of the underlying investments is less than expected, you can end up with a contract that will lapse or require you to put in additional dollars to keep it in force.

Disability insurance is a risk management tool to protect your income. If all or most of your income is from a job, you should consider what would happen to you and your family (if you have one) if your income was significantly reduced or eliminated. If you lose your job, you always stand a good chance of getting another one. But what happens if you can't work due to accident or illness? The best of financial plans will fall apart if your ability to earn a living is significantly reduced or eliminated. Disability insurance can be obtained to pay you a percentage of your income for a set period (2–5 years) or for your lifetime. Premiums can vary greatly, so make sure you shop around.

You should also make sure that you have adequate health insurance. If you become sick and have to have medical care, your health insurance will help cover most of the expense. In addition to your medical insurance, you should also look to purchase long-term care insurance.

Long-term care (LTC) insurance is insurance that helps cover the expense of nursing home care, assisted-living care, or other types of care associated with aging. Instead of having to pay these expenses out-of-pocket, you are able to shift that burden to your LTC insurance provider. LTC benefits can be provided for a set period (2–5 years) or for your lifetime. The amount you pay in long-term care premiums will be based on these factors:

- Benefit Period – How long they will pay
- Elimination Period – How long before they pay
- Daily Benefit – How much they will pay

The longer you want them to pay any benefits, the higher your premiums. The quicker you want them to start paying benefits, the higher your premiums. The more in benefits you want them to pay, the higher your premiums. You should also look for a contract that offers inflation protection so that your benefits keep up with increases in long-term care costs. You should also look for an LTC contract that allows home health care.

With long-term care insurance, the younger you are, the lower your premiums will be. I recommend that you look at purchasing long-term care insurance no earlier than age 50. By that time, you should have a better idea as to how much coverage you will need. If you have done a good job of saving and investing, you may not need that much coverage, if any at all.

The Role of Stewardship

As you develop your financial plan, you should ask yourself, "How have I managed what God has already given me?" Some of you may be wondering why such a question is relevant to the financial planning process. Jesus gives us the answers in a parable.

What Have You Done With Your Talents?

Whenever there is a discussion about stewardship, the parable of the talents is usually the passage of scripture that is used as an example. Let's take a closer look at that passage, which is Matthew 25:14–30:

14 For *the kingdom of heaven is* as a man travelling into a far country, *who* called his own servants, and delivered unto them his goods.

15 And unto one he gave five talents, to another two, and to another one; to every man according to his several ability; and straightway took his journey.

16 Then he that had received the five talents went and traded with the same, and made *them* other five talents.

17 And likewise he that *had received* two, he also gained other two.

18 But he that had received one went and digged in the earth, and hid his lord's money.

19 After a long time the lord of those servants cometh, and reckoneth with them.

20 And so he that had received five talents came and brought other five talents, saying, Lord, thou deliveredst

unto me five talents: behold, I have gained beside them five talents more.

21 His lord said unto him, Well done, *thou* good and faithful servant: thou hast been faithful over a few things, I will make thee ruler over many things: enter thou into the joy of thy lord.

22 He also that had received two talents came and said, Lord, thou deliveredst unto me two talents: behold, I have gained two other talents beside them.

23 His lord said unto him, Well done, good and faithful servant; thou hast been faithful over a few things, I will make thee ruler over many things: enter thou into the joy of thy lord.

24 Then he which had received the one talent came and said, Lord, I knew thee that thou art an hard man, reaping where thou hast not sown, and gathering where thou hast not strawed:

25 And I was afraid, and went and hid thy talent in the earth: lo, *there* thou hast *that is* thine.

26 His lord answered and said unto him, *Thou* wicked and slothful servant, thou knewest that I reap where I sowed not, and gather where I have not strawed:

27 Thou oughtest therefore to have put my money to the exchangers, and *then* at my coming I should have received mine own with usury.

28 Take therefore the talent from him, and give *it* unto him which hath ten talents.

29 For unto every one that hath shall be given, and he shall have abundance: but from him that hath not shall be taken away even that which he hath.

30 And cast ye the unprofitable servant into outer darkness: there shall be weeping and gnashing of teeth.

The key to understanding this parable is in the very first verse, verse 14. Contrary to how it is often presented, this parable is about helping you to understand what the kingdom of heaven is all about.

To be sure, it is not about making money. Jesus used talents (money) to get his point across because back then, as it is now, it was easier to get people's attention if you talked about money. In addition to its core message about stewardship, there are many financial lessons that can be learned as well.

Should you ever decide to take a long trip to a far away place, you won't pack up all of your possessions and take them with you. You will probably ask a family member or neighbor to watch things for you while you are gone. In this parable, the man does exactly that and calls his servants together to deliver his goods into their care.

In verse 15, he gives one servant five talents, another two talents, and another one talent. In biblical times, a talent was a sum or measure of money that had been weighed. For example, a talent of silver weighed about 100 pounds. These measures varied from country to country. Our version of talents would be the currency and coins that form the medium of exchange in our world today. It is important to understand that the handing out of these talents was not based solely on financial knowledge or investment skill. It was based primarily on each servant's ability to take care of his lord's possessions. In this case, the possessions of the kingdom of heaven consist of the love, peace, and joy of God, and his care, governance, and possession of all things on earth.

Now we know from verses 16 through 18 that the servant that got five talents went and traded with the exchangers (bankers) and gained another five talents, for a total of ten talents. We also know that the other servant did the same and doubled his talents to end up with four. However, the servant that received the one talent went and dug a hole in the ground, and hid the talent.

In verses 19 through 23, we read where the man returns from his long trip. He has been away for a long time and now gathers his servants together to get an accounting (reckoning) of the goods that he left in their care. The first two servants gave reports detailing how they doubled the talents that were entrusted to their care. The lord was pleased and told them what a wonderful job they had done. Then they received more good news. Since they had been faithful over a few things, the lord was going to allow them to govern (rule;

steward) over many things. Because of their faithful service, these servants received a promotion! Before, they were entrusted to care for a few things. Now, they are entrusted to care for much more.

But wait. What about the other servant? Well, I can imagine he is standing in the back, head down, and feet shuffling. His mind is racing, trying to think of some way to make his report sound better than it really is. Unfortunately, his report starts off on shaky ground because he begins it with an excuse. This servant begins by telling the lord in verses 24 and 25 that he didn't do anything with the talent that he had been entrusted with because he knew that the lord was a tough (hard) man, and that the man reaped the benefits of others' efforts (... reaping where thou hast not sown, and gathering where thou hast not strawed). Because he didn't want to take a chance and lose his lord's money, he dug a hole in ground and hid the talent there.

This servant is a real piece of work! Not only did he make excuses, he insulted his lord. First, he accused the lord of being a hard or tough master. I find this difficult to believe because of the kind and gracious manner in which the lord treated the first two servants. Then, he implies that the lord unfairly reaps the benefits of the work of others. Again, I would disagree. It was his lord's money. He provided the capital and resources, so he should be the one who benefits the most. The other servants didn't seem to have a problem with this. That's because they knew that the job at hand was to do one thing, and one thing only: Take care of their lord's stuff! Because they did such a good job, ultimately, they were taken care of.

The final insult was the one that just tore me up. In verse 25, he concludes his report by telling his lord that the talent he hid in the ground is still there (...lo, *there* thou hast *that is* thine). This fool didn't have the common decency to at least dig the money out of the ground and return it to his lord. It's almost as if he said, "That's what I did with your money. You go get it if you want it." How ungrateful can someone be?

Needless to say, the lord was not pleased and he made his feelings known in verse 26. He further chastises the servant for not investing his money with the bankers or traders (exchangers), and generating an investment return (interest; usury). As punishment, he removes the one talent from the lazy servant's care and gives it to the servant with the ten talents. Finally, the lord kicks him out, so that he can hang out with others who are sad, unhappy, and miserable, because they are no longer under the care of their lords. He, along with others, is on the outside looking in, with plenty of time to think about his actions.

I really love this parable because there are so many lessons to be learned from it. First and foremost, Jesus is teaching us about the finer points of stewardship. The purpose of stewardship is for you to use, nurture, and improve the gifts and talents that are in your care, so that God can be further honored and extend his reach through you to those in need.

There are many gifts, talents, and blessings that God may entrust to your care in your lifetime. Sometimes they are given to you because you need them. Sometimes they are given to you because you want them. Nevertheless, they are given to you according to your ability to handle them. In some cases, you will possess the necessary skills to handle them yourself. In other cases, you have the good sense to hire someone to help you manage the resources as best as possible. Sometimes, they are given to you because He wants to test you. The purpose of the test is to provide a critical evaluation of your skills. This is very different from being tempted. When someone tempts you, they are usually trying to get you to do something wrong. God tempts no man. If God decides to test you, the test is for your benefit, not His. If you do well, you will be ready to move from Stewardship 101 to Stewardship 202.

The servant that received one talent could have doubled his like the others. His master certainly felt he had the ability to do so, or he wouldn't have given him the talent. But for some reason, the servant didn't do it. Maybe he thought it was too much work. Maybe he was ·jealous, and he didn't want to go to the trouble of increasing the talent for someone else's benefit. Even though he didn't lose the talent, he was judged harshly because he didn't do the right thing with it. He was negligent in its care. To understand why this is so important, let's look at a financial concept called the time value of money.

The time value of money says that a dollar received today is worth more than a dollar to be received in the future. For example, consider the lottery. Suppose you are the grand-prize winner in a lottery that had a jackpot of $10,000,000. The lottery commission gives you the following options: $400,000 per year for 25 years or a lump sum payment of $4,776,056. If you are like most other lottery winners, you will take the lump sum. Why? Because you could die tomorrow, and when you die, the payments stop. Your family gets nothing. You also know that most lottery commissions invest their funds very conservatively. If you do a good job of investing, you might be able to earn a higher rate of return, which might allow your lump sum to grow to $10,000,000 or more in 25 years or less. If you just take the annual payments, you lose the opportunity to earn interest on the additional dollars you would have received in the lump sum. This is what we call an opportunity cost.

When we take the blessings that God has placed in our care, and misuse or abuse them, we lose the opportunity to do more with them. Stewardship of all that God has blessed us with is a serious matter, and like each of the servants in this parable, we will be periodically judged on how well we have done. These gifts and talents are God's investment in you. With respect to all that God has entrusted to your care, what kind of return will you be able to offer?

Another lesson of this parable is that as Christians, we have to learn that it's okay to take risks, just as long as they are prudent risks. How long did it take for the servants to double the investment? Did it take five weeks or five years? We don't know, but let's use something called the Rule of 72 to put things in perspective.

The Rule of 72 is a simple mathematical concept that can help you estimate how long it will take for your investment to double in value. It can also be used to help you determine what rate of return is required to make an investment double within a certain period of time. Table 5-1 shows how the formula works.

For example, if you have an investment that has a 3% rate of return, take 72 and divide it by 3 and the result is 24. It will take about 24 years for your money to double if it is earning 3% per year.

Table 5-1

Rule of 72: How does it work?

If I'm earning 3% on my savings account, how long will it take for my money to double?

72 ÷ 3 = 24 It will take about 24 years for money to double.

I want to double my money in six years. What rate of return will I have to earn?

72 ÷ 6 = 12 I will need to earn about 12% per year for my money to double in six years.

You can also use it to determine what rate of return will be required to make your money double within a certain period of time. For example, if you would like to double your money in 6 years, take 72 and divide it by 6 and the result is 12. This means that in order for you to double your money in 6 years, you would need to average earning 12% each year. Using the Rule of 72 is a quick way to determine if a particular rate of return will be adequate for your investment goals or realistic for a given time period. The formula works best for periods of two years or longer.

Now in the case of the servants in the parable, let's assume that it took five years for them to trade with the exchangers. Using the Rule of 72, if we take 72 and divide by 5 years, the results is 14.4. This would mean that the servants would have had to earn on average about 14% per year to make their talents double within five years. I can tell you from experience that 14% per year is not a return that you would get from a low risk investment.

When it comes to money, many of us act like the lazy servant. The first mistake that we make is that we adopt a mindset of ownership instead of stewardship. When you have a mindset of ownership, you have a tendency to want to protect and preserve what you have accumulated. However, from a spiritual point of view, you must realize that since you own nothing, you also do not own the decision to selfishly use what God has blessed you with. God has instructed us through His Word as to how He wants us to care for His possessions. Develop a healthy spirit so that you can learn to listen to God. Doing so will allow you to give a good report when it is your time.

Finally, I am often asked why was the one talent of the lazy servant given to the servant with ten, instead of the servant with four? Doesn't the servant with the four talents need it more? Isn't that unfair?

I come from a family of three boys. As with most siblings, I thought I was supposed to get everything that my brothers got. If my Mom gave my brother a piece of candy, I was supposed to get a piece too. If my Dad poured one of my brothers a glass of soda, I was supposed to get a glass filled with the same amount of soda. One day I was complaining to my Mom that she was doing more for one of my brothers than she had done for me. She continued to let me ramble for a few minutes, then very politely told me that "I may not treat you all the same, but I treat each one of you fair." I thought about what she said, and then it hit me. Fairness should not be based on equality. Fairness should be based on utility: who will use it the best, or who could use it the most.

If my brother already had a glass full of soda, and my glass was empty, should my Dad have poured the same amount into my brother's glass that he used to fill mine? Of course not! My brother's glass was already full. If my Dad had poured more into it, the soda would have spilled because the glass could hold no more. This would have been a waste of soda. I got some soda because my brother's glass had enough soda already. In the case of the servants, the one that had the most talents got more because he was best equipped to do more with it. To give it to one of the other servants may have meant that the talent would not have been put to its greatest use or possibly wasted. God may not treat us all the same, but He treats each one of us fair.

The role of stewardship in your financial plan is very important and requires serious thought. If you do not have a healthy attitude toward stewardship, your financial planning efforts will not be successful. As you set your financial goals for the future, make sure that they are built with an attitude of stewardship, not ownership.

Chapter 6
Debt Management

Debt problems are not a function of social class. They exist for all kinds of people from all walks of life. There are many people who are looking good, smelling good, and riding nice. However, some of them are like ducks in a pond. It looks like smooth sailing above the water. But if you looked underwater, you'd see that their feet are paddling like crazy to keep them afloat! Through my many years of experience in banking and finance, I have just about seen it all. Excessive debt can happen to anyone.

How do you get into debt?

Why do people go into debt? Quite simply, you go into debt because you do not have enough money to pay for something that you want or need now. Therefore, you must borrow the money from a friend, your family, or lending institution to pay for it. Sometimes, there are events that occur that leave us no choice but to rely on the charity of others or to borrow money. As a Christian, the decision to borrow is important and should be weighed equally with the decision of how you are going to pay it back. You should only borrow money if you have a sure and stable source of repayment.

Types of Debt

There are several types of debt, but I will focus on the three that are used the most: installment debt, revolving debt, and mortgages. Debt can be either secured or unsecured. Secured debt involves some type of collateral being held to cover (secure) the loan. Unsecured debt is where the only thing backing your loan is your promise to pay. Installment and revolving debts can be secured or unsecured. Mortgages, by definition, are secured only.

Installment debt is debt that is taken out for a set term, such as

36 months (three years). You make periodic payments (usually monthly) on the loan until you reach the end of the term. If the payments have been made on time, you should pay the loan off in the term agreed to in the loan documents. Typical installment loans are car loans and personal loans.

Revolving debt is debt in which the money you borrow becomes available again once you pay any or all of it back. Theoretically, as long as you make your payments on time, you can use and reuse the credit line as much as you want. Hence the term "revolving." Remember that revolving debt is a spinning door that leads to nowhere. Pay it back, charge again. Pay it back, charge again. This form of debt is the most prevalent form of debt available, and it is the most dangerous. Credit cards and lines of credit are examples of revolving debt.

A mortgage is a debt where real estate is pledged to the lender as security for the payment of the debt. Mortgages are available for a variety of properties:

- Residential – Single family homes, condominiums, town-homes, etc.
- Rental Property – single family homes, duplexes, apart-ment buildings, etc.
- Commercial Property – office buildings, shopping centers, and other large projects

Most mortgages have terms of 15 to 30 years. The interest rate charged on a mortgage can be fixed or adjustable. Because the government of the United States wants to encourage home ownership, mortgage interest in most cases is tax deductible. This helps lower the cost of borrowing. For many people, their mortgage will be the largest debt they incur in their lifetime.

How Things Get Out Of Control

Debt is not bad. It is the improper use of debt that is bad. The trouble with debt, especially revolving debt, is that once you get into trouble, things can quickly spiral out of control. Here's how.

The very force that can work to help you build financial wealth is the same force that can plunge you into financial despair. That force is compound interest. Compound interest is where your interest earns or accrues interest. With most credit accounts, your interest is compounded daily. This means that interest is calculated on the balance owed each day within your statement cycle and is posted (added) to the balance on the closing date or when a payment is posted to the account, whichever comes first. At this point, the interest becomes part of your balance owed. During the course of a year, your statement cycle will run anywhere from 28 days to 31 days. The number of days in a cycle determines how much interest is added to the account. Because of this, your annual interest rate will be different from your effective interest rate. The annual interest rate is the stated rate that is on the agreement that you signed when you opened the account. The effective interest rate is the actual rate of interest that you pay because the interest that you are charged on the account accrues interest.

Let's say you have a credit card with a balance of $2,000 and the interest rate is 18% per year. Because the interest charged on your account accrues interest, the effective interest rate is 19.8%. Your typical payment on this card might be 2% of the outstanding balance with a minimum payment of $10. In this example your monthly payment will start off at $40. Whenever you make a payment on your account, it is divided into two categories. The first is principal, which is the actual amount of money that you borrowed to make your purchases. The next is interest and fees.

Interest accrues on your balance daily. Each month, on the closing date, the interest that has accrued since your last payment is posted to the account. Using the above information, your account activity for the month would look like this:

Beginning Balance	$2,000.00
Accrued Interest	$29.80
Adjusted Balance	$2,029.80
Payment on Account	$40.00

New Balance $1,989.80

In this particular example, 75% of your payment went to pay for interest and the remaining 25% went toward principal or the actual amount that you borrowed. If you continue to pay the minimum payment due each month until the entire balance is paid off, take a look at how long it will take for you to pay it off:

Original Amount Borrowed	$2,000.00
Total Interest Payments	$5,073.20
Total Payments	$7,073.20
# of Monthly Payments to	
Payoff Credit Card	377
Or	
Years to Payoff Credit Card	31.42 yrs.

Your eyes are not playing tricks on you. Yes, if you just pay the minimum payment due each month for this credit card, it will take you over 30 years to pay it off. That's longer than it would take you to payoff a typical mortgage on a house. The reason it takes so long for you to pay it off is that your minimum payment goes down as your balance goes down.

Who in their right mind would pay the minimum payment due each month? Well, there are plenty of people who do that all the time. I can't tell you how many times I have had clients tell me that they have been paying on an account "forever" and the balance seems to go nowhere. After some investigation, it is usually because they were paying the minimum payment due on a credit card with a high interest rate.

What would have happened if you had kept the payment constant at $40 per month? Your numbers would then look like this:

Original Amount Borrowed	$2,000.00
Total Interest Payments	$1,724.54
Total Payments	$3,724.54

# of Monthly Payments to Payoff Credit Card	94
Or	
Years to Payoff Credit Card	7.83 yrs.

This is a big improvement over the first example, but it is still taking too long to payoff this credit card debt. Your objective should be to pay as much as you can so that you can liquidate the debt as quickly as possible. Now, let's take a look at what happens when you make a late payment on the account.

Using the same information in the previous example, let's assume that you owe $2,000 on this credit card and the card has a $2,000 credit limit. You mail them the minimum payment of $40, but your payment arrives one day after the payment is due. Your account activity will look like this:

Beginning Balance	$2,000.00
Accrued Interest	$29.80
Late Payment Fee	$29.00
Less Payments Received	$40.00
New Balance	$2,018.80

All of this seems rather routine except for one thing: Your balance is now over the credit limit of $2,000, so your account will be assessed an overlimit fee of $39. This brings your account balance to $2,057.80. In order to correct the problem, you must send $57.80 to bring your balance back down to $2,000 plus the regular minimum payment of $40, for a total of $97.80. This is more than double what you would have sent if the payment had gotten there on time. If you really couldn't afford to send the $40 in the first place, how are you going to be able to send $98.22? This is an example of how individuals get into financial trouble.

When you have pushed your debt load to the limit, you have very little room for error. One little mistake like the one in the previous example can push your financial situation out of control. Job loss, temporary layoffs, or unexpected expenses will only make things worse, but at a faster rate.

The Promise to Pay

Typically, when you borrow money from a bank, credit union, or any other type of financial institution, you will sign some type of credit agreement or promissory note. By signing that form, you are making a promise to pay back what you borrowed, plus any interest due based on the terms of the agreement. Even when you borrow money from family and friends, you are making a verbal promise to pay the money back.

As stated earlier, circumstances may arise that will keep you from fulfilling your promise to pay. Hopefully, your lender will try to work with you to come up with an alternative plan to repay the debt. However, it is a sin to intentionally break your promise to pay. It is written in Psalms 37:21 that "The wicked borroweth, and payeth not again: but the righteous sheweth mercy, and giveth." This scripture speaks to the ways of the wicked in two ways. First, the wicked often live by borrowing and are usually overburdened by debt. Therefore they can't pay back their debts because they don't have the ability to do so. Next, the wicked will also borrow with no intent to ever repay the debt. They have the ability to pay it back; they just won't do it. All of this is sin and goes against God's laws and principles.

The words of Solomon in Ecclesiastes 5:5 encourages us to think carefully before we take on debt:

Better *is it* that thou shouldest not vow, than that thou shouldest vow and not pay.

If you make a promise to pay, you are expected to honor that promise. If you think that there is a chance that you might not be able to honor that promise, then it is best that you not borrow the money at all.

When Debt Becomes A Burden

How can you tell if you have become overburdened with debt? There are usually a few telltale signs:

- Frequent late payment notices
- Calls at home and your job from bill collectors
- Putting off doctor's appointments to save on co-payments
- Frequently returned checks due to insufficient funds
- Increasing inability to meet your family's basic needs of food, clothing, and shelter
- Continued use of savings to pay your bills

If you are experiencing one or more of the above on a regular basis, it is likely that you have a debt problem. Recognize it for what it is and begin the process to change it.

Christians should have a natural aversion to debt. Excessive debt can get in the way of your relationship with God. Consider Proverbs 22:7:

The rich ruleth over the poor, and the borrower is servant to the lender.

When you are overburdened with debt, you are a financial slave. If you don't believe me, try missing a few payments and see what happens! Your creditors (masters?) will respond in a variety of ways to compel you to pay. Scripture further tells us that you cannot serve two masters, for you will love one and hate the other (Matthew 6:24). Constantly dealing with debt problems can cause you to lose focus on how to live as God would have you to live. There is tremendous pressure and stress when you are overburdened with debt. This can spill over into other areas of your life. It can affect your performance at work. It can affect your relationship with your family and friends.

Some people experience some or all of the signs of being overburdened with debt, but don't believe that they have a problem. The typical excuse that I hear is "everybody runs a little behind on their bills." In today's world, running a little behind on your bills has become a way of life for many people. The world would love for you to believe that this is normal. Don't fool yourself. If late payments and bill collectors are commonplace in your life, there is a problem and you need to try and fix it. It won't be easy, but the problem can be fixed.

Strategies for Getting Out of Debt

There have been times when I have met with clients to develop a strategy to eliminate their debt, and they will sometimes have the look of a deer staring at the headlights of car as it heads toward them, down a dark highway. They are dazed and confused as to what is coming, and paralyzed with fear. If they don't move or take action, they may meet a much worse fate, never knowing what hit them.

There is a four-step process to getting out of debt:

- Turn It Over To God
- Develop A Plan
- Increase Your Cash Flow
- Be Patient

Turn It Over To God

The very first step that you must take to get out of debt is to turn the problem over to God. You must recognize that you can't do it alone, and that you need His divine guidance and wisdom to help you make good decisions about how to proceed. God has all power to solve any problem. You must have complete confidence in Him. You will not see results without faith.

When you turn your problem over to God, it doesn't mean that there isn't anything else for you to do. In fact, it usually means you will have a lot of work to do. As I said before, God is a God of nature. He speaks to us in the natural and supernatural occurrence of events. You will have to make some sacrifices. You may have to face embarrassment and shame. You will have to focus more on things that you need instead of things you want. It will be a humbling experience, but God will lead you in the right direction.

Develop A Plan

To reduce or eliminate your debt, you must develop a plan. First and foremost, you must change the behavior that got you into this position in the first place. Sure, there are unexpected things that happen that can cause you to get into debt. But for many, debt problems are a result of constant overspending, access to easy credit, and poor financial planning. There is an old saying that says that the definition of insanity is doing the same thing over and over, but expecting different results each time. If you want to get out of debt, change the habits that helped put you there.

As you continue to develop your plan to get out of debt, make a list of all of your bills and expenses. Group all household and living expenses together. This list should include such items as telephone, cable or satellite television, electricity, or any other utilities. It should also include such items as groceries, gas for your car, dry cleaning, etc. Then group all of your installment and revolving debt together. Finally, make sure you include other expenses such as dining out and entertainment. Figure 6-1 is an example of a budget worksheet that you could use help develop your plan.

Once you have put your list together, you should scan the list and place an "A," "B," or "C" by each item. A-rated items are those that are absolutely necessary for you to physically survive. For most people, these will be items that revolve around food and shelter, such as groceries, rent, or your mortgage. B-rated items are those that are necessary for you to earn a living. These will be things like car payments, gas for the car, auto insurance, or other transportation expenses such as bus, train, or cab fare. C-rated items are those others items in your budget that are for the comforts of life. These are things like cable television, dining out, consumer electronics, etc. The purpose of this rating system is to get you to prioritize your spending. Don't let your car get repossessed, or get evicted from your apartment, or have your home foreclosed upon, trying to keep your

Table 6-1

Sample Budget Worksheet

Instructions:

Place the letter A by any expenses that are necessary for you to live. Place the letter B by any expenses that are necessary for you to work. Place the letter C by any expenses that are optional

INCOME
Salary/Wages _____
Commissions _____
Bonus _____
Business Income _____
Interest/Dividends _____
Total Income _____

EXPENSES
____ Mortgage/Rent _____
____ Utilities _____
____ Auto Loan _____
____ Credit Cards _____
____ Personal Loans _____
____ Cell Phone _____
____ Food and Grocery _____
____ Clothing _____
____ Laundry/Dry Cleaning _____
____ Medical _____
____ Child Care _____
____ Gasoline _____
____ Auto Insurance _____
____ Cable/Satellite TV _____
____ Restaurants _____
____ Church Contributions _____
____ Personal Care _____
____ Emergencies _____
____ Other Expenses _____
Total Expenses _____

cable television connected!

As you develop your plan to reduce your debt, and eventually become debt-free, you should examine your current cash flow with several objectives in mind. If you don't have any savings set aside to cover emergencies and unexpected items, take the monthly payment from the bill you just paid off and begin to put it into a savings account. Do this so that you can reduce the likelihood that you will have to go into debt again when something comes up.

Once you feel that you have enough in your savings to cover emergencies, you should take the money available from a bill that has been paid off, and apply it as an extra payment on another bill. This strategy not only allows you payoff a bill faster, but it saves you money on interest charges as well. Let's look at an example.

David and Mary have been paying their bills on time, but it seems that they can never get ahead. They want to reduce their debt, but they aren't sure how to do it. Here is what they owe:

Debt Type	Interest Rate	Monthly Pmt	Balance
Car Loan	7.50%	$309.26/mo.	$9,942.00
Dept. Store	18.00%	2% or $25 min.	$426.32
Line of Credit	18.00%	3% or $15 min.	$1,119.56
Credit Card	14.99%	2% or $10 min.	$6,194.87
		Total Debt	**$17,682.75**

Based on the minimum payments on all of their debts, they are currently paying out about $490.26 per month. If they just pay the minimum payment that is asked for every month, it will take them 400 months (33.33 years) to pay everything off. The total of all of their payments would be $29,005.49, of which $11,475.99 is interest. After reviewing their budget, David and Mary believe that they can apply $500 per month toward paying off their bills. After doing some research, they determine that they should attack the bills by paying the ones with the highest interest rates first, and then apply any dollars freed up from paid-off accounts to the remaining balances. David and Mary put together the following debt plan with estimates of when they will payoff a bill and the interest they will save:

Debt Type	# of Months to Payoff	Interest Paid	Interest Saved
Dept. Store	12	$35.45	$25.73
Line of Credit	24	$253.71	$536.93
Car Loan	36	$1,113.79	$0.00
Credit Card	45	$2,421.51	$7,088.87
Plan Totals		$3,824.46	$7,651.53

This debt plan looks like a good and works for several reasons. First, they were able to find an extra $9.74 per month to put towards their bills ($490.26 + $9.74 = $500). Although this doesn't seem like much, every little bit helps. Next, by keeping their monthly debt service payments at $500 per month instead of paying minimum payments each month, they were able to payoff these bills in 45 months instead of 33.33 years. Since they were used to paying $500 per month, David and Mary stayed committed to using all of those funds for paying off debt. Once they paid off the department store account, they took those funds and applied them toward the line of credit. The line of credit was soon paid off and they applied those funds to the credit card. Finally, when they paid off their car, they used those funds to help finish paying the credit card. Best of all, by being committed to reducing their debt, they saved $7,651.53 in interest, which is a lot of money. Now they can focus on possibly buying a home or investing for their family's future. They didn't get out of debt overnight, but they were able to do it much faster than if they had never sat down and developed a plan.

You can do what David and Mary did. In fact, here are some other things you can do to further reduce your interest expense and become debt-free. First, contact your creditors and try to get them to lower your interest rate. If it is a credit card account, some lenders will lower it with just your phone call. If it is any other type of debt, you may have to refinance the debt to get a lower rate. Either of these steps will be dependent on how well you have paid on the account for the last year or so. If you have made several late payments, do not expect them to lower your interest rate. As you get your debts under control, remember that this can be a strategy to further improve the situation.

Next, if you are substantially behind on your bills and have been delinquent in paying them for some time, you may want to try to negotiate a final settlement. Many creditors will settle for an amount that is less than the current amount that is due just to get the account off of its books. However, this debt reduction tactic requires that you have access to cash in order to pay the amount that you and your creditors settle upon. Also, if the settled amount represents a discount of more than $600 from the actual balance owed, the creditor is required to generate a Form 1099-C. You will be required to report the discount on your tax return as income, and pay taxes on it.

The steps that I just described for getting out of debt are basically what a debt management or credit counseling company will do for you. By doing it yourself, you can save on the fees that some of the companies charge. If you feel like you need the counseling services that some of these companies offer, or for some reason you think that it will work better for you to just have one payment for your bills, these companies can help. However, you should proceed with caution before signing up with any of these firms.

Most of these companies are non-profit organizations, which might lead you to believe that they are performing some type of public service. Many years ago, most of the companies were truly service oriented, and offered credit counseling, education programs, and budgeting services in addition to debt management programs (DMPs). However, in recent years, there has been an explosion in the number of debt management companies. Although you would expect that since there are more debt management companies, more programs and services are now available. Unfortunately, many of these companies offer fewer services and in fact, some offer DMPs only.

Which leads me to ask why are there so many debt management companies around now? Are there that many people wanting to help others with credit problems? More importantly, are they really willing to do it and not make a profit? Sadly, the answer is no.

Even if you are a non-profit organization, you have to get funding from somewhere to pay for the staff and overhead for the organization. There are grants available from various foundations to help fund financial literacy programs, which provide similar services to what these debt management companies offer. But most of these debt management companies get there funding from two sources: you and your creditors. Here's how it works.

The debt management process is really controlled by creditors. Through the years, there has been an informal creditor policy to rebate part of the payments collected in a DMP to the debt management company. This is what has been commonly referred to as "fair share." Many years ago, this rebate was as much as 15% of the amount collected. However, this figure now averages about 8%. Even though the fair share contributions are voluntary, they are nevertheless expected by the debt management company.

Creditors made these payments because the debt management companies performed a valuable service for them. In addition to collecting payments (debt management companies are really a form of collection agency), the credit counseling and education services offered were of benefit to creditors as well. These services were a form of intervention that could help avoid bankruptcy, which could cause creditors to lose even more money. They could also help clients get back on track so that they could become good customers of the creditors in the future.

Since fair share fees have declined, many debt management companies have been forced to reduce or eliminate services. To make up the gap in funding, they have also begun to charge for their services. Many have a sliding scale that is based on your ability to pay. When you sign up for a DMP, you usually pay some type of set up fee. This fee varies, but can be as much as your entire first-month payment into the program. Then, built into your consolidated payment is something called a voluntary contribution. The term "voluntary" may be questionable because it is not entirely clear that you have a choice in paying the fee. This fee varies as well, but can be as much as 10% of your monthly payment.

I don't have a problem with paying a fee for services rendered. What I do have a problem with is a for-profit company masquerading as a non-profit organization. Many of these companies characterize these fees as charitable contributions when they are not. Only amounts over and above the value of the services rendered can be characterized as charitable contribution. In most cases, the fees charged are for services rendered only.

Some of these companies generate millions of dollars in excess of their expenses, and provide no other services to their clients outside of DMPs. Sweetheart deals with affiliated companies allow the owners to extract these profits through less than arm's length transactions. Need counseling? Sorry, they don't provide that or if they do, it'll cost you. Need help in developing a budget? Sorry, they don't provide that either or if they do, it'll cost you. Want to attend a seminar? Sorry, they don't provide that at all. You get the picture.

The appeal of these firms is very strong. They typically claim to be able to cut your payments in half, sharply reduce your interest rates, or significantly reduce the amount of time needed to payoff your debts. But can they?

Sharply reducing your payments can only be achieved by reducing your interest rates, extending your term, or both. When offered any of these solutions, make sure that any reduced payment is enough to pay both principal and interest. Next, you should make sure that any refinance of your debt does not significantly extend your terms. This could lead to you paying more in total payments over time. Finally, since debt management companies can only deal with unsecured debt, some of them may arrange for your debt to be refinanced with an affiliated company. High interest rates and hidden fees can drive up your costs, and leave you in worse shape than when you started.

Next, there is nothing magical about reducing the amount of time needed to payoff your debts. Creditors will sometimes reduce or waive fees, which will allow you to pay the debt off faster. Some of them will "re-age" the account, which has the effect of taking all of the past due payments and fees and putting them at the end of the term. This brings your account current and stops all of the late fees and penalties from accruing. Finally, if you can lower your interest rate and pay more than the minimum payment due, you will pay the debt off early because more of your payment is going to reduce the principal.

Bottom line, you need to understand what you're getting into. If you have really bad credit, it is unlikely that these companies will be able to do much to improve your situation. If your credit is pretty good, but you're just struggling to pay your bills, you can probably save yourself a lot of money by tackling the problem yourself. Many of the debt management strategies offered by debt management companies are available directly to you from the creditor if you just ask.

Again, not all of these companies are bad. Some of them do a good job of providing a complete package of debt counseling and management, and they are worth the fees that they charge. Just like anything else, make sure you do your homework before you get one of these companies to help you get out of debt.

Increase Your Cash Flow

I know that increasing your cash flow is easier said than done. Nevertheless, it is an important part of trying to reduce your debt. Cash flow is a function of your income and expenses. Therefore, you can increase your cash flow by increasing your income or decreasing your expenses.

As we discussed in the previous section, you should take the cash that's available once you payoff one of your debts, and apply it to another. However, you should also look for other ways to increase your income. This will give you more money to use for debt liquidation. Here are some suggestions for increasing your income:

- Make sure you're being paid what you are worth at your current job. Check out job salary surveys at your local library or on the Internet. One of my favorite websites is Salary.com. This site provides basic salary information at no charge, and more detailed information for a fee. They also offer articles on salary negotiation. Use this information to negotiate a better increase at your present job, or a competitive salary at your next one.
- Ask your current employer for overtime. Maybe they have

some special projects or assignments that need to be completed. You could do the work, save your employer the expense of hiring someone from a temporary agency, and earn some extra money.

- Look for a second job. I know this is difficult when you already have a job, but the extra money earned can really make a difference. If you are in a profession that lends itself to freelance work, taking on a few extra projects can help out in the same way.

As I said before, you can also increase your cash flow by decreasing your expenses. This is one of the hardest aspects of trying to get out of debt because it means we have to spend less money. It is our spending behavior that got us into debt in the first place, and behaviors are the hardest thing to try to change.

Reducing my spending was the hardest thing I had to do when I began my plan to reduce my debt. I hated it because in order for you to reduce your spending, you have to know where you spend all of your money. I would do a budget, and it would tell me how much extra money that I should have left over to make extra payments on my bills. However, what I actually had left over was much lower. Where was my money going?

To find out where my money was going, I decided to write down what I purchased every time I spent money. This was a pain in the neck to do, but it really opened my eyes. I used to think that there were money gremlins that would wait until I went to sleep and quietly take money out of my wallet. They would only take a few dollars—just enough so I wouldn't notice. However, once I started tracking my spending, I soon found out that there were no gremlins. I found the enemy, and the enemy was me.

Here's what typically happened. I would get $100 dollars out of my account to use as my spending money for the next two weeks. This money was to cover daily lunches, snacks, newspapers, magazines, or other items for general entertainment. To my dismay, it seemed that my $100 dollars never made it to the end of the two-week period.

It seemed like every other day, at least one of my children was asking for $10 to pay for some field trip or other activity at their school. Whenever I had to pick up my children from school, and take them to an after-school activity, they would profess to be starving and near death. To keep from having to explain to my wife why our children fainted under my watch, I would stop at a fast food restaurant to get them a snack. There were other times when, on my way from work, I would get a call from home to pick up that "one thing" we needed from the grocery store. Unfortunately, it seemed that I could never leave the grocery store with just that "one thing." Before I knew it, my $100 was gone, and I still had two or three days left in the two-week period.

I also discovered that I was spending a lot of money on eating during the day. I usually spent about $4.50 on my lunch each day, and about $1.50 on drinks and snacks. That worked out to be about $30 per week just for eating during the day. But when I looked at it on a yearly basis, I couldn't believe that I would end up spending over $1,500 on eating during the day. That seemed like way too much money to spend on lunch and snacks, but that's exactly what I was doing. I decided it was time to make a change.

The key to reducing your spending is learning how to be organized. My money kept disappearing because I was spending money on unplanned things that I soon forgot about. Once I learned where my money was going, the problem was fairly easy to fix.

The first thing that I did was to relentlessly encourage my kids to let me know, in advance, when they had an activity that required money. That way I could work it into my budget. The next thing that I did was to make a grocery list, stuck to it, and tried not to go to the grocery store but once a week. When the kids had activities after school, I tried to pack something for them that morning. This kept me from having to stop at fast food restaurants. All of these steps saved me about $750 over the course of a year.

None of this will work if you continue spending as you did before, or worse, create new debts. Remember, keep your spending down, get your income up, and you'll be debt-free before you know it.

Be Patient

This is probably the most important of the four steps. You didn't get into debt overnight, so you shouldn't expect to get out of debt overnight. Develop a realistic debt plan that you can handle and stick to it. I have often heard people pray for God to give them patience. God will not give you patience. However, He will allow you to go through situations that will give you the opportunity to learn patience. In James 1:3–4, we are told of the value of patience in our Christian walk:

3 Knowing *this*, that the trying of your faith worketh patience.
4 But let patience have *her* perfect work, that ye may be perfect and entire, wanting nothing.

As you try to work through your debt plan, your faith will be tried. There will be many things that will come your way, tempting you to abandon your plan. This is how you develop patience. Stay on course. Verse 4 speaks to letting patience "do her thing" in preparing you for your eternal reward. In doing so, your desires for earthly possession decrease because you know that they cannot compare to what awaits you in Heaven. Learning to distinguish between your wants and needs is a wonderful blessing, especially when you are trying to reduce your debt, or become debt free. Patience will be a wonderful companion to guide you through this journey. Embrace her and hold her hand.

Strategies For Staying Out Of Debt

The best strategy for staying out of debt is to try to pay for as much as possible with cash. Recognize debt for the potential problems it can cause in your life and stay away from it. Again, Solomon offers some good advice in Proverbs 27:12:

A prudent *man* foreseeth the evil, *and* hideth himself; *but* the simple pass on, *and* are punished.

This scripture very simply tells us that if you see something heading your way that is bad for you, you need to run and hide! It is foolish (simple) to keep going on, doing the same things you were doing before, knowing that you will get hurt (punished). Excessive debt is an evil that we should all try to avoid.

Here are some other tips to help you stay out of debt:

- Build up an emergency reserve to help cover unexpected expenses
- Avoid impulse purchases. Don't go shopping just to kill time, or shop for groceries while you are really hungry. You'll end up buying something you hadn't planned to buy. Don't spend money on little things just because they cost only a "few dollars." Little things can add up.
- Use lump sums wisely. Tax refunds, inheritances, or monetary gifts should be used to liquidate or eliminate debt, rather than spent on additional purchases.
- Make a budget and stick to it. A budget is your spending plan. It will help keep you on track. If it's not in the budget, don't spend it.
- Pray. It is written in Proverbs 16:9 that "A man's heart deviseth his way: but the LORD directeth his steps." Ask God to guide your steps so that your spending decisions will be wise ones.

Staying out of debt is a lifelong battle that we all will have to face. Remember, man cannot serve two masters, for he will love one and hate the other. Staying debt free allows you to completely focus on your relationship with God. Make staying out of debt a lifelong goal.

What About Bankruptcy?

As a Christian, your promise to repay any money that you have borrowed should be taken very seriously. However, as a matter of last resort, you may have to consider bankruptcy.

Bankruptcy is a legal proceeding authorized by the federal government to provide individuals and businesses relief from the burden of excessive debt. It also provides an orderly process through which the net proceeds from the liquidation of your assets can be distributed among your creditors.

There are two things that you should do before you file bankruptcy: think and pray. Especially in times of financial difficulty, you need to be in constant prayer. Ask God for wisdom and wise counsel so that you will make good decisions. As you go through these difficult times, prayerfully consider all options. Bankruptcy is not a solution for all financial problems.

One of the first things you may need to do is lose some of your pride. I have seen too many situations where people in financial difficulty failed to make a proper decision because their pride got in the way. Solomon told us in Proverbs 16:18 that "Pride *goeth* before destruction, and an haughty spirit before a fall." While it is always important to maintain your dignity, losing some of your pride early in the process may give you the opportunity to solve your financial problems in ways other than bankruptcy.

This may mean that you have to sell your house. I know that you may have a certain standard of living that you want to maintain, but be aware that bricks, mortar, and personal possessions do not make a house a home. A smaller home, an apartment, or a grass hut can provide the same nurturing environment as your previous home if it is filled with love. Don't be afraid to sell your car. Sure, people may wonder why you're driving a less expensive car, or riding the bus to work, but at least you don't have that payment hanging over your head. The bottom line is that you can always reacquire these things once your financial situation improves.

Some of your creditors may be willing to work with you because they do not want to see you file for bankruptcy. It's not necessarily because they care about your plight, but mainly because they have a better chance of recovering more of the delinquent balance when they negotiate a payment plan on their own instead of through a bankruptcy court settlement. If you are not confident in handling this process on your own, seek out a reputable credit counseling organization.

If it still boils down to filing bankruptcy, there are two types that are available to individuals: Chapter 7 and Chapter 13. Each bankruptcy type is named after the section or chapter of Federal statutes that govern them. Chapter 7 bankruptcy is often referred to as a "straight" or "liquidation" bankruptcy. Chapter 13 is often referred to as "wage earner" or "repayment" plans. Because bankruptcy is a legal proceeding, I recommend that you consult a qualified bankruptcy attorney.

There are advantages and disadvantages to filing for bankruptcy. The advantages are as follows:

- It stops most legal proceedings and collection efforts from your creditors. This is important because it reduces some of the stress of the situation. Also, if your employer keeps getting requests to garnish your wages, you could lose your job.

- If you are filing Chapter 7, most of your debts will be discharged, which gives you a chance for a "new start." Your assets will be liquidated to help pay creditors. Your existing creditors will have no claim on your future assets or income. If you are filing Chapter 13, you get some time to work out your debt problems under reasonable terms (usually 3 to 5 years). If you file Chapter 13, and your financial situation worsens, you may be able to petition the courts to convert your filing to Chapter 7.

- Depending on how you file, and the state you live in, you may be able to exempt some of your assets from creditor claims.

- Because you will have difficulty in obtaining credit when you emerge from bankruptcy, you will have to learn to pay cash for everything. Because Christians should have a natural aversion to debt, this may be an opportunity for you to learn behaviors that will help keep you debt free.

The disadvantages are as follows:

- Bankruptcy is just as much of an emotional issue as it is a financial one. It can affect your self-esteem. More importantly, you need to examine the behaviors or circumstances that may have contributed to your financial problems, and put steps in place to correct them.
- A bankruptcy filing can remain on your credit report for up to ten years. It also becomes a matter of public record. This can make it difficult to obtain credit in the future. Also, if you are able to obtain credit, it may be at significantly higher interest rates.

You can recover from bankruptcy. It is not the end of the world. Use the situation as an opportunity for self-examination. Have an honest discussion with yourself regarding the financial mistakes that you may have made, and develop a plan to minimize the likelihood that you'll have to go through it again.

The Credit Report: Your Financial Scoreboard

Your credit report is a report that shows how you have handled any accounts where you have borrowed money. Put another way, it is your financial scoreboard. Potential and existing creditors look at your credit report to determine what kind of credit risk you are.

Many credit bureaus now use a credit scoring system to evaluate your credit history. One of the more popular systems in use today is one developed by Fair, Isaac & Company (FICO). The FICO® credit score is an evaluation of how you have you have handled credit in the past. The credit scoring system doesn't mark you as being a good or bad credit risk. It just computes a score. Lenders use the score to determine whether you are a good or bad credit risk. In fact, the credit score is just one of many factors that a lender will use to determine if you are credit worthy.

To generate your FICO® Score, the information in your credit file is evaluated in the these five categories:

- Payment History
- Amounts Owed
- Length Of Credit History
- New Credit
- Types of Credit Use

Your payment history is your track record. Any late payments in your payment history will bring your score down. The more late payments you have, the more your score will be negatively impacted. Also, the more recent the late payments, the more your score will be negatively impacted. Any accounts with a good payment history will raise your score.

Delinquent payments, judgements, and collection items usually stay on your credit report for seven years. Paying off a delinquent account or closing a delinquent account will not remove it from your file. However, once you start paying your bills on time, the delinquent items in your file will have less impact as time goes on.

Your credit score is also affected by the total amount of debt that you owe to your creditors. Owing money on a credit card is not necessarily a bad thing. A balance owed on many different accounts is a bad thing, and will probably lower your score.

The length of your credit history is important too. How long have you been borrowing money? Has it been for a few months or many years? The longer your credit history, the better it is. If you have a long credit history, your potential lender can see how you have handled your accounts through a variety of economic conditions, or personal circumstances.

Your score is also based on the amount of new credit that you have secured. Several new credit accounts may be a red flag to a potential lender that you may be about to overextend your self. Finally, your score will also take into account the types of credit that you use. Do you have a lot of credit cards, or is there more of a balance between credit cards, a mortgage, and installments loans?

The following is a list of things that can lower your FICO® Score:

- Serious delinquency
- Serious delinquency, and public record or collection filed
- Derogatory public record or collection filed
- Time since delinquency is too recent or unknown
- Level of delinquency on accounts
- Number of accounts with delinquency
- Amount owed on accounts
- Proportion of balances to credit limits on revolving accounts is too high
- Length of time accounts have been established
- Too many accounts with balances

If your credit request is denied, the lender may use up to four of the above reasons to explain why.

I am often asked whether you can simply pay someone to fix your credit and magically make your credit problems go away. The answer is no! In reality, the only way that you can repair your credit is to start paying your bills on time. There are some companies that claim that they can repair your credit for a fee. In most cases, they send letters challenging the validity of the credit item in question. The creditor has 30 days to respond to the letter. If they don't respond, the credit bureau will remove the item. Most companies respond within the 30-day period.

These are all things that you can do yourself, so it makes little sense to pay someone to do it for you. More important, no amount of letter writing will remove items that are there legitimately. If you have bad credit because you really did not pay your bills on time, don't waste your time or money on sending letters. Just start paying your bills on time and payoff any judgements or collection items that are showing as unpaid. Taking care of these items will help nurse your credit rating back to health.

Excessive debt takes away from your ability to build financial wealth. Poor credit makes it even harder and raises the cost of living in many areas of your life. Looking for a better paying job? If you have poor credit, you may not get one because many companies will now check your credit report before they hire you. Would you like to buy a home? Your credit score will have significant influence on you being approved and the interest rate you are offered. A poor credit score could increase your costs for borrowing by 25% or more.

Your credit score is now being used to determine whether you can get home or auto insurance. More and more companies are beginning to use it to determine how and if you will able to use services that are important for you to make it day-to-day. If you have to pay double what other people are paying for normal living expenses, you will soon begin to feel as if you can't make any progress. If you have good credit, make sure you keep it that way. If your credit history could use some improvement, make sure you take the steps now to improve it.

Chapter 7
Investing

Why Should You Invest?

You should invest because doing so allows you to achieve one or more of your financial goals. Whether it is for retirement, your child's education, buying your first home, or starting your own business, do it because it is something you need to do. You should never invest just because you see others doing it and you think that it will help you get "stuff" like them.

The attraction of financial wealth is strong. Most of our images of success are associated with being rich. When you are wealthy and the world knows it, people automatically think of you as being smart, glamorous, or famous. These are all things that stroke the ego and can make you feel good. Given all that we know about financial wealth, who wouldn't want to be rich? But things are not what they always seem. Financial wealth also breeds some other attributes: envy and greed.

The following verses in Psalms 73:2–3 warn us of the folly we face when we invest just because we are envious of what others have accumulated:

> 2 But as for me, my feet were almost gone; my steps had well nigh slipped.
> 3 For I was envious at the foolish, when I saw the prosperity of the wicked.

The foolish, as referenced here are those who do not fear God. These tend to be people who are very full of themselves. Oftentimes they are successful and proud of the many things that they have achieved, and the many possessions they have obtained. They attribute all that they have to their hard work and luck. They are wise in the ways of the world, but are spiritually foolish because they do not

100

recognize God's grace and mercy. Unfortunately, we sometimes see the many things that they have, contrasted with the many things we don't have, and envy begins to set in.

You're living right. You're doing all that God has commanded you to do. But it seems that others that aren't quite as "righteous" as you are enjoying a life of prosperity. The temptation is that if the wicked are investing and appear to be prosperous, then maybe you should try it too. Don't be fooled. Any investment program that is not guided by the Word of God ultimately will not be successful. When you decide to invest, make sure that it is for the right reasons.

Greed is also a big factor in not only deciding whether or not to invest, but also in how we invest. Consider the following:

1 Timothy 6:9–10
9 But they that will be rich fall into temptation and a snare, and into many foolish and hurtful lusts, which drown men in destruction and perdition.
10 For the love of money is the root of all evil: which while some coveted after, they have erred from the faith, and pierced themselves through with many sorrows.

Money is not the root of all evil. It is the *love of money* that is the root of all evil. If you ask most Christians whether or not they would ever worship a false god, they would emphatically tell you no. However, there are many Christians who are involved in unspiritual activities simply because of an anticipated financial reward. Yes, there is no golden calf or other graven image that they are bowing down to, but they are spiritually bowing down to the almighty dollar.

Understanding greed and how it can affect your financial decision making is an important step in limiting its impact. We are all bombarded with messages that are designed to appeal to our personal level of greed. How many of the following headlines have you seen recently?:

• Get rich now

- Follow these easy steps on your road to riches
- Retire rich today!
- Five easy steps to financial independence

Some of these headlines are so enticing, that it is really hard not to at least check them out to find out more. Before you do, let me share some things with you.

Economics is the study of the production, distribution, and consumption of goods and services. More simply stated, it is the study of supply and demand. It was also one of the courses that I took as an undergraduate at the University of Georgia that I absolutely despised. My feelings about Economics could be summed up in one word: boring. Many years later, I decided to attend graduate school at Wake Forest University and soon discovered that I had to take economics again. Although I was older, and hopefully wiser, I still dreaded having to take Economics again. This time, however, it wasn't so bad. In fact, I learned a few things.

There are some economic facts that you just can't get around in this world. First, capital that is ready to be invested will seek the easiest path with the highest return in accordance to an acceptable level of risk. Those who invest first can sometimes make above normal or abnormal profits. However, if the path to these high profits is easy, the investment will attract more and more investors. As more and more investors pour into the investment, the level of profitability begins to decline, until it becomes normal or below normal. This led me to one of many realizations. First, if it were really that easy to make exceptional returns on an investment over a long period of time, everyone would be doing it because it is easy. Next, the only way to sustain above normal or abnormal profits is to make it hard for others to do what you are doing, or engage in an activity that is illegal. Hoping you're not interested in illegal activities, legal examples of this would be investments that are monopolistic, have a high barrier to entry, or are protected by patents.

I have learned through the years that there are a lot of smart people in this world. There is very little, if anything, in the investing world that is not already known. New investments or investment strategies are usually modifications of something that is already in existence. If this so called new thing turns out to be very profitable, you can be sure that many others will start to use it. Eventually, these fast and easy profits will get harder and harder to come by. Building financial wealth usually takes hard work, time, and patience. Greed makes you think that there are shortcuts. Get rich quick programs are usually well-organized schemes to separate you from your money. This is what the Apostle Paul is telling us in 1 Timothy 6:9. An excessive desire to be rich can cause you to fall prey to investment scams or extremely risky investments (...into temptation and a snare, and into many foolish and hurtful lusts). If the investment goes bad, as it usually does, it can lead to financial difficulty or ruin (...which drown men in destruction and perdition).

What Are the Risks of Investing?

There is a difference between risk and uncertainty. Risk is the chance that something might happen. Risk is something that can be measured. Uncertainty is a much different animal. Uncertainty is having no knowledge as to whether or not an event will happen. Uncertainty is very difficult to measure. Therefore, it can have a very stifling effect on markets and individual investment decisions. The risks of investing come in four forms: volatility, loss of principal, loss of opportunity, and fraud. Let's discuss each one.

Volatility describes how the price or value of your investment will fluctuate over time. Various investments will fluctuate in different ways. More conservative investments such as savings accounts, money market funds, and certificates of deposit fluctuate very little or not at all. Other investments, such as stocks, can fluctuate a lot. Volatility is based on two types of risk: systematic and unsystematic.

Systematic risk is risk that relates to the entire market in general. If the market is up, then your investment will go up in value. It's not because your investment did anything special. Think of it as water in a bathtub and your investment is a toy boat. If you let water out of the tub, the toy boat (your investment) will float lower with the lower water level. Add water to the tub, it will rise to the higher water level.

Unsystematic risk is risk that is specific to your investment or the industry that your investment participates in. Your investment is in a car traveling down a highway. There are other investments similar to yours, riding in the same car. If the car breaks down, it's probably not going to affect other cars traveling down the same highway. If the car crashes, all riders (investments) in the car may suffer injuries of varying proportions, or worse death (bankruptcy?). Finally, it could be that your investment gets a case of "car sickness" and all other riders are just fine.

The next type of risk is loss of principal. When you invest, you can lose some of your principal either through the assessment of fees or penalties, or by selling the investment for less than what you paid for it. Volatility, as manifested through systematic or unsystematic risk, can put you in a position to suffer a loss of principal.

Another type of risk is the loss of opportunity, or what we sometimes call opportunity cost. Anytime you make an investment decision, you must weigh the expected gain from your investment decision against the investment potential of your other investment options. Suppose you decided to purchase a three-year CD for $1,000 with an interest rate of 4%, compounded daily. At the end of the three-year period you will have earned $127.49 in interest. Let's also assume that at the same time, you had the choice to invest the same amount into a mutual fund that you felt pretty sure would pay you 8% per year for the same term. If the mutual fund did generate returns of 8% per year, compounded daily, your earnings would have been $271.22.

Choosing the CD over the mutual fund potentially "cost" you the opportunity to earn an additional $143.73 in earnings. What you have to ask yourself is "Was it worth it?" Was it worth it to have the safety of the CD? Possibly, because the mutual fund could have earned much less than 8%, or suffered losses instead of gains. But the mutual fund could have earned much more than 8% as well. How much will the lower rate of return on the CD impact your success in achieving your financial goals? If you have a particular goal that requires a rate of return of at least 6%, and you're consistently purchasing investments with rates of return that are lower than that, eventually you will be faced with a dilemma. You will either have to start choosing investments with much higher rates of return, therefore exposing you to more risk, or you will have to extend the time needed to achieve your goal. The opportunity to earn or lose on a particular investment is an important factor that should be considered when choosing any investment.

Another type of risk is fraud. This is simply where someone lies, cheats, or misleads in order to steal your money. This type of thievery has been around since the beginning of time, but as technology progresses, the sophistication of fraud progresses as well. More than ever, you need to be on guard to help prevent fraud from happening to you.

How do you become a victim of fraud? In some cases, it happens without your knowledge. Examples of this are embezzlement and identity theft. But fraud can also take place with you as a willing participant. These types of frauds are usually in the form of investment or business "opportunities."

Christians tend to be more susceptible to scams and hustlers because they believe they should be more trusting. Crooks know this because many of these frauds are committed under the guise of Christians helping Christians. In fact, it has been said that of all the scams that are out there, more money has been stolen in the name God than any other way. However, do not allow your trust to be abused because of lack of knowledge on your part.

When I meet someone who has been the victim of a scam, they are often embarrassed and feel stupid. There are some people who are taken advantage of just because they didn't know better. However, most people who are scammed are people who would be classified as having more than adequate intelligence. The reason why this group of folks gets scammed is that they think that they know better. They let their guard down because they were looking for the obvious. They know that if it sounds too good to be true, it probably is. Rookie scamsters typically put together schemes that fall into this category, with little success against the "smart" people.

The seasoned scammer takes a totally different route. He (or she) will spend a lot of time making the scam seem reasonable. They will be very nice and pleasant. They will seem very interested and concerned about you. They will even kneel down with you to pray. This is all part of a strategy to gain your confidence (This is where the term "con man" comes from, which is a shortened form of "confidence man."). This is why I will hear the victim of this type of scam say that they checked everything out, and they don't understand what went wrong.

The bottom line in protecting yourself against this type of fraud is to never let your guard down. A common theme in many scams is the sense of urgency. Scamsters try to make you feel like if you don't make a decision right now, you will miss out on an opportunity of a lifetime. It is this rush to make a decision that can cause you to not think things through. Just remember this simple rule: The bigger your potential loss, the more thorough you should be in checking out the investment.

As your relationship with God grows, He will continue to bless you with knowledge. This knowledge will help you to become wise to the ways of the wicked. The following is a discussion of some common scams, and some tips on how to deal with them.

Unlicensed individuals selling securities – In most cases, you have to be licensed to sell securities. Securities are investments such as stocks, bonds, promissory notes, mutual funds, etc. When considering an investment, make sure the person offering the investment is licensed. You can call your state securities regulator to verify that a person is licensed or registered to sell securities. You can also check with the National Association of Securities Dealers. An unlicensed individual who is trying to sell you an investment may be a red flag. Make sure you check things out before you invest.

Internet fraud – The wide reach of the Internet, and its perceived anonymity, is used by scammers to "pump and dump" thinly traded stocks, peddle bogus investments, and publicize pyramid schemes. Some of these scammers set up websites that appear to be legitimate businesses, but are nothing more than a means to steal your money. Many states have set up Internet surveillance programs that watch for fraud or investigate investor complaints. However, many of these programs are understaffed and overwhelmed, as the number of suspicious websites along with investor complaints has exploded.

The Internet is a wonderful resource for information. The convenience and speed at which business can be conducted is amazing. However, none of these things relieve you of your responsibility to thoroughly check things out. Just remember that the same speed and convenience that can make your Internet experience pleasurable is available to crooks to help them steal your money.

Pyramid schemes – These are always popular because they appeal to people's desire to make quick and easy money. They usually promise investors high returns, and participants are encouraged to recruit new people to join their organization or "network." Some pyramid schemes are pure scams where early investors are paid from the funds received from new investors. As the pyramid expands, it becomes increasingly difficult to recruit new investors. Funds to pay existing investors begin to dry up and the pyramid collapses.

Other pyramid schemes are built upon businesses that sell a real product or service. Some of these are often referred to as multilevel marketing (MLM) programs. While there are some legitimate multilevel marketing programs, you should study them carefully before you join. Be wary of any program that requires you to pay money upfront to participate in the "opportunity," or requires you to purchase expensive training materials or minimum levels of inventory.

Additionally, the collapse of a MLM program that is really a pyramid scheme can take years because of its ability to continually recruit new people to take the place of the ones who drop out. For most pyramid schemes, 96% of the participants are in the bottom two levels. As long as the 4% in the top levels can continue to replace the dropouts in the bottom two levels, the pyramid will survive and they will continue to rake in the cash. This can go on for years and involve millions of people and billions of dollars.

Because of the potential devastation to you, your family, friends, or co-workers, additional care is required to avoid participating in a multilevel marketing program that is really a pyramid scheme. You could lose your life savings. You might decide to quit your job to pursue the "opportunity" full-time, only to soon find out you've made a big mistake. You could lose the trust and respect of your family, friends, and co-workers because you got them involved in something that turned out to be a scam. If someone has just about convinced you that this is an "opportunity of a lifetime," ask him or her for proof. Request a disclosure from the company showing the average payout to their distributors by percentile (highest 1% to the lowest 1%). Better yet, ask a current participant to show you their Schedule C from their federal tax return. This information will help you determine if the MLM is worth getting involved with.

Investment seminars and courses – These seminars and courses are often marketed through newspaper, radio, and TV ads, infomercials, and the Internet. They generate a lot of excitement and promise you information that will "change your life." There is usually a lot of talk about "getting rich," and secret techniques that have been "proven" to build wealth beyond measure. However, if you really want to know how to get rich like them, you have to buy some of the tapes, books, or videos that they have for sale. Bottom line, the only people getting rich are usually the ones running the seminar or teaching the course.

What is Your Time Horizon?

In managing your money, you should think of having three buckets in which to place your money. The first bucket is your short-term bucket. These are funds that you need for things that will happen within the next two years. This is money that you need for your day-to-day expenses, monthly bills, annual expenses, or emergency cash. The best types of investments for this bucket are checking accounts, savings accounts, money market funds, treasury bills, and short-term CDs. The next bucket is the medium-term bucket. This is for things that you might need within the next two to five years. This is money that you may need for things such as a down payment on a house, or the purchase or replacement of a

Table 7-1

What Is Your Time Horizon?
Make sure you put your investment dollars in the right bucket according to your goals.

Short-Term Horizon: 0–2 years

Short Term

Best Investment Choices: Checking Accounts, Savings Accounts, Money Market Funds, Treasury Bills, Treasury Notes, Bonds, and Certificates of Deposit

Medium-Term Horizon: 2–5 years

Medium Term

Best Investment Choices: Money Market Funds, Treasury Notes & Bonds, Municipal Bonds, Corporate Bonds, Mutual Funds, and Stocks

Long-Term Horizon: 5 years +

Long Term

Best Investment Choices: Treasury Bonds, Municipal Bonds, Corporate Bonds, Mutual Funds, and Stocks

vehicle. Or it could possibly be funds that you do not have a specific purpose for right now, but you want to be able to get to the funds with minimal restrictions or minimal risk to principal. Your best investments for this bucket are CDs, short-term bonds, conservative blue-chip stocks or mutual funds. The last bucket is the long-term bucket. This is for funds that you need for any long-term goal such as retirement, college education for your children or grandchildren, or just building up funds for your nest egg. Once you have defined your goals, it is just a matter of placing your funds in the proper bucket.

Asset Allocation

Asset allocation is the process through which investment resources are tactically assigned to various classes of assets, such as cash, stocks, bonds, precious metals, real estate, etc., in order to reduce risk. Now if that sentence didn't make any sense to you, that's okay. That was just my fancy way of saying "Don't put all of your eggs in one basket," which is something that I'm sure you have heard your parents or grandparents say.

Asset allocation isn't new. Solomon gave us some insight to the concept of asset allocation in Ecclesiastes 11:2:

Give a portion to seven, and also to eight; for thou knowest not what evil shall be upon the earth.

Verses 1 through 6 in this chapter actually refer to giving generously to the poor, or the less fortunate. In the first part of verse 2, Solomon encourages us to give a portion of our wealth to the seven (needy persons). If an eighth needy person shows up, give to him too. The reasoning behind such generous giving is found in the second part of the verse. We truly do not know when evil and hard times will come our way. Economic recessions and corporate downsizings may cause you to lose your job. An unexpected illness or injury may bring financial hardship. Your investments may lose significant value because of market conditions or corporate fraud. Any of these situations may cause you to have to depend on the generosity of others for help. If you have shown mercy and compassion to others in their time of need, it is very likely that they will show you the same in your time of need as well. Such giving is an investment in the lives of others and is sure to bring you many happy returns.

Asset allocation works the same way. When you spread your

investments among many different assets classes, one class of investment that is performing well can help offset another investment class that is not. The key to successful asset allocation is diversification. To diversify means to spread out or to use different types. In investing, you can diversify not only among assets classes, but within assets classes as well.

For example, you could decide to invest all of your money in stock. Your assets would be 100% allocated to stock, but they would not be diversified. If you were to put 25% of your money in cash, 50% in stock, and 25% in bonds, your asset allocation would be diversified because you have spread your money across three different asset classes.

As I mentioned before, you can diversify not only among assets classes, but within asset classes as well. For example, within the asset class of cash, you could invest in money market funds, bank savings accounts, and short-term CDs. If money market rates start going down, the fixed rate on your CD can help offset the lower rate. If you invest in real estate, you might divide your investment between residential and commercial rental property. This type of diversification can be done with stocks, bonds, mutual funds, and other types of investments as well.

How you allocate your investments will depend on several factors. A study by Brinson, Hood, and Beebower found that 93.6% of investment returns are attributable to asset allocation.[1] The remainder is due to market timing, securities selection, and choosing the right money manager. The real question is which sector or asset-class should your funds be in at a particular point in time. Investors need to understand the risks associated with the investments that they own or wish to purchase and measure them against their own fears. It is only by doing so that you will be able to build a portfolio that will meet your needs and help achieve your goals.

The best bottom-line explanation of diversification that I ever

---

[1] Determinants of Portfolio Performance, Brinson, Gary P; Hood, L. Randolph; Beebower, Gilbert L; Financial Analyst Journal; Jan/Feb 1995, pg. 133-138

heard comes from Nick Murray. Mr. Murray has been in the investment business since 1967 and has written several books for financial professionals and individual investors. Memorize this sentence and repeat it often. It will serve you well:

> "Diversification is the conscious choice not to make a killing
> in return for the all-important blessing of never getting
> killed!"

We've all heard about someone who made a "killing" (very high rate of return) on an investment. Maybe it was Joe down at the barbershop. Or maybe it was Sue who works in the purchasing department at work. We've all heard about someone who made a lot of money on some type of investment and is financially secure forever more. While some of these stories are probably true, it has been my experience that they are usually, at best, incomplete. Why? Because people love to talk about their winning investments. However, they hate to talk about their losing ones.

By its very nature, the bigger the potential "killing" in an investment, the bigger the chance that it might get "killed." As I stated before, investments that have a high potential rate of return usually have a high degree of risk associated with them. Put too much of your money in just one of these things, and your financial goals may be at the morgue waiting for you to identify their lifeless bodies.

Diversification helps you achieve a level of consistency that improves the likelihood that you will achieve your financial goals. When market conditions are good, you might not make as much money as others claim they are making, but you will make money. More importantly, when markets are bad, you probably won't lose as much money as everyone else. In fact, you might continue making money!

Successful financial planning is all about managing your investments in such a way that the odds of getting from point A to point B in your financial life are increasingly in your favor. Asset allocation is all about reducing risk. By limiting or eliminating your exposure to high-risk investments, or overexposure to one type of investment, you improve your chances for investment success.

That's the beauty of diversification through asset allocation. If you safely make it from point A to point B, you win. Your financial journey is not a race with others, so it doesn't matter how Joe or Sue did it. If you can reach your goals without taking a lot of risk, you will have peace of mind. That's a blessing that even King Solomon would be thankful for.

Your Investment Options

Once you are ready to invest, you have to decide which investments will best help you achieve your goals. As you begin to invest, you will start to assemble a portfolio. An investment portfolio is nothing more than a collection of investments. There are many investment options that are available and I will discuss some of the more popular ones. Make sure you understand the pros and cons of each, which are usually found in the prospectus. A prospectus details the features of an investment, such as stocks, bonds, and mutual funds. For each investment discussed in this chapter, I will try to answer these four questions:

- What is a (*name of investment here*)?
- How do you make money with it?
- What are the risks?
- What else do you need to know?

Savings Account

What is a savings account? – A savings account is an account that you open at a bank, savings & loan, or credit union.

How do you make money with a savings account? – While your money is deposited in the account, they will pay you interest. The amount of interest paid will vary, depending on the type of account, how much is deposited in the account, and general market conditions.

What are the risks? – There really isn't any risk at all. This type of account is usually insured up to $100,000 and is considered to be very safe.

What else do you need to know? – Even though your typical savings account may be insured, that insurance will not protect you in all circumstances. Account insurance, such as that provided by the Federal Deposit Insurance Corporation (FDIC), is meant to cover a bank failure that happens every once in a while. If there were massive bank failures occurring at the same time, it is unlikely that FDIC insurance would be able to cover all depositors at the same time. In circumstances such as this, you would probably receive a settlement that represented some percentage of your account balance.

Certificates of Deposit

What is a certificate of deposit? – Banks, savings & loans, and credit unions issue certificates of deposit (CDs). In exchange for tying you money up for some set period of time, the bank will pay you interest at a rate that is usually higher than what you would get in a regular savings account. CDs usually have a set term that can range anywhere from 7 days to 20 years. The interest rate is usually fixed for whatever time period your CD is set for.

How do you make money with CDs? – You make money on a CD by earning interest. The interest on the CD is handled one of two ways. One way is to have the interest earned on the CD to be paid to you as cash on a monthly, quarterly, semi-annually, or annual basis. The other way is to have the interest that is earned to be paid back (reinvested) into the CD. This is usually the best method because your interest earns interest and you get a bigger return.

Let's say you invested $500 into a 5-year CD and the current interest rate on that type of CD is 4.69%. That means for every $100 that you invest in this CD, they will pay you $4.69 per year. Since you invested $500, you would earn five times that amount or $23.45. Now remember that you can take your interest as cash when it's paid or you can have it paid back into the CD. Let's assume that you decided to have it paid back into the CD. After the first year, your CD would be worth $523.45, which is the original amount you invested plus the interest earned. After the second year, your CD would be worth $548.00. But wait a minute! That is an additional $24.55. Why is the second year's interest greater than the first year? Because not only did you earn interest on your original investment, you earned interest on your first year's interest as well. This is what we call compound interest. So at the end of the five-year term, your CD would be worth $628.78. If you had taken your interest out each year, you would have earned just $117.25. But since you let your interest earn interest, you were able to earn an additional $11.53. That's the power of compound interest and it can work on just about any investment.

What are the risks? – CDs are generally regarded as being safe. However, you can lose money on them. If you cash a CD in before its maturity, you may have to pay an interest penalty. If the CD has a term that is less than one year, the interest penalty will be the equivalent of three months worth of interest. If the term is one year or longer, the interest penalty will be six months worth of interest. If there is not enough interest in the CD to cover the penalty, the remaining balance of the penalty will be deducted from your principal. If you purchase a CD, make sure that it is with money that you are sure you won't need until after the CD matures.

What Else Do You Need To Know? – The interest you earn on a CD is taxed in the year that it is earned. So even if you are rolling your interest back into your CD, you still have to pay taxes on it. Interest from CDs is taxed the same as regular income.

Money Market Funds

What is a money market fund? – Money market funds are mutual funds that invest in a variety of fixed-income investments that have a maturity of 395 days or less. Because the maturities of these investments are relatively short, they do not fluctuate in value that much, if any at all. Money market funds are very stable and typically pay a higher rate of interest than regular savings accounts.

How do you make money with a money market fund? – A money market fund pays dividends that are based on the interest received by the investments being held in the money market fund portfolio. Because money market funds strive to maintain a per share price of $1.00, they act just like a regular dollar denominated savings account. If you invested $1,000 in a savings account that paid interest at a rate of 4% per year, compounded daily, you would earn $3.29 in interest in 30 days. Your new account balance would be $1,003.29. If you invested $1,000 in a money market fund that yielded 4% per year, compounded daily, you would earn $3.29 in dividends in 30 days. You would then own 1,003.29 shares, each worth one dollar apiece, for an account value of $1,003.29.

What are the risks? – Money market funds are not insured. Even though the fund company will strive to maintain a per share price of $1.00, there is no guarantee they will. If they can't, you may get back less than what you've invested.

What else do you need to know? – Money market fund failures are rare, but they can happen. Also, make sure you pay attention to fees, because the higher the fees, the lower your dividend yield. Before you invest, make sure you read the prospectus to get an idea of what the underlying investments are.

Bonds

What is a bond? – A bond is basically a loan. As an investor in a bond, you are loaning the issuer of the bond your money. The issuer of the bond then agrees to pay you interest either for as long as you own the bond or until it matures. The interest paid on the bond is based on the face value (par value) of bond, which is the amount of principal owed to you when the bond matures.

Bonds can be purchased in several different ways, depending on the type of bond. Bonds can be purchased when they are first issued via a bond offering. One or more brokerage firms usually manage the bond offering. The brokerage firms solicit orders from individual and institutional investors. Their role is to try to sell most, if not all, of the bonds that are available. The more bonds that are sold by the brokerage firms, the more money they will raise for the issuer. Bonds can sometimes be purchased directly from the issuer or through an auction. Bonds can also be purchased through the secondary market.

The secondary market is where previously issued securities are traded. Think of it as a used car lot for bonds. It consists of various exchanges where buyers and sellers can trade bonds that were previously issued. If you bought a bond when it was first offered (a new car), and you want to sell it before it matures, you will sell it in the secondary market (the used car lot). If you purchased a bond in the secondary market (a used car), and you want to sell it prior to maturity, you will sell it in the secondary market (the used car lot).

How do you make money with bonds? – You can make money with bonds two ways. The first way is with the interest that the bond pays. The interest on the bond can be paid monthly, quarterly, semi-annually, or at final maturity. At final maturity, you receive your last interest payment and your original principal. The other way that you can make money on a bond is through capital gains. You realize a capital gain when you sell the bond, prior to maturity, for more than what you paid for it.

Bonds typically fluctuate in value based on what interest rates are doing in the market. The market rate is the rate that is established for your type of bond by the buyers and sellers in the secondary market. It is based on the yield of similar bonds with similar maturities. The other rate that you should pay attention to is the coupon rate. The coupon rate is the rate at which interest is paid on the bond. The term "coupon" comes from the fact that bonds used to be issued in certificate form. Attached to the bonds were coupons that represented each interest payment. On the due date of an interest payment, the bond owner would cut out or "clip" the coupon from the bond certificate. He could take it to the bank and exchange it for cash or deposit it to his account. Most bonds today are sold as "book entry." Book entry bonds exist only as an electronic entry in the books of the issuer. There is no physical certificate for the bond

The primary point to remember is that if market interest rates go up, bond values go down. If market interest rates go down, bond values go up. If your bond is worth more than the face value of the bond, it is said to be trading at a premium. If the value of the bond is less than the face value, it is said to be trading at a discount.

What are the risks? – If market interest rates move against you, your bond will decline in value. If you have to sell the bond and the price is below what you paid for it, you will suffer a capital loss. The longer the maturity, the more sensitive the bond will be to changes in interest rates.

Also, if the issuer of the bond gets into financial trouble, they could default on the bond and not pay the interest that is due to the bondholders. The issuer of the bond could also go bankrupt, which could significantly reduce your chances of getting all of your original investment back.

What else do you need to know? – There are basically three classes of bonds: Government, Corporate, and Municipal.

The U.S. Treasury issues government bonds and they come in several varieties. The government bond that most people are familiar with is the U.S. Savings Bond. U.S. Savings Bonds are issued by the U.S. Treasury and are backed by the full faith and credit of the United States Government. The most common form of the savings bond is the Series EE. You purchase the bonds for half of the face value. The bonds will pay interest for up to thirty years. The rate of interest for the bonds is set every six months. Depending on how market interest rates are moving, the rate of interest for savings bonds can change or stay the same.

This leads us to a common misconception about savings bonds. Many people think that savings bonds will double (reach their face value) within a set period of time. Actually, the amount of time it takes for a bond to reach face value will depend upon the average interest rate earned on the bond, or its minimum interest rate, whichever is greater. For example, if market rates for the life of the bond never exceed the guaranteed minimum rate (currently at 3%), it could take about 24 years for the bonds to reach face value. If the interest rates earned on the bond averaged 6%, it would only take about 12 years for the bonds to reach face value.

Another type of savings bond is the I-Bond. The rate of interest paid on the I-Bond is indexed for inflation. The rate is calculated by taking a base and adding the inflation premium to it. Like the EE bonds, I-Bonds pay interest for up to thirty years.

Interest on the bonds is earned, but not paid until you cash them in. Because of this feature, EE bonds and I-Bonds are often referred to as accrual securities. Once you cash them in, you will have to recognize the interest earned for tax purposes. Also, interest earned is exempt from state taxes, but taxable at the federal level.

Another type of government bond is the treasury bill. Treasury bills are government bonds that have a maturity of one year or less. They usually have maturities of three months, six months, and one year. Treasury bills are purchased at a discount to their face value. For example, if you purchased a $10,000 one-year treasury bill that yielded 5%, it would cost you $9523.81. The difference between the face value of the bond ($10,000) and the purchase price ($9,523.81) is your interest earned ($476.19).

Other types of government bonds are treasury notes and bonds. Treasury notes and bonds have maturities of 2 years or longer. Interest is paid every six months on the bonds. When the bonds mature, you will receive your last interest payment and the face value of the bond.

Corporate bonds are bonds issued by corporations. This is a riskier type of bond in that it is backed by the ability of the corporation to pay the money back to you, the investor. To help investors determine the level of potential risk in a bond, there are organizations called rating agencies that assign a letter grade to a corporation's bond. A rating of "Aaa" is higher than "Aa", which is higher than "Bbb". The ratings scale will vary according to the rating agency.

Municipal bonds are bonds issued by government entities such as states, cities, and government agencies. The unique feature about municipal bonds is that the interest received is exempt from federal taxes and is also exempt from state taxes if you buy bonds from the state in which you reside. Municipal bonds are also graded by rating agencies.

Annuities

What is an annuity? – An annuity is a contract between you and an insurance company. In exchange for the money you invest in an annuity, the insurance company promises to pay you regular payments for the rest of your life, or for a lesser period of time that you may specify.

There are two types of annuities: immediate and deferred. An immediate annuity is an annuity that "immediately" starts making guaranteed payments to you for the period you specify, based on the amount that you invest. A deferred annuity is an annuity that accumulates earnings and "defers" making guaranteed payments to you until later, whenever you specify that you are ready to receive those payments. Deferred annuities are also referred to as tax-deferred annuities because the taxes that are due on the earnings are deferred until they are actually withdrawn from the annuity.

Immediate and deferred annuities are further subdivided into two categories: fixed and variable. Fixed annuities are called such because they offer "fixed" rates of return for a given period while you own the annuity. Rates are usually fixed for an initial guarantee period that can range from one year to ten years. After the initial rate guarantee period, rates are set for one-year terms and adjusted annually thereafter. Variable annuities get their name because the amount of the guaranteed payments that you will receive depends on how well the underlying investments perform. In addition to fixed-rate options, variable annuities allow you to invest in money market funds, stock funds, and bond funds.

How do you make money with annuities? – You make money with annuities two ways. You make money with an annuity from the accumulation of earnings from the underlying investments. The other way that you make money from any annuity is from the deferral of taxes on your earnings. The longer you can put off paying taxes on your earnings, the longer those earnings can earn more for you. Tax deferral can really add up over long periods of time. By having control over when you make withdrawals, you are choosing to pay taxes when it may be most beneficial to you.

What are the risks? – Annuities are long-term investments. Once you have invested in one, it may be difficult to get to most of your money without having to pay a surrender charge. A surrender charge is a penalty that you will pay if you withdraw more than what is contractually allowed within the surrender period. For most annuities, this contractual amount is 10% of the contract value. While there are some annuities that do not have surrender periods, the standard surrender period for most annuities is seven years. The surrender charge usually starts out at about 6–7%, and declines each year until it reaches zero.

What else do you need to know? – Be careful as to what portion of your portfolio you invest in an annuity. Annuities are meant to be long-term investments. Because of surrender charges and penalties for withdrawals before age 59 ½, you should not commit short-term funds to this type of investment.

Annuities, especially variable annuities, can be expensive products to own. Many variable annuities offer riders that can add various features to your contract. A rider is an addendum to the basic annuity contract that provides for some other feature, such as minimum rates of return, nursing home coverage, or guaranteed principal return. However, these riders add additional costs to the annuity. The more riders you have on an annuity contract, the lower your rate of return will be.

Stocks

What is a stock? – A stock is a security that represents a fractional share of ownership in a company. This ownership interest is sometimes called equity. Equity is defined as the net difference between what a company owns minus what it owes. For individuals, this is what we refer to as net worth. This owner's equity is divided into units called common stock. Because the holders of stock share in the ownership of the company, they are sometimes referred to as shareholders, as well as stockholders. Your percentage of ownership in a company depends on two things: the number of shares you own and the total number of shares that are outstanding.

Preferred stocks are stocks that in some ways act like bonds. They usually pay a fixed dividend regardless of the corporation's earnings. The value of the preferred shares can sometimes increase, which gives you the opportunity to earn money through capital appreciation as well. In the event that the company is liquidated because of bankruptcy, preferred stockholders are paid after bondholders but before common stockholders.

Blue chip stocks are stocks of large corporations that are consistently profitable. The term "blue chip" is derived from the game of poker, where the blue chips are the most valuable ones. There is no official list of blue chip stocks, and stocks that are currently considered to be blue chip can lose that designation if their financial condition deteriorates.

How do you make money on stocks? – You make money on stocks through dividends and capital gains.

Dividends represent cash payments from the net income of the company you own stock in. Dividends are usually paid to all shareholders of record on a quarterly basis.

Not every stock pays a dividend. Even if a stock pays a dividend, the company can decide at a later date to either reduce the dividend or eliminate it completely. However, the benefit of a dividend is that it allows you to recover some of your investment while you hold the stock.

If you sell a stock for more than what you paid for it, that is a capital gain. It doesn't matter whether you hold the stock for one year, one month, one day, one hour, or one minute. If you sell it for less than what you paid for it, that is a capital loss.

What are the risks? – You can lose money. In fact, you can lose all of your money. Stock prices are a function of supply and demand. If there are more people who want to buy a stock than people who want to sell that same stock, then the stock price will go up. If you have more sellers than buyers, the stock price will go down. If the company that you are invested in falls on hard times, the stock price may go down because you will have more sellers than buyers. If the company that you have invested in goes bankrupt, you will probably lose all of your money. Stocks move up and down in price every day.

In fact, they fluctuate every minute of the day. Companies can also deliberately try to hide problems, or intention-ally engage in fraud. When exposed, the stock of the company often declines, which can cause you to lose money.

What else do you need to know? – Who buys stock? Buyers of stock are usually individuals like you and me, or institutions such as pension funds, mutual funds, or large corporations. How do you buy stock? Stocks are usually purchased through a brokerage firm. The brokerage firm will charge you a fee or commission to buy the stock, and they will also charge you a fee or commission when you sell it. Some companies allow you to buy stock directly from them through something called a Dividend Reinvestment Plan (DRIP). If this plan is available, you can buy shares directly from the company you're investing in at little or no cost. Once enrolled in the plan, any divi-dends paid by the company can be automatically reinvested to buy more shares.

How much does it cost to buy stock? It can cost anywhere from $5 per trade to tens of thousands of dollars per trade. It really depends on how much stock you're buying and who you're buying it through. Trading through an online brokerage firm via the Internet is usually the least expensive way to buy stocks. However, online and discount brokerages are primarily geared toward the do-it-yourselfer. If you need assistance, then you will probably buy your stock through a full-service brokerage.

Mutual Funds

What is a mutual fund? – A mutual fund is an investment where individual investors send their money to an investment company. The mutual fund pools the money it receives and decides where and how it will be invested. Mutual funds can invest in stocks, bonds, cash, and other types of investments as well. Mutual funds may invest in just one type of investment, or many. When you invest in a mutual fund, you own shares in the mutual fund. The mutual fund will own shares of stock in various companies, or it may own the bonds of various companies or governments. Your investment in the mutual fund gives you an indirect investment in the securities that the fund owns. You can decide which mutual fund you want to invest in, but you cannot tell the mutual fund specifically how you want your money to be invested.

How do you make money with mutual funds? – You make money with mutual funds through capital gains, dividends, or interest.

What are the risks? – While it is technically possible to lose all of your money with a mutual fund, it is not likely. Most mutual funds are diversified, and they can own a few securities or very many. In order for you to lose all of your money, every investment in the portfolio would have to eventually go bankrupt. Again, while this is possible, it is not likely. The key thing to remember is that mutual funds fluctuate in value everyday. If you have to sell your shares in the mutual fund at a price that is less than what you paid for them, you will lose money.

What else do you need to know? – There are two types of mutual funds: open-end and closed-end. An open-end mutual fund is one that issues as many shares as investors demand. When investors buy shares, the fund issues new shares. When investors withdraw money, the fund redeems shares. The price of a share in a mutual fund in calculated by dividing the total net assets of the fund by the number of mutual fund shares that are outstanding. This figure is also called the net asset value (NAV). The total net assets of a mutual fund consist of the combined value of all of the investments being held by the fund. The net asset value is calculated at the end of each trading day.

Closed-end funds are funds that have a fixed number of shares and their shares trade throughout each trading day. Closed-end fund shares are usually issued in an initial public offering. The price of closed-end shares is primarily influenced by the supply and demand of the shares. If there are more buyers than sellers, the price of the shares will go up. If there are more sellers than buyers, the price will go down. If the price of a share of a closed-end fund is greater than its net asset value, it is said to trade at a premium. If the price is less than the net asset value, then it is said to trade at a discount.

124

There is also a hybrid type of mutual fund is the exchange-traded fund (ETF). ETFs are mutual funds based on a portfolio of securities designed to track the performance of a certain index. Even though they are mutual funds, they can be bought and sold throughout the trading day.

Open-ended funds are further divided into two categories: no-load and load funds. No-load funds are funds that do not charge any type sales charge for buying or selling the fund. A load fund has a sales charge that you are assessed either when you buy the fund or when you sell it. You buy a load fund because you are working with a financial advisor who is providing you with advisory services. The sales charges are paid as a percentage of the amount invested. Once the sale charge is paid, part of it goes to the mutual fund and the other part goes to your advisor's firm, who then pays him. How you pay your sales charge depends on what class of mutual fund you buy. Load funds come in just about every alphabet designation from A to Z. However, let's look at three of the most common.

A front-end load is usually associated with Class A shares. The typical sales charge on Class A shares starts out at 5.75% of the amount invested. Most mutual funds offer breakpoints, which are discounts in the sales charge based on the amount in vested. For example, if you invest less than $50,000, your sales charge on Class A shares might be 5.75%. If you invest more than $50,000 up to $100,000, your sales charge drops to 4.50%. The sales charge gets lower and lower until you invest $1,000,000, where investments of this amount or more are not subject to a sales charge. Class B shares are sometimes referred to as back-end loads. With B shares, you aren't charged a sales charge when you first invest. All of your investment goes to work right away. If you sell any or all of your shares after you buy, you may be subject to a deferred sales charge (back-end load). Deferred sales charges usually decline each year and disappear totally after five to seven years.

Whether you purchase load or no-load funds, there are behind the scenes fees that you will have to pay, just because you own the fund. These fees are part of something called the expense ratio. The expense ratio can consist of up to three parts:

- Management Fee
- Other Expense
- 12b-1 Fee (Distribution)

The management fee is the fee paid to the company actually making the investment decisions for the mutual fund. In most cases, this is the mutual fund company that sponsors the fund, but this function is sometimes contracted out to another investment management firm (the sub-advisor). The fee that goes towards other expenses covers trading and administrative costs. The 12b-1 fee is called a distribution or marketing fee. It goes to the brokerage firm that sold you the fund to cover marketing and ongoing service. If you have a financial advisor that sold you the fund, he will share in the fee with his firm. As your mutual fund grows or declines in value, so will the amount that your advisor is paid to service your account. 12b-1 fee payments can start anywhere from one month to thirteen months after you buy the fund, and will continue to be paid as long as you own the fund.

Since the expense ratio reduces the gross return on the mutual fund, you should try to invest in mutual funds with reasonable annual expenses. Usually, the lower the expense ratio the better. However, you should still compare funds across several areas and look for consistency. There are some mutual funds with very low expense ratios, but awful long-term performance. There are also some (but not many) funds with high expense ratios and excellent long-term performance. Make sure you do a complete review of any fund before you invest any money.

If you are a do-it-yourself investor, you should buy no-load funds. But if you need help and are going to buy load funds, which class of shares should you buy? Table 7-2 is an example of a table that you would find in a prospectus of a mutual fund that carries a load. This table assumes a hypothetical initial investment of $10,000 and an annual growth rate of 5%. The purpose of such a table is to show the investor his estimated total cost of investing for each period shown.

If you are only going to be investing in a fund for five years or less, Class B or C shares could be a very cost-effective choice,

---

Table 7-2

Mutual Fund Costs Over Various Periods

	1 Yr.	3 Yrs.	5 Yrs.	10 Yrs.
Class A	$661	$843	$1,040	$1,608
Class B	$667	$817	$1,092	$1,743*
Class B (no redemption)	$167	$517	$892	$1,743*
Class C	$267	$517	$892	$1,944
Class C (no redemption)	$167	$517	$892	$1,944

*Reflects the conversion of Class B shares to Class A shares, which pay lower 12b-1 fees. Conversion occurs no more than eight years after purchase.

---

especially if you think that markets will be rising after you initially invest. However, once you get beyond five years, Class A shares are usually the least costly in terms of total expenses.

Given that most investors consider themselves to be long-term investors, you would think that most purchasers of loaded mutual funds would buy Class A shares. However, the prevailing class of shares sold to investors is Class B. Here are some reasons why:

- Class B shares are sometimes presented by financial sales-persons as "not costing you anything," because all of your initial investment goes to work right away. Subsequently, some investors believe that their B shares are low cost like no-loads. This is not true.
- The typical Class B fund will have a 4% dealer reallow-ance (commission). This reallowance is fronted by the mutual fund company and is recouped through the higher fees or the deferred sales charge. There are no discounts for larger fund purchases; therefore, advisors can earn a higher commission on Class B shares than Class A shares for purchases of $100,000 or more.

Before you purchase any loaded mutual fund, make sure you understand how that class of fund is going to be most cost effective for you, based on your investment goals and time horizon.

Finally, there are two major debates concerning mutual funds. One of them is loaded funds versus no-load funds, and the other is actively managed funds versus passively managed funds (index funds). Let's examine the load versus no-load argument first.

No-load funds will usually have slightly higher performance because in most cases, their fee structure is lower. This leads me to the central issue of this particular argument, which is cost.

If you read most of the articles and literature against loaded mutual funds, they usually try to make the point that it makes no sense to pay someone to "help you pick a good mutual fund." Everything you need to know is available for little or no cost on the Internet, in magazines, or in books. If the sole purpose of a load were to only pay for assistance in picking a fund, then this argument would be irrefutable. However, the purpose of a load is to compensate your advisor for all of the services that he or she may provide. These services should include helping you plan for your retirement, your child's education, or any of the other financial planning issues that you'll face in your lifetime. The higher fees that you pay when purchasing a loaded mutual fund should only be paid if you need financial advice and guidance, and your total cost of investing is equal to or less than your perceived value of the financial advice that you are receiving. Your total cost of owning a loaded mutual fund consists of not only the cumulative fees paid for your particular holding period, but the lost earnings you could have had if you had invested in an alternative fund. To further understand, let's look at an example.

The ABC fund is a pure no-load fund. The only fees that you will pay for this fund is a 0.50% management fee, and a 0.25% fee for other expenses. Total annual expenses for the ABC fund is 0.75%. The ABC fund has a sister fund called the XYZ fund. This fund is managed in exactly the same way as the ABC fund, but it charges a front-end load of 5.75%. It also charges a 0.25% 12b-1 fee in addition to the 0.50% management fee, and the 0.25% fee for other expenses. Total annual expenses for the XYZ fund is 1.00%.

If both of these funds are invested and managed in the exact same way, their gross returns before expenses should be the same. Let's assume that an investor in either of these funds will earn 10% per year before expenses. Table 7-3 shows that the net return for the ABC Fund is 9.25% and the net return for the XYZ Fund is 9.00%.

Table 7-3

How Expenses Affect Your Return

	Gross Return	Annual Expenses	Net Return
ABC Fund	10.00%	0.75%	9.25%
XYZ Fund	10.00%	1.00%	9.00%

If you had invested $10,000 in the loaded XYZ Fund instead of the no-load ABC Fund, how much would it have truly cost you over a holding period of ten years? Table 7-4 calculates the difference and shows that purchasing a loaded mutual fund through a financial advisor would have cost you $2,025 in potential earnings. This works out to be an average additional cost of $203 per year.

Table 7-4

Impact of Loads on Investment Growth Over Time

	Net Investment	Net Return	Holding Period	Ending Balance
ABC Fund	$10,000	9.25%	10 years	$25,129
XYZ Fund*	$9,425	9.00%	10 years	$23,104
			Difference:	$2,025
		Average Additional Costs Per Year:		$203

* net investment after a 5.75% front-end load

Were the extra costs of the loaded mutual fund good or bad? Well, as usual, it depends. To have access to a financial advisor for about $203 per year is a pretty good deal, in my opinion. In fact, if it were not for loaded mutual funds, many investors could not afford financial advice and guidance. Many fee-based financial planners charge at least $500 for a two-hour consultation. If you need a financial plan, you could pay $1,000 to $2,500 or more. For an investor with only $10,000 to invest, the ten-year cost to invest under this arrangement would be prohibitive. That's why many fee-based financial planners will not accept clients with less than $100,000 to invest.

Unfortunately, minimum balances for new accounts are creeping up in the brokerage world as well. Many firms have adopted client minimums of $25,000 or more. This will increasingly become the norm, as financial advisors are under constant pressure by their firms to produce ever-increasing levels of revenue. Because of production quotas, many advisors will have no choice but to turn small investors away. Nevertheless, it is misleading to frame the debate of loaded mutual funds versus no-load funds solely within the context of fees. The added fees do have a purpose. The fees are not hidden, as some suggest. They are listed in the prospectus under the section entitled "Fees and Expenses." The key is to find a loaded mutual fund with reasonable fees, and make sure you are getting the other services you are entitled to. If you aren't, either get a new advisor, or start managing your money yourself and buy no-load funds. If you need help and still want to invest using no-load funds, make sure you take into consideration your advisor's fee plus the expense ratio of the no-load funds.

The other major debate concerning mutual funds is that of actively managed mutual funds versus passively managed funds (index funds). Actively managed mutual funds are ones in which the portfolio managers believe that they can consistently generate returns that are above the benchmark that they are measured against. Passively managed funds are those where the portfolio managers simply want to try to match their benchmark at the lowest cost possible. Both actively managed and passively managed funds can be load or no-load.

With regard to fees, passively managed funds are usually less expensive to own. In general, they don't have to pay high-priced portfolio managers, and their trading costs are lower because they don't trade as often as actively managed funds. This lower fee structure can lead to higher returns for the passively managed fund.

With regard to performance, there are several factors that can negatively affect the performance of actively managed funds versus passively managed funds. First, the performance of an actively managed fund is quite dependent on its portfolio manager or managers. If the portfolio manager leaves the firm, or if a significant number of the portfolio managers on a managing team leave the firm, performance can be adversely affected. Next it is statistically difficult to win every year. To put this in perspective, think about professional team sports.

There are some teams that are consistent performers. They are always near the top in terms of most games won, and they even win the championship every once in a while. In fact, they may be able to win the championship two or three years in a row. If so, they are recognized as one of the best teams ever. But, even for these top teams, rarely are they able to win a championship for 10, 15, or 20 years in a row. Team dynamics, such as changes in player personnel, injuries, or schedule changes, can make such winning streaks virtually impossible. With actively managed mutual funds, such success is equally elusive. That is why approximately 75% of them will underperform their relative benchmark in any given year.

So with their higher fees and likely underperformance, why would anyone ever want to invest using actively managed mutual funds? Well, there are a few more things that you should consider.

Most of what has been written about passively managed funds versus actively managed funds is based on data that compares the average rate of return of all of the funds in each group. However, this can be misleading because when you take a simple arithmetic average of a group of numbers, it treats all of the numbers as if they were of equal importance. There are thousands of mutual funds and the vast majority of them are actively managed funds. When you calculate a simple arithmetic average, the returns of the funds where most investors have their money are disproportionately affected by the many smaller funds in the group where less money has been invested. Therefore, you do not get an accurate picture of returns generated for the typical investor.

Most investors migrate to the more popular offerings because they want to own the funds that are the most recommended. Not only do these popular funds hold most of the assets, but most of the mutual fund shareholders as well. To evaluate actively managed funds versus passively managed funds based on where the majority of the money is invested in each, let's examine the two groups by using something called the 80:20 Rule.

The 80:20 Rule, also known as the Pareto Principle, originated from Vilfredo Pareto. Mr. Pareto was an Italian economist who was studying the distribution of wealth in different countries in the early 1900s. As he conducted his research, he discovered an interesting phenomenon. Approximately 80% of the wealth in most countries was consistently controlled by 20% of its people. Since then, the 80:20 Rule has been applied to many other things. For example, 80% of the collections at your church will typically be given by 20% of the members.

Using data from the February 2003 Morningstar Principia Database, I searched for stock mutual funds that had been around for at least ten years through February 2003. Since the S&P 500 is a popular index on which many passively managed mutual funds are based. I only looked at funds that were categorized as Large-Cap Blends. This is how Morningstar categorizes the S&P 500 Index. There were 198 funds that met these criteria, of which 166 were actively managed and 32 were passively managed. The simple arithmetic average was 6.87% for the actively managed funds and 8.03% for the passively managed funds. Total assets for the combined groups of funds were $417.6 billion. Table 7-5 is an 80:20 Rule analysis of the funds in my search.

As you can see, the 80:20 Rule held up fairly well. For the actively managed funds, 80.6% of the total assets in this group were represented by 19.3% of the funds. For the passively managed funds, 83.6% of the total assets in this group were represented by 15.63% of the funds. What this tells us is that the performance of these particular funds will be representative of how most of the dollars in each group is invested. Now, let's compare the rates of return for each group.

Table 7-5

80:20 Analysis of Large-Cap Blend Active and Passive
Mutual Funds (for the ten years ending February 2003)

Type of Fund	# of Funds	% of Total Funds	% of Total Assets
Active	32	19.28%	80.60%
Passive	5	15.63%	83.57%

Source: Morningstar Principia – Feb 2003

Again, to try to make the comparison as fair as possible, I looked at the load-adjusted returns. This would take into account all fees and sales charges that would affect the net return of each fund. Also, the rates of return shown are weighted, based on the total assets of each fund. This means that funds with more money in them have a bigger impact on the group average. Table 7-6 is a summary of what I found:

Table 7-6

80:20 Analysis – Summary of Returns

Type of Fund	Weighted Avg. Return	Range of Returns Low	High
Active	9.06	4.71	14.15
Passive	8.50	7.98	8.71

Source: Morningstar Principia – Feb 2003

As you can see, when we isolate the few funds that hold the most assets, the actively managed funds generated a weighted-average rate of return of 9.06%, which is higher than the 8.50% weighted-average return generated by the passively managed funds. The only other thing that we can do to further analyze these returns is to adjust for taxes. However, tax rates will vary among investors, and that data was not readily available. Since passively managed funds tend to be more tax efficient, my guess would be that adjusting for taxes would narrow the gap some between the two types of funds.

After examining this data, it was my conclusion that it is possible for the majority of dollars invested in actively managed large-cap blend funds to earn a higher weighted-average rate of return than similar passively managed funds. Although more research is needed, this analysis convinces me that passively managed funds aren't always the way to go.

There is one more reason why I don't believe investors should always purchase passively managed mutual funds, as some would suggest. If ever there came a day when the majority of investors decided to put all of their money into passively managed funds, the underlying stocks in funds would experience a tremendous rise in price. However, the subsequent rise in price would not be because these stocks were worth more. The rise in price would simply be because the demand for these stocks far exceeded the supply, which would cause most of the stocks in the index to be overvalued. This would immediately become a situation that an actively managed fund manager could exploit for profit. Soon, actively managed funds would collectively start to show better returns than passively managed funds. Because most investors chase performance, the performance of passively managed funds would probably start to suffer as investors sold those funds to buy the "better" performing actively managed funds. Because of this scenario, it is my belief again that passively managed funds aren't always the best choice.

Although we have been looking at average rates of return, the more appropriate number to look at is the annualized return. The annualized return measures how much you actually made on the investment from point A to point B. Because of this, it is quite possible to have a fund that has the highest average return in a group, but a lower annualized return than other funds in that same group. To demonstrate, let's take a look at three hypothetical funds.

The Grand Poobah Index fund (GPI) is a popular passively managed fund that many investors regard to be the gold standard of all mutual funds. Its fees and expenses are lower than most of its peers, and it consistently has higher returns than 75% or more of them in any given year. However, there are two actively managed funds (AM-I and AM-II) that have gained your attention, and you are considering making an investment in them instead. Take a look at Table 7-7, which shows the last ten years of data for each fund. The data in the table has been manipulated to make a point. But, as you can see, making a decision about passive or active mutual funds based on average returns could lead you into choosing the wrong fund.

Table 7-7			

Mutual Fund Returns: Average vs. Annualized			
	GPI Fund	**AM-I Fund**	**AM-II Fund**
Year 1	10.00%	9.50%	15.00%
Year 2	10.00%	9.50%	7.25%
Year 3	10.00%	9.50%	7.25%
Year 4	10.00%	9.50%	7.25%
Year 5	10.00%	9.50%	7.25%
Year 6	-10.00%	-5.00%	7.25%
Year 7	10.00%	9.50%	7.25%
Year 8	10.00%	9.50%	7.25%
Year 9	10.00%	9.50%	7.25%
Year 10	10.00%	9.50%	7.25%
Average Return	9.00%	8.05%	8.03%
Annualized Return	7.81%	7.96%	8.00%
Growth of $10,000	$21,212	$21,509	$21,589

* all investment returns are hypothetical and not indicative of any particular security's return

The GPI fund was very consistent, earning 10% in every year except Year 6 when it lost 10%. However, that year of losses significantly impacted the annualized return of the GPI fund, dropping it to 7.81%. The AM-I fund was very consistent too, earning 9.50% in every year except Year 6 when it lost 5%. The portfolio manager of this actively managed fund was able to sidestep some of the market decline (through luck or skill) by increasing the cash position of the portfolio.

This is something that the passively managed fund would not have necessarily been able to do. Nevertheless, that year of outperformance allowed the AM-I fund to post a higher annualized return than the passively managed GPI fund. Additionally, this was accomplished even though its higher fees and expenses caused its returns in the other years to be less than that of the GPI fund.

Finally, if you look at the AM-II fund, it looks like a terrible performer. Except for Year 1 and Year 6 (through luck or skill), this portfolio manager has significantly underperformed the GPI fund. However, because the year of outperformance was early in the evaluation period and of significant magnitude, the AM-II fund was able to post the highest annualized return of all three funds.

What you actually earn on an investment is dependent upon the timing of cash flows in and out of it. How much you initially invest, how much you periodically add, and how much you periodically withdraw, will affect your actual annualized return. This is a very individualized process, so what applies to you may not necessarily apply to others. You should not base your decision to purchase a mutual fund solely on published rates of return.

Bottom line: Does the **average** passively managed mutual fund outperform the **average** actively managed mutual fund? Yes it does. Does the **typical** passively managed mutual fund investor outperform the **typical** actively managed mutual fund investor? Probably not, with the likely answer being that the returns are very similar. The decision to use a passively managed fund versus an actively managed fund is highly dependent upon your financial goals. I don't believe that either type of fund is definitively better than the other. Also, there is no rule that says you can't use both. Do your homework, ask questions, and you'll make a good decision.

Chapter 8
Smart Ways to Save for College

College is not for everyone, and there are other alternatives for advanced learning and skill development. Additionally, getting a college education is no guarantee for financial success. However, it is an undeniable fact that our society places increased value on a college education and tends to compensate those who acquire one with more income than those who do not.

Historically, getting a college education has been a good investment. In 1975, a full-time, year-round worker with a bachelor's degree had an annual salary that was 50% more than a full-time, year-round worker with only a high school diploma.[2] By 1999, the differential had increased to an 80% advantage for the worker with a bachelor's degree versus the worker with the high school diploma. For those workers with masters or professional degrees, they earned 80% more in 1975, and 160% more in 1999. This can add up to be a lifetime earnings differential of $1 million or more.

Even if your children do not attend college, I suggest that you always encourage them to pursue opportunities for learning that will help them acquire new skills. This, along with more work experience, will allow them to qualify for better jobs, which can help them close the income gap with college graduates.

Sources to Pay for College

If college is something that you at least want your child to have the opportunity to consider, you need to start thinking about it as early as possible. There are basically four sources of income that will be available to you or your child to help pay for college, and they are:

---

[2] U.S. Census Bureau, The Big Payoff: Educational Attainment and Synthetic Estimates of Work-Life Earnings, July 2002, page 3. Data based on full-time workers 18 years old and over.

- Scholarships and Grants
- Loans
- Work
- Personal Savings

Scholarships and Grants

The ideal situation is to have your child receive a scholarship for all or part her education. Scholarships are usually awarded to students who exhibit exceptional academic or athletic talent. They are also awarded to students based on financial need or their inter-est to pursue a particular field of study. Grants are usually based on just financial need. Additionally, your local church, civic group, or social organization may offer scholarships or grants with less stringent eligibility requirements. The best thing about scholarships and grants is that they do not have to be repaid.

There are lots of scholarships and grants available for all kinds of students. You just need to put in some effort to find out about them. Unfortunately, there are a lot of companies that promise to help you get scholarships and grants for your children, but are only out to steal your money. Between your high school guidance counselor, your local library, and the Internet, you can find out about most scholarship programs that are available. Invest your time, not your money. In most cases, you should stay away from fee-based scholarship or grant matching services. Many of them promise more than they can deliver. The reality is that you shouldn't have to pay money to get money. Legitimate programs do not charge application fees.

Additionally, some scholarship and grant matching services are nothing but fronts for identify theft rings. If the application asks for your social security number, or personal financial information such as bank account numbers and credit card number, it could be a scam. They can take this information and apply for new credit cards in your name or access your bank account and withdraw funds. Don't let your desire to find scholarship money for your child override your good judgement. Be careful.

Loans

If your child is not able to qualify for a scholarship and you have not saved enough money on your own to pay for her education, you may have to consider obtaining a loan. As I mentioned earlier in the book, the decision to borrow money must be weighed carefully against the decision of how you're going to pay it back.

The only way to avoid the need to borrow is to save, and start saving as early as possible. Just because you think that you will be able to qualify for student aid in the form of loans doesn't mean that you should automatically apply for them. Borrowing money to pay for college can leave you or your children with a tremendous amount of debt that may take years to repay.

In the 2001-02 school year, students received almost $90 billion in financial aid, of which approximately 46% of this amount was in the form of federal government loan programs Most student loan programs offer low interest rate loans and favorable repayment terms. In most cases, you don't have to start making payments on your loans until you have been out of school for a year. If you find that the payments from all of your loans are too much to handle, you may be able to consolidate them into one. Additionally, your lender may extend the term of the loan to help lower your payments.

Again, I cannot stress how important it is to handle student loan debt properly. If you have to take out a student loan, make sure that you use some of the debt reduction strategies discussed in Chapter 6 when it is time to start paying the loan back. The faster you payoff your loan, the more interest you will save. Also, you or your child should be careful not to take on any additional debt after college. Once you start making payments on your student loans, you may find that you don't have much money left over for anything else if your existing debt level is too high.

---

[3] Trends in Student Aid 2002, The College Board, www.collegeboard.com

Work

If you have not been able to save enough for your child's education, and a scholarship is not likely, you may want to consider encouraging your child to get a job while he or she is pursuing their college degree. This can be a very difficult option for your child, but it has several benefits.

First, for your child to successfully work and study at the same time, he will need lots of self-discipline. He will have to be organized and focused. Fortunately, these are skills that will help your child become a better student and a better employee. In fact, many corporate managers have told me that they pay extra attention to job applicants who worked their way through college because they tend to be self-starters and more mature.

Additionally, if your child is able to work through college, he may be able to obtain real work experience that may give him an edge over the competition for jobs when he graduates. This is especially important when recent corporate layoffs flood the market with more experienced workers who are more than willing to accept an entry level job rather than not work at all. Also, you should investigate co-op programs, which combine in-class learning with paid work experience. Also, if your child is able to get a job at a company, he may be able to qualify for tuition assistance from their employer after he has been there for a minimum amount of time.

All of this may mean that your child does not graduate in four years, but that's okay. It will be a blessing that he was able to obtain his degree without going into debt. Also, I believe his achievement will mean much more to both of you because he had to work so hard for it.

Personal Savings

If you have decided that a college education is a good investment in your child's future, or even your own, what is the best way to save for it? Fortunately, there are many choices for you to consider. In fact, recent changes in the tax laws have made some of these choices even more appealing. Let's discuss some of them.

U.S. Savings Bonds – U.S. Savings bonds are a very popular and easy way to save for your child's education. Many of you probably received savings bonds as birthday gifts, Christmas presents, or prizes in a contest. However, many people are not aware that U. S. Savings bonds have an additional feature that allows you to exclude up to $10,000 of interest earned from taxes if used to pay for eligible tuition and required course and administrative fees. Expenses incurred from institutions such as vocational schools, colleges, and universities that meet federal assistance standards are eligible. This feature was added in 1990 when the Treasury Department introduced the Education Bond Program. Series EE bonds issued January 1990 or after, and Series I bonds are eligible for the program.

In order to get the tax benefits, the bonds must be purchased in your name. Grandparents can't claim the exemption unless the grandchild is a dependent. Your children can be named as a beneficiary, but they can't be named as a co-owner. This program also requires that you be at least 24 years old when the bonds are purchased. The bonds have to be cashed in the same year that you incur the educational expenses. Also, if you cash in more bonds than your actual educational expenses, the amount of interest that is tax-exempt is pro-rated. A key point to remember is that the total amount of qualified expenses is reduced by the amount of any scholarships, fellowships, employer-provided educational assistance, and other forms of tuition reduction. Also, the cost of books and room and board are not allowed as qualified expenses. There are income limitations to the tax benefit, so make sure you consult a tax advisor.

Custodial Accounts – Custodial accounts are also very popular in their use as a tool to save for a child's education. Depending on the state you live in, your custodial account will fall under the Uniform Gifts to Minors Act (UGMA) or the Uniform Transfers to Minors Act (UTMA). Both types of accounts have similar functions. As custodian, you control the account until the child reaches the age of majority, which is age 18, 21 or 25, depending on your state.

These accounts offer a lot of flexibility in that you can invest in just about any investment that is available. As a custodian, you are the fiduciary for the account. A fiduciary is someone who has the responsibility of managing the account for the sole benefit of the account beneficiary. As the fiduciary, you are governed by the Prudent Man Rule. The Prudent Man Rule states that you must invest the money in this account as any prudent (wise) man would. Therefore investments or investment strategies that could be perceived as extremely risky could leave you legally liable for losses. That's right, your child could sue you if you mismanage the account!

As custodian, you can spend money on anything that is for the child's benefit. In addition to education expenses, you can use it for things like computers, books, or even a car. However, if you are a parent who is also the custodian, you will have an added restriction of not being able to spend money in the account for food, clothing, shelter, and medical expenses. These are things that are considered to be part of your parental responsibilities.

Another downside of the custodial account is that you lose control of the account once the child reaches the age of majority. So if your child decides that he or she wants to buy a Harley-Davidson Low Rider® instead of attending Harvard, there is not much that you can do. Clients often ask if they can just withdraw the money from the account if they feel their child will not handle it responsibly. The answer is no. Once you contribute money to a custodial account, it irrevocably belongs to the child.

A custodial account is considered to be an asset of the child, therefore it can negatively impact eligibility for financial aid. So, the choice to use a custodial account to pay for college expenses will boil down to three things: 1.) You know that you won't qualify for financial aid, or 2.) The amount you will save in a custodial account will not significantly affect your child's eligibility for financial aid, and 3.) You are fairly confident that your child will handle the funds responsibly whether he or she goes to college or not.

Coverdell Education Savings Account – This account is what was originally known as the Education IRA. In 2001, the name was changed to the Coverdell Education Savings Account in memory of the late Senator Paul Coverdell. Senator Coverdell was a congressman who championed the cause to improve the original Education IRA.

Anyone can contribute to an Education Savings Account (ESA). Most people contribute to an ESA for their children or grand-children, but the accounts can be set up for someone who is not related to you as well. The beneficiary of the account has to be less than 18 years old when the account is set up.

The original ESA had an annual contribution limit of $500. With recent changes in the tax law, that annual limit has been increased to $2,000. Contributions to the account are made with after-tax dollars, so you do not get any tax break for your deposits. However, as long as your withdrawals are made for qualified educa-tion expenses, any withdrawals that include earnings are made free of taxes and penalties. At first, the Education IRA could only be used to cover expenses for college or other types of higher education. Now they can be used to cover qualified education expenses for kinder-garten through high school as well.

What are qualified education expenses? Beginning in 2002, withdrawals can be used to pay for elementary and secondary school expenses such as tuition, fees, books, and supplies. Other qualified expenses include room and board, uniforms, and other expenses for supplemental items that are required by the school being attended. Additionally, expenses incurred by special-needs students for special services may qualify as a qualified educational expense.

An added bonus of the ESA is that it can also be used to cover the purchase of a computer. It can also be used to purchase related computer equipment, educational software (sorry, sports and game software do not count!), and even Internet access. As long as the ben-eficiary uses them while he or she is in school, they will be treated as qualified expenses.

As a donor to the ESA, you do not have to have earned income in order to contribute to the account. However, if your modified adjusted gross income (AGI) is $95,000 to $110,000 ($190,000 to $220,000 AGI for joint filers), the contribution amount is reduced. If your AGI exceeds the top end of the ranges, then you are not allowed to contribute to the account at all. These earnings restrictions may change, so make sure you consult your financial or tax advisor before you set up an account.

A child can have more than one ESA. However, the $2,000 contribution limit is an aggregate amount. For example, if your child has two separate ESAs, you could choose to contribute $2,000 or less to one account, or split the contribution up between the two. However you choose to do it, the total contribution between both accounts cannot exceed $2,000. If your child or other beneficiary has more than one ESA, make sure you coordinate contributions between all donors.

529 Plans – 529 Plans are named after Section 529 of the Internal Revenue tax code. These plans are designed and operated by state govern-ments and allow you to set aside funds to pay for college expenses. There are two types of 529 plans: prepaid and savings.

529 prepaid plans are plans that allow you to lock in tomorrow's cost of tuition by paying for it today. These plans are either sponsored by a state government, or by a particular college or university. Some are very basic and cover tuition only. Others are more flexible and will cover tuition, and room and board. Most prepaid plans allow you to purchase units that represent a portion of your future college costs. A certain number of units will pay for a semester of college expenses. The more units you buy, the more expenses you can cover. The cost of these units will fluctuate according to your child's age.

One caveat of investing in prepaid plans is that the success of the plan is dependent upon the sponsor's ability to invest the cash at a rate of return that is equal to or greater than the rate of increase for tuition. Unfortunately, the two don't always move in the same direction. More importantly, if tuition costs are steadily rising while investment yields are dropping, a funding gap can occur. When this happens, the sponsor may have to dramatically increase the cost of units, or significantly alter the terms of the plan. If you are already participating in a prepaid plan or plan to do so in the future, make sure you stay on top of the plan's performance.

The 529 Savings Plans do not lock in tomorrow's college costs at today's prices like a prepaid plan. What the 529 Savings Plans offer is a greater choice of investments that may give you the opportunity to earn a rate of return that exceeds expected increases in college costs. Some of the investments offered in a 529 Savings Plan are very stable, so your risk of loss is minimal. However, there are some investments in the plan that could be volatile, and therefore subject to loss of principal. When you invest in a 529 Savings Plan, you'll also need to invest some time and energy into monitoring and reviewing the plan. If you don't have the time or energy, enlist the help of a good financial advisor to help you.

The 529 Savings Plan also offers some additional advantages over the prepaid plan. The 529 Savings Plan can be used at any accredited institution of higher learning in the U.S. There are no income limits to participation. A 529 Savings Plan is considered to be an asset of the person who establishes the account. Therefore you will always control the account, even after the beneficiary reaches the age of majority. This allows you to change beneficiaries, or withdraw funds for other uses (subject to taxes and/or penalties). Additionally, if you are the child's parent and you apply for financial aid for your child, only about 6% of the value of the account will count as being available to pay for your child's educational expenses for that year.

529 Plans are a great way to save for your child's education. Whether they are appropriate for your situation will depend upon your unique circumstances. For more information on 529 Plans, I recommend the website Savingforcollege.com, which is found at www.savingforcollege.com. There is also a book entitled *The Best Way to Save for College – A Complete Guide to 529 Plans 2003-2004 Edition* by Joseph Hurley, CPA. Mr. Hurley is also the founder of Savingforcollege.com, LLC.

Other Choices for College Funding – Another choice in savings for your child's education is to just accumulate funds in your name. With this option, you will always maintain control of the funds. If your child does not attend college, or some other form of higher learning, you will be able to use the money for something else. The downside to doing this is that any interest, dividends, or capital

145

gains received will be taxed at your tax rate, which may not be as favorable as some of the other options.

If you are paying college expenses out-of-pocket, be aware that there are numerous tax breaks and credits that allow you to reduce your overall costs. Because many of the tax credits have restrictions based on income and filing status, I won't go into full detail as to how they work. However, if you're interested, be sure to ask your tax professional for more information or consult *IRS Publication 970, Tax Benefits for Education*. Here are the highlights:

- You can withdraw funds from an IRA without penalty to pay for higher education expenses for yourself, your spouse, your child, or grandchild. While you won't have to pay an early withdrawal penalty, you'll still owe income taxes. Withdrawals are limited to $10,000 over your lifetime.
- The Hope Scholarship is a $1,500 tax credit that is available for the first two years of college. If you owe taxes, you may be eligible for a tax credit equal to 100% of the first $1,000 of tuition and fees paid, and 50% of the second $1,000. This credit has several restrictions, such as filing status, modified adjusted gross income (MAGI), and student enrollment status. There are others. Make sure you understand them all before you claim the credit.
- The Lifetime Learning Credit is a family-based tax credit because it is available on a per taxpayer basis. It is available for members of your family who are beyond the first two years of college, or who may be taking courses to improve or upgrade their job skills. This credit has some of the same restrictions as the Hope Scholarship credit.
- If you do have to obtain student loans, you may be able to deduct up to $2,500 of interest paid each year within the first five years of repayment. This deduction has restrictions based on filing status and MAGI, and is only available for interest incurred on loans that were used to pay for tuition, books, fees, equipment, room, and board.

The decision to attend college is a big one. While it may be something that you really want for your child, it is your child that is going to have to do the work to graduate. If your child is not really ready to go to college, you may be making a potentially costly mistake. You can end up wiping out most of your savings, staring at a mountain of debt, or both.

There is nothing wrong with considering some alternatives. Maybe your child would be better off attending a junior college or community college first. Maybe your child could work a year before starting college. This might allow him or her to mature a little more because he or she has experienced the "real world." This can also give your child some insight as to what he or she really wants to do. However, be careful not to allow your child to waste too much time looking. Our children often need our direction and guidance more than they are sometimes willing to admit. Don't be afraid to give them a little nudge when it appears that they may have stalled. King Solomon gave us some good advice on this subject in Proverbs 22:6:

Train up a child in the way he should go: and when he is old, he will not depart from it.

As you prepare for your child's future, the most important thing that you can do is spend as much time as is needed to teach your child the Word of God. It will serve him or her well throughout their lives. Next, seek wise counsel to help you make good decisions about saving for their future education needs. Finally, be prayerful in all that you do. If you can do all of these things, you will have a plan that will help your child get through all of life's lessons with high marks.

Chapter 9
Securing a Worry-Free Retirement

Saving for retirement is a common goal that many of us share. In fact, a financially secure retirement is usually the number one goal that people list when developing their financial plan. Unfortunately, it is also the goal that most people are inadequately prepared for when they reach retirement age.

Why do so many of us miss the mark when it comes to retirement? One reason is that it is so easy to procrastinate. Retirement is something that most of us would like to do as soon as possible, but tomorrow is always the day we'll start to prepare for it.

Sources of Retirement Income

There are many different ways that you can save for your retirement. The goods news is that you are not limited to any one option. The bad news is that since there are so many options, choosing the right ones can be overwhelming.

Retirement income can be divided into four categories:

- Social Security
- Personal savings
- Non-Qualified
- Qualified

Many financial planners often describe these four categories as representing the legs of a four-legged stool. The stool is your retirement. If one of the legs is weak or unstable, the stability of the stool (your retirement) is in jeopardy. Now, I'll discuss the two most used categories in more detail.

Social Security

Social Security came into existence with the passing of the Social Security Act of 1935 (originally called the Economic Security Act). After the severe Depression of the early 1930s, many state governments, local communities, and charities found it increasingly difficult to help those who were in need.

Social Security was established as a national social insurance program to help reduce the risks of not having enough money to sustain yourself when you reach retirement age. Our government recognized that if something weren't done, many of the elderly poor would eventually become their responsibility. So, they established a retirement insurance program for qualified workers to help them provide for themselves.

Social Security is a pay-as-you-go program. Money collected through payroll taxes on today's workers are used to pay benefits for current retirees. In 2002, the Social Security Administration (SSA) paid retirement and survivor benefits to roughly 39.1 million people, while 152.7 million workers contributed to the program.[4] The average monthly benefit paid in 2002 was $895. How much you get as a Social Security benefit will primarily be a function of how long you worked, and how much you have paid into the system.

As the number of retirees drawing benefits has increased, SSA officials have begun to worry that there may come a time when there are not enough workers paying into the system to pay the benefits expected by retirees. While no one knows if future benefits will be reduced, or worse, eliminated, Social Security will still be a retirement option for you to consider. Just don't depend on it as your primary means to support yourself during retirement.

Qualified Plans

A qualified retirement plan is one that has "qualified" for special tax treatment because it adheres to certain rules and guidelines set

---

[4] 2003 Annual Report of the Board of Trustees of the Federal Old-Age and Survivors Insurance Trust Funds.

forth by the Internal Revenue Service or the Employee Retirement Income Security Act (ERISA). Once a qualified retirement plan is set up, it will offer the following tax benefits:

- Your employer can take a tax deduction for an allowable contribution to the plan on your behalf in the year that the contribution was made.
- Any contributions that you make to the plan may be excluded from your taxable income in the year the contributions were made. Also, you will not have to pay any taxes on the contributions or the earnings on those contributions until they are withdrawn.
- Funds in a qualified retirement plan are held by a trust. The trust is exempt from paying taxes on the earnings from those funds.
- Plan participants or their beneficiaries are allowed to transfer their balances from one qualified plan to another without triggering a taxable event.

Because of the tax preferences given to qualified plans, they have become the primary means through which individuals save for retirement. Qualified plans can be further sub-divided into two categories: defined benefit plans and defined contribution plans.

Defined Benefit Plans. Many years ago, your retirement was something that was taken care of for you. You would work at the same company for 20 or 30 years, retire, get a gold watch, and collect your pension. Add in your Social Security check, and you had a comfortable retirement.

But now, things are different. Increasingly, employers and the government have been sending you a message: Your retirement is your responsibility. To better understand this, let's take a look at just how much things have changed.

As I stated earlier, there used to be a time when your employer would set aside funds for your retirement. Such plans are called defined benefit plans. A defined benefit plan is one in which your employer provides a predetermined retirement benefit to you (or your beneficiaries) based on a set formula. This formula can be based on many factors, but age and years of service are usually included in the calculation. Your employer puts money into the plan on your behalf, and they have full control as to how those dollars are invested. This retirement benefit is usually paid as a fixed percentage of your income or a specific dollar amount.

When you retire, your employer will calculate the value of your pension and offer you the following payment options:

- Single-life annuity
- Joint-life annuity with 50% survivor benefit
- Joint-life annuity with 100% survivor benefit
- Period-certain annuity
- Lump-sum distribution

If you accept any of the annuity options, the retirement payments received will be guaranteed according to the option selected. A single-life annuity will get you the biggest payment, but it poses the biggest risk to you or your family. Single-life payments are based on your life only. When you die, the payments stop. Your family or heirs get nothing. The joint-life annuity with a 50% survivor benefit will pay you the full pension payment for as long as you live. If you die before your beneficiary, they will get 50% of your retirement payment. Once your beneficiary dies, the payments stop. The joint-life annuity with 100% survivor benefit works the same way, except it pays the same benefit (100%) to your beneficiary as it does to you.

A period-certain annuity guarantees that, between you and your beneficiary, it will pay a set benefit for a minimum period of time. For example, if you chose a ten-year period certain annuity with a monthly benefit of $750, it would pay you $750 per month for ten years. If you should die within the ten-year period, your beneficiary will continue to receive the $750 monthly payment until the end of the ten-year term. If you live beyond ten years, you will continue to get the payments for as long as you live. When you die, the payments stop, and your heirs get nothing.

Lump-sum distributions are where the full value of your pension is paid to you in one big payment. If the distribution is made directly to you, it will be subject to income taxes. Also, if you are under age 59 ½, the distribution may be subject to early withdrawal penalties. To avoid the taxes and penalties, you should roll your distribution over into another qualified plan (IRA, 401(k), etc.).

Some people also try to take their lump-sum distribution and payoff all or most of their bills. The idea is that since most or all of their bills will be paid off, they won't need as much income to live on. The problem with this line of thinking is that the added tax liability and possible penalties make this an expensive option that rarely makes sense. If you do need some of your pension money to pay bills, consider spreading the distributions over several years to minimize the tax burden. Consult your tax advisor to help you devise a strategy that will work best for you.

Recently, many companies have begun to switch from traditional defined benefit plans to a new type of defined benefit plan called the cash balance plan. Traditional defined benefit plans are meant to reward long-term employees. The longer you work at your company and the more money you make, the larger your pension benefit will be. A cash balance plan is really dependent upon your salary only. For example, a cash balance plan might be set up to credit your pension account at a rate of 5% of your annual salary plus interest.

The benefit of a cash balance plan is that it allows your pension benefits to build up at a steadier rate and earlier in your working life. Additionally, your plan balances are eligible for rollover to another qualified plan should you change employers. Generally, this was not the case with traditional defined benefit plans.

Why would a company switch from a traditional defined benefit plan to a cash balance plan? The primary reason is cost. Cash balance plans have a more stable cost pattern. The amount of money that a company has to put into its pension plan to pay retirement benefits to current and future retirees is based on a long-term expected rate of return. As long as the actual rate of return is equal to or greater than expected rate of return, pension liabilities are said to be fully funded. When the actual rate of return is less than the expected rate of return, the pension will have an unfunded pension liability.

Traditional defined benefit plans got hit with a one-two punch from 2000 through 2002. The stock market went into a three-year decline and interest rates declined to levels not seen in 40 years. Because actual rates of return were way below expected rates of return, many companies found themselves facing huge unfunded pension liabilities. Although a rise in interest rates and positive stock market returns could erase some of the deficit, many companies are choosing to convert their traditional defined benefit plans to cash balance plans to help deal with the issue. Some companies converting to a cash balance plan will see an immediate decrease in their pension liabilities. In most cases though, a conversion to a cash balance plan will not lower pension liabilities, but will just make them more predictable.

So what does this mean for you? Cash balance plans do offer the following advantages:

- **Easy to Understand**. If you can add, multiply, and divide, you can figure out how much your pension is worth.
- **Safety**. Your account will receive pay credits and interest each month, regardless of the ups and down of the stock market. Also, your pension will be guaranteed by the Pension Benefit Guaranty Corporation (PBGC), which is a federal agency that protects the benefits of American workers.
- **Portability**. If you stay at your job for least five years (the typical vesting period), you can take the lump-sum value of your pension with you should you change employers. You can take it as cash (subject to taxes and penalties) or roll it over into an Individual Retirement Account (IRA) or your new employer's qualified plan. Since cash balance plans are conservatively invested, you may be able to successfully invest the funds within the IRA, and earn a higher rate of return than you would have in the cash balance plan.

Are there any disadvantages to cash balance plans? Yes, there are, and it is primarily in the conversion process. If you are in your 20s, you'll come out ahead in a conversion. If you have less than five years to retire, and you've been with your employer for twenty or more years, you probably won't notice that much of a difference. However, if you have 10 to 15 years to go until retirement, and you already have ten or more years of service, you may end up with a significantly smaller pension under a cash balance plan than you would have had under the traditional defined benefit plan.

Companies are handling these situations in a variety of ways. At first, some companies were recalculating their employees pension benefits solely on the new cash balance formula. For older employees, this was a major issue because it usually meant that their pension benefit could be reduced as much as 45%. Fortunately, due to employee protests and lawsuits, many of these companies have backed off of a retroactive recalculation of pension benefits when converting to a cash balance plan. Most companies are now letting employees over a certain age have the option of staying in the old plan or carryover the vested portion of the pension under the old plan into the new cash balance plan. Under this situation, their pension benefit will not be reduced, but will probably grow more slowly than it would have under the old plan.

If you become aware that your employer is considering converting to a cash balance plan, don't just ignore it. This is a major event that could seriously affect your retirement. Make sure you ask questions and factor any changes into your retirement plan.

Defined Contribution Plans. There are still some defined benefit plans in existence, but many of them have given way to defined contribution plans. A defined contribution plan is one where the amount that you can put into the plan is defined, but the amount that you will get as a retirement benefit is not. How much you get as a retirement benefit will be dependent upon how much you contribute to the plan, how much your employer contributes to the plan as a matching benefit (if anything at all), and the investment performance of the total dollars contributed to the plan. There are many types of defined contribution plans, with the most popular being the 401(k) and 403(b) plans. Of particular note is the new Individual

154

401(k) plan. This type of defined contribution plan is meant to cover individual business owners and their spouse who also works for the firm. Sole proprietors, doctors, lawyers, accountants, consultants, hairdressers, real estate agents, and other types of independent contractors may find this type of plan especially attractive.

Why is it that most companies now offer defined contributions plans instead of defined benefit plans? There are many reasons, but the primary one is cost. Defined contribution plans are usually less expensive to administer. Additionally, companies are not required to contribute to the plan. When they do, it's usually in the form of a matching contribution. For example, a company may offer a 50% matching contribution, up to a maximum of 3% of your salary. Since employee participation in defined contribution plans usually runs between 65% and 80% of eligible employees, companies can save on the amount they spend on employer contributions.

Contributions to a defined contribution plan can usually be made on a pre-tax or after-tax basis. When contributions are made on a pre-tax basis, your income tax deductions are calculated on your salary after the deduction for your contributions. For example, suppose your annual salary is $30,000 per year. Your total deductions for state and federal taxes run about 15% of your pay, or $4,500. You decide to contribute 6% of your pay to your 401(k) on a pre-tax basis. This works out to be $1,800. When your employer recalculates your income tax deductions, they work out to be $4,230, which is $270 less than they were before you started contributing to your 401(k). This happens because your taxes were calculated on $28,200 in salary, which is your $30,000 salary less the $1,800 in pre-tax 401(k) deferrals. Even though $150 per month is being deducted out of your paycheck, your take home pay is only decreased by $127.50, because of the lower taxes.

When you make contributions to your defined contribution plan on an after-tax basis, your account balance will grow at the same rate as would if the contributions were before-tax. The difference is that you don't get the tax savings out of your take home pay. In the previous example, your take home pay decreased by $127.50 instead of $150, which saved you $22.50 per month. Ignoring future pay increases, if you were to invest that $22.50 each month at 8% for 20 years, it would grow to $13,253.

Should you ever contribute after-tax dollars to your defined contribution plan? There are some circumstances where it can make sense. For example if you are very sure that you are going to retire before age 59 ½, an after-tax contribution can come in handy, and here's why. Should you retire before age 59 ½, you will be too young to collect Social Security. Your only source of income will be your pension, your personal savings in taxable accounts, and any non-qualified or qualified accounts that you may have. There are methods to receive periodic income from qualified and non-qualified accounts without having to pay an early withdrawal penalty. Additionally, these funds will still be subject to income taxes. If you have some bills that you would like to payoff, complete some home improvements, or take a nice retirement vacation, you may find that your choices to pay for these things may be somewhat limited.

However, if you have a defined contribution plan where you have made after-tax contributions, you may be in luck. If you rollover your plan assets to an IRA, any after-tax contributions that you made to the plan are prohibited from being deposited into an IRA. Therefore, you will receive that chunk of money without any tax consequences, because you have already paid taxes on it. These funds can be a useful resource to help you transition into retirement, and take care of some of those things you wanted to take care of.

While I always advise clients to contribute whatever they can afford to their defined contribution plan, I also encourage them to try to at least contribute the percentage that will get them the maximum company match. The company match is free money, and I don't know of anyone who should turn down free money. More importantly, the company match makes such a big difference in your retirement future that you really can't afford not to get as much of it as you can.

For example, let's assume at age 35 you had the opportunity to participate in your employer's defined contribution plan. You decided to contribute 6% of your annual pay, and your employer made a matching contribution of 3% of your annual pay. Your current salary was $30,000 per year and you expected it to increase by 3% per year. Assuming an 8% rate of return, here are some numbers for you to consider:

Value of account after 30 years	$449,706
Total matching contributions	$42,818
Earnings attributed to matching contributions	$106,519
Total wealth forgone if you did not participate in the plan	$149,337

Why would anyone not want an extra $149,337? Those dollars could really make a difference in the quality of your retirement. If you haven't been participating in your employer's plan because you never bothered to sign up, do it now. If your current financial situation just doesn't allow you to participate in your employer's defined contribution plan, you need to make improving your situation a priority. Time passes by very quickly. Before you know it, you'll be staring at retirement and not sure how you are going to make it. Take the time now to understand how your plan works and use it to your advantage.

Finally, you should be aware that your employer has certain obligations to you that it needs to uphold with respect to the defined contribution plan. Most plans are what we call participant directed. This means that you have some say in how the funds deposited in your account are invested. It also means that most of the responsibility and liability for your investment performance rests with you, as long as your employer has complied with Section 404(c) of the Employee Retirement Income Security Act (ERISA).

Section 404(c)of ERISA has three basic requirements:

- The plan must offer a "broad range" of investment choices
- The investment choices selected must be sufficient to permit the participant to materially affect the potential return and risk of his account
- The investment choices selected must be able to allow the

participant to diversify the account enough to minimize
the risk of excessive losses

In theory, your employer could meet the requirements of Section 404(c) by offering a stock fund, a bond fund, and a money market fund. However, the investment landscape has changed quite a bit through the years, and three investment choices may not be enough to allow you to materially affect the risk and return of your account, or guard against excessive losses. Additionally, investments such as stock mutual funds will vary according to size (large, medium, or small capitalization) and style (growth or value). Not only must you be able to diversify across asset classes, but you must also consider investment style and size.

To comply with the spirit of the law in this new investment environment, I believe employers must offer more choices. While there is no magic number, I believe anywhere between 8 to 12 choices is a good. Anything more than 12 can be confusing and over-whelming for the employee. Additionally, your employer should engage in the following:

- Develop and/or implement an Investment Policy State-ment (IPS)
- Conduct an annual due diligence review of the plan
- Provide ongoing investor education programs

The purpose of the Investment Policy Statement (IPS) is to detail how your employer is going to evaluate the plan. Your benefits department should be able to provide you with a copy. If they don't have one, it's not a reason to panic, but you should probably "encourage" them to develop one. If they don't have an IPS, they probably aren't conducting annual due diligence reviews of the plan either. The purpose of the review is to make sure the investments in the plan are adequate performers, and that the fees and expenses associated with the plan are reasonable. Lastly, they should be providing ongoing opportunities for investment education. Many employees don't manage their plan properly because they just aren't sure what to do. While many plan providers and sponsors offer brochures, along with online resources, these just aren't enough. If your employer isn't sponsoring investment education, try to encourage them to do so. There is nothing like being able to learn and interact with a live person to answer your ongoing investment questions.

What should you do if your employer isn't engaged in any of the previously mentioned activities? ERISA section 409(a) indicates that any person who is a fiduciary with respect to a plan and breaches any of the responsibilities, obligations, or duties with respect to that plan, shall be personally liable to make good any losses to the plan resulting from such breach. They may also be subject to any other remedial relief that the court may deem appropriate. This is just a fancy way of saying that if your employer's defined contribution plan is so crummy that it makes it really hard for you to manage your retirement money the right way, you may be able to sue them to recover the lost earnings.

Now, let me say that I don't recommend anyone rushing out to sue their employer for any losses they've experienced in their defined contribution plan. Besides the obvious effects that such a move could have on your career advancement opportunities, it could also lead to very awkward moments in the company cafeteria. However, if you feel that this is a serious issue with your employer, I suggest that you approach it from the point of view of trying to help "educate" them. It has been my experience that many members of a company's employee benefits committee don't even realize that they are personally and financially on the hook for any losses incurred by the plan if there is a breach of their fiduciary duties. In fact, many of them don't even know what an IPS or due diligence review is. If this is something that is important to you, approach it the right way and everyone can win in the end.

Individual Retirement Accounts (IRAs). The Individual Retirement Account was first introduced in 1981 as a tax-favored way to encourage people to save for their retirement. As the name states, it is a retirement account for individuals. Therefore, there is no such thing as a joint IRA. Contributions to an IRA can be made before-tax, after-tax, or both, depending on your income and other factors.

You can contribute to an IRA as long as you have earned income (salary, wages, etc.), and the amount contributed doesn't exceed the annual contribution limit or 100% of your annual compensation, whichever is less.

Through the years, the tax code has been changed and modified such that there are many different types of IRAs today. Most IRAs are self-directed. This means that you control what investments are made in your account. The many different types of IRAs will fall under two categories: deposit and brokerage. A Deposit IRA is an IRA that invests only in deposit products offered by banks, credit unions, and savings and loans. Examples of investments offered in a Deposit IRA would be savings accounts, money market savings accounts, and certificates of deposit (CDs). A Brokerage IRA is an IRA that allows you to invest in things such as stocks, bonds, mutual funds, money market funds, etc. There are also IRA accounts that will let you invest in real estate, partnerships, and other more sophisticated investments. Because of the complicated nature of these investments, make sure you consult your tax advisor before setting up one of these IRAs.

Under the umbrella of a Deposit or Brokerage IRA, there are several types of IRA accounts that you can open. On your own, you can set up a traditional IRA or a Roth IRA. With a Traditional IRA, you must have earned income (wages, salary, etc.) in order to contribute to the account. You can make contributions to the account up to age 70 ½. For the 2003 tax year, the annual contribution limit is $3,000. If you are age 50 or older, you may contribute up to $500 more as a catch-up contribution. This was written into the tax code to allow individuals who haven't saved as much as they should to accelerate their rate of savings for retirement. Under current tax law, the contribution limits are scheduled to increase to $4,000 per year in years 2005–2007, and to $5,000 per year in year 2008. Beginning in year 2009, the annual contribution limit will be indexed, and increase according to increases in the cost of living. Catch-up contributions will increase to $1,000 per year from year 2006 and beyond. As with any other tax laws, these are subject to change, so make sure you consult your tax advisor before you open an account or make a contribution.

Now, if you don't have any earned income, you may still be able to save for retirement by opening what is called a Spousal IRA. As the name may suggest, you have to be married to set up this type of IRA, and you must file a joint tax return. With the Spousal IRA, contribution limits and catch-up provisions are the same as a regular IRA. Also, the total contribution between your IRA and your spouse's IRA cannot exceed the contribution limit or 100% of your spouse's income, whichever is less.

With Traditional IRAs, contributions may be tax deductible depending on whether you are an active participant in a retirement plan at your job, your tax filing status for the year you are going to make a contribution, and your modified adjusted gross income (MAGI). For more details on the deductibility of your contributions, consult your tax advisor or *IRS Publication 590*.

With Roth IRAs, your contributions are not tax deductible. Contributions can be made even after you have reached the age of 70½. Additionally, you are never required to take any money out as long as you live. However, after age 59½, any withdrawals that you make are completely tax-free and without penalty. This is the big benefit of the Roth IRA.

In my opinion, the beauty of the Roth IRA is that it allows you to limit your tax liability to your contributions only. If you are a Roth IRA contributor for a long period of time, the tax savings can be phenomenal. For example, let's assume that at age 25 you decided to contribute $2,000 per year to a Roth IRA, and your average rate of return for the next 35 years was 8% per year. At age 60, you would have contributed $70,000 to the account and it would be worth about $345,000. Your original investment of $70,000, plus the $275,000 of investment earnings would be available for withdrawal with zero tax liability.

Some other types of IRAs are SIMPLE IRAs and SEP IRAs. The Savings Incentive Match Plan for Employees (SIMPLE) IRA is designed for sole proprietors or small businesses with fewer than 100 employees who do not maintain another retirement plan. The employer establishes the eligibility requirements. However, all employees who have earned at least $5,000 during the previous two years and who are expected to earn at least $5,000 in the year that the plan is established must be allowed to participate. For tax year 2003, employees can contribute up to $8,000 or 100% of their compensation, whichever is less, on a pre-tax basis.

Employees age 50 or older can defer up to $1,000 more as a catch-up contribution. The employer is required to make an across the board 2% contribution for all eligible employees or a dollar-for-dollar matching contribution of up to 3% of the employee's W-2 compensation. As an exception, the employer is allowed to lower the match to not less than 1% for two years out of any five-year period. The SIMPLE IRA is attractive to both the employer and employee for several reasons. Small business owners like it because it allows them to offer a competitive retirement benefit with minimal administrative burden. Also, employers get to take a tax deduction for their contributions to the plan. Employees like it because it allows them to save more for retirement than what is allowed through a Traditional or Roth IRA. They also like it because contributions are 100% vested immediately. Also, because the SIMPLE IRA is self-directed, the employee controls how it is invested.

The Simplified Employee Pension (SEP) IRA is an IRA that is established by the employer for the employee. The employer makes a direct, tax-deductible contribution to the SEP IRA. Employees are not allowed to make salary deferral contributions. Employer contributions are discretionary each year, but must cover all employees who are at least age 21, who have been employed in three of the preceding five calendar years, and who earned in excess of $450 in 2003. The employer has the option to make eligibility requirements less restrictive if they choose to. The maximum contribution that an employer can make to a SEP IRA is the lesser of $40,000 or 25% of annual employee compensation. Contributions are immediately 100% vested.

Many of the changes governing IRAs were put into place with the passing of the Economic Growth and Tax Relief Act of 2001 (EGTRA). Maximum contribution limits and catch-up provisions will increase periodically through 2010. Unfortunately, EGTRA has a sunset provision that states that all of the changes granted by this act will expire at the end of 2010. Beginning in 2011, all rules governing IRAs will revert to what they were in 2001 unless Congress passes further legislation to extend the changes or make them permanent. Make sure you consult your financial or tax advisor to help you determine what type of IRA is right for you.

When Would You Like To Retire?

Initially, when I ask my clients when would they like to retire, the usual answer is "tomorrow!" However, after more thought, the real answer to this question isn't always easy to come by. When to retire is just as much an emotional issue as it is a financial one.

Emotionally, you have to figure out when you will be ready to retire. Some of us are really connected to our work. In such cases, our work defines who we are. It is where most of our friendships are developed and maintained. It is where we have invested most of our emotional capital. You love to work, and you are not sure what to do with yourself when you are not working. If your work environment has assumed too much prominence in your life, it will be very difficult for you to walk away. In such cases, retirement will be a traumatic experience.

For others, retiring will present no emotional issues at all. It's not that you didn't like your job (well, maybe it is!), but there are others things in life that you are emotionally connected to. Being able to retire will allow you to spend more time on those things. In fact, you are so ready to retire that you tell your co-workers to skip the retirement luncheon because you'll be too busy cleaning out your desk so that you can leave on time!

If you are married, retirement presents another set of issues that you have to consider. For some, retirement means finally being able to spend more time traveling and doing other things with your spouse. For others, the fact that you now have more time to spend with your spouse is the problem. On more than one occasion, I have received a phone call from a client telling me that ever since they retired, their spouse has been driving them crazy.

The complaints vary. He follows me everywhere I go. She never lets me go anywhere. He thinks I'm his maid. All she wants to do is go shopping. We never go anywhere. We're always going somewhere. When you were working, you never had the opportunity to experience these wonderful habits or personality traits. However, since you've retired, they have reared their ugly heads.

While some of these complaints may indicate relationship problems that existed long before you retired, I think they highlight the importance of honestly discussing your retirement expectations with your spouse. Doing so not only helps you to decide when to retire, but also helps you to emotionally prepare for it as well.

What's Your Strategy?

There are two phases to your retirement strategy. The first phase is the accumulation phase. This is where you try to save as much as you can for your retirement, and earn as much as you can on what you have saved. The next phase is the distribution phase. This is where you take money out of your retirement account to use as you see fit. These distributions can be in the form of periodic payments (monthly, quarterly, etc.), occasional withdrawals as needed, or both.

In the accumulation phase, there are several issues that you will need to address. First, you will need to determine how much to save for your retirement. This involves making some decisions about when you want to retire and how much it will cost to support your desired retirement lifestyle. Once those decisions are made, you will calculate how much you can afford to save towards your retirement goal and what average rate of return you will need to achieve to reach the goal. Your required average rate of return will be the primary driver in the selection of investments for your retirement portfolio. For example, if the required average rate of return needed to achieve your retirement goal is 10% per year, you will probably need to focus on using investments that give you the best opportunity to earn that kind of return, such as stocks or stock mutual funds. If your risk tolerance dictates that you are only comfortable investing in CDs and bonds, your likely rate of return will not be enough to allow you to achieve your retirement goal. You will either need to allocate more funds toward savings for your goal or lower your expectations for your retirement lifestyle. Or let's suppose that all you need to achieve your retirement goal is an average rate of return of 3% per year. Investing in stocks or stock mutual funds may offer you the opportunity to earn more than 3% per year, but it will also expose you to more risk. You could end up losing money and have to postpone your retirement plans. If 3% per year is all you need, investing in CDs and bonds may allow you to earn that rate without exposing your portfolio to a lot of risk, and therefore increase the likelihood that you will achieve your retirement goal.

There are several risks that you will face as you plan how you will use your retirement savings during the distribution phase. They are as follows:

- Risk of inflation
- Risk of outliving your money
- Investment risk (loss of principal)

Inflation risk is the risk that increases in the cost of living will exceed any increases in your income. Inflation risk is why most of us expect our employers to at least give us a cost of living increase in our pay each year. When you retire, inflation risk should be more of a concern because much of your income will be fixed over time (hence the term, "fixed income"). Usually, the only income payment that you receive during retirement that is periodically adjusted for inflation is Social Security. Pension and annuity payment usually aren't adjusted for inflation. Any adjustments for inflation in your distributions from your retirement savings will primarily be dependent upon the investment success of your portfolio.

When the rate of inflation exceeds the rate of growth in your portfolio, you will have what is called a negative real rate of return. What this means is, even though your portfolio is growing over time, you are actually losing money because the dollars you are earning today can't buy as much as they used to. Back in 1982, I can remember paying about $1 for a loaf of bread. In 2003, I typically paid about $2.25 for that same loaf of bread. This represents about a 4% per year rate of inflation. However, if I invested $1 back in 1982, and had an average rate of return of 3% per year for the same period, my dollar would only be worth about $1.86. In order to buy that same loaf of bread, I'm going to have to earn a much higher rate of return, or spend some of my principal.

This leads to a major problem that retirees face when developing their strategy. Many retirees think that since they are retired, they can't afford to take any chances with their investments. The natural inclination is to put their money in the safest investments that they can find. But, if your investment return is not keeping up with the rate of inflation, you may have to start spending your principal to meet your living expenses. If this goes on too long and you are blessed to live a long time, then you will face the risk of outliving your money.

When this happens, retirees sometimes get desperate because they know they need to earn more on their investments. This desperation to earn a higher rate of return can lead them to take on more risk, knowingly or unknowingly, than they should. Additionally, there are unscrupulous investment advisors and salespeople who are very aware of some retiree's desperation to earn more and will actively try to take advantage of them.

To protect yourself, you should first remember that there is no such thing as a no-risk, guaranteed investment with a high rate of return. To get higher rates of return, you usually have to accept higher levels of risk. Higher investment risk usually means a higher level of fluctuation in your principal. One bad investment decision can have the effect of wiping out most, if not all, of your portfolio. If this were to happen, the quality of your life during retirement could be permanently affected. Don't let your desperation to earn more on your portfolio cause you to make a poor decision. Proper diversification can help reduce your investment risk.

When you retire, there are several questions that you will need to have answered. How much income should you withdraw from your retirement savings each year? Should it be a fixed dollar amount or a fixed percentage of your balances? Should you try to live off your investment earnings only or should you plan to spend some, or all, of your principal? How do you allow for lump-sum withdrawals? Here are some answers:

How much income should you withdraw from your retirement savings each year? Obviously, you should only withdraw what you need. However, the real issue here is determining how much you can safely withdraw from your retirement savings without going broke. In general, you should only withdraw 50% of what you think you can earn over the long-term. For example, if you think you can earn an average rate of return of 8% per year during your retirement years, you should only withdraw 4% of your portfolio value for income. This should provide enough cushion for your portfolio so it can withstand most prolonged market declines while generating the necessary income to support your living expenses. In some cases, you may be able to go as high as 60% of your long-term expected rate of return. However, I would only attempt this if I were fairly confident that the investment climate was going to be extremely favorable in the near future. If things don't work out as planned, you could significantly impair your portfolio's ability to generate the income that you'll need.

Should you withdraw a fixed dollar amount or a fixed percentage of your balances? By withdrawing a fixed dollar amount, you'll know what to expect each payment period. However, if the actual rate of return on your portfolio begins to stay under your expected rate of return for too long, your rate of withdrawal will be too high, which may lead to you running out of money. When you set your withdrawals as a percentage of your balances, you will never run out of money. However, your periodic payments will fluctuate with the value of your portfolio. If your portfolio suffers a serious decline, your periodic withdrawals may not be enough to meet your living expenses.

Should you try to live on your investment earnings only or should you plan to spend some, or all, of your principal? When you retire, you'll probably have your pension and Social Security as sources of income. If you still need additional income, I typically will recommend that you try to live on your investment earnings. This is the safest route to take, and it will allow you to better deal with the financial uncertainties of retirement. However, if your investment earnings alone aren't enough to fill your income gap, you may have to spend some of your principal. It is at this point that you are making a bet. You're betting that your financial situation will improve, or you will die, before you run out of money. Since neither death nor poverty are desired outcomes, I strongly encourage you to start saving for retirement as soon as possible.

How do you allow for lump-sum withdrawals? After you retire, situations will arise where you will need large chunks of money. This could be auto or home repair, medical emergency, or helping a family member out financially. When you retire, try to set aside a chunk of money for these emergencies or special expenditures. If you don't have a chunk of money that you can set aside when you first retire, try to save some of your retirement income to slowly build up your cash reserves. Remember, too many unplanned lump-sum withdrawals will lead to reduced income from your portfolio, or the premature liquidation of your portfolio.

Finally, there are plenty of workbooks, as well as calculators on the Internet, that can help you figure out how much you will need for retirement. They will also guide you in answering some of the questions we just discussed. However, a major flaw in most of these tools is that they rely on what I call straight-line calculations. The assumption is made that the rate of return on your portfolio will be constant. For most people, this is next to impossible to achieve. To better plan your retirement, or any other financial goal, you should consider something called Monte Carlo simulation.

Monte Carlo is a technique that is used to help determine the range of outcomes for a particular event. It is usually applied to some type of mathematical model. Most retirement or financial planning models assign a value to each variable in the model. Examples of variables in a retirement planning model would be the rate of return, monthly contributions, monthly distributions, expected tax rates, and lump-sum distributions. There are many more variables that could be added to this list. When you change one variable, you have to recalculate the entire model. As long as there aren't many variables, this may not take too long. But, what if your model has just 10 different variables? I hope you have lots of pencils, because you would have over 3.6 million different outcomes.

Computer software using Monte Carlo simulation can make quick work of such calculations to help you come up with a range of outcomes based on the values you have assigned to your variables. Using this software can help you determine the probability of achieving any of your goals. I liken the output of these programs to a weather report. If you knew there was a 70% chance of rain tomorrow, you probably would not plan on attending a picnic because you would be relatively sure that it would get rained out. If the chance for rain were only 10%, you would probably plan on attending the picnic. It could still rain, but the likelihood would be very small. With Monte Carlo simulation, you can determine if the outlook for your retirement plan is rainy with a chance of storms, or clear and sunny. This type of software is readily available either as a standalone program, Microsoft® Excel Add-In, or web-based calculator. If you are not the type to tackle something like this on your own, a good financial advisor will know how to apply Monte Carlo simulation to your financial plan.

We've discussed all of the different options you can use to save for your retirement. We've also discussed the different issues you need to be concerned whether you are in the accumulation or distribution phases of your plan. Now that you have the pieces, you can pull everything together for a winning retirement plan. So, where do you go from here?

The best strategy for securing a worry-free retirement is to start early. Back in Chapter 5, we talked about the time value of money, which states that a dollar received today is worth more than a dollar received tomorrow. The other concept that comes into play is compound interest. If at age 25 you were to start investing $100 per month for your retirement, and you could earn 8% per year on your portfolio, you would have about $58,902 by the time you were age 45. If you stopped contributing to the account at age 45, and just let it continue to grow at a rate of 8% per year, you would have about $290,199 when you reached age 65. The total that you contributed to the account was only $24,000. Your total investment earnings were $266,199. But, what if you couldn't start saving for your retirement until age 45? You know that you're behind, so you decide to save $200 per month until age 65. Assuming you could earn 8% per year, your portfolio would only grow to $117,804. Your contribution would have been $48,000 and your total investment earnings would be $69,804. In fact, in order to have the same ending value of $266,199, you would have to invest about $452 per month beginning at age 45. The total amount that you contributed to the portfolio is about $108,480, which is 4½ times as much as you would have had to put in if you started at age 25. The reason for this is that you started putting money into your retirement account sooner rather than later (time value of money). Also, once you put money into the account, it had a longer period to grow and allow the interest and dividends to earn more interest and dividends (compound interest).

For most people, you should prioritize saving for your retirement as follows:

- Take advantage of your 401(k) or 403(b) plan at your employer, especially if there is a company match.
- If you don't have a 401(k) or 403(b) plan at work, and you

qualify to make deductible contributions to an IRA, consider opening a Traditional IRA.

- Open a Roth IRA, especially if you are under the age of 50. The tax-free earnings could really come in handy when you retire.
- If you've maxed out what you can put into your 401(k) or 403(b), consider annuities, or a tax-efficient mutual fund.

Securing a worry-free retirement is a lot like building a car. You want to use the right pieces according to the features that are right for you. If you are young, or if you are an aggressive investor, your retirement portfolio might be like a sports car. The ride may be rough, but it will get you where you need to go and get you there fast. If you are older, or if you are a more conservative investor, your retirement plan might be more like a big family car. It's not very fancy, nor does it have a lot of power, but it safely gets you to your destination. Put the wrong parts (individual investments) in either of these cars (portfolios) and you may crash on your road to retirement.

Chapter 10
The Real Deal on Real Estate

There are two ways to invest in real estate, and that is either directly or indirectly. When you directly invest in real estate, your interest in the property is represented by a legal document called a deed. A deed is a signed legal document that represents the transfer of property and shows the legal right to possess it. When you indirectly invest in real estate, your interest in the property is represented by your ownership in the entity that owns the real estate.

Is Real Estate Your Biggest and Best Investment?

I often hear people say that buying a home is the biggest investment you will make in your lifetime. For most people, this is a true statement. I also hear people say that buying a home is the most profitable investment that you can make in your lifetime. I'm here to tell you that for most of you, this is not true.

Why should you purchase a home? Is it because you need a tax deduction? I hope not, because buying a home because you need a tax deduction is about as bad as having children because you need a tax deduction. In both cases, you will spend a lot more than you get in tax benefits. Mortgage interest is a tax deduction, not a tax credit. If it were a tax credit, $1 of mortgage interest would reduce your tax liability by $1. Since it is a tax deduction, $1 of mortgage interest only reduces your tax liability according to your tax rate. For example, if your federal tax rate is 27%, $1 of mortgage interest will reduce your tax liability by 27¢. Real estate taxes are deductible as well, so they have the same effect. The deductibility of these two items serve to reduce your cost of being a homeowner.

However, there is also another angle that must be considered. The deductibility of mortgage interest and real estate taxes is only relevant if you itemize deductions on your tax return. Taxpayers are automatically given a standard deduction to reduce their taxable income. For the 2002 tax year, those deductions were as follows:

Single	$4,700
Married filing jointly	$7,850
Married filing separately	$3,925
Head of Household	$6,900
Qualifying widow(er)	$7,850
(deductions are increased if you are age 65 or older, or blind, or both)	

The deductibility of mortgage interest and property taxes favors those individuals with big mortgages or who live in areas of the country with high property taxes. If you are able to itemize, the deductibility of these items help to reduce your cost of home owner-ship. It doesn't eliminate it, but it does reduce it. The key question is what will it cost you to get the tax break? Let's look at an example.

Joe, age 30, is single. He is currently renting an apartment for $500 per month, but is considering buying a home. Joe makes $28,000 per year, and has about 5% of his pay deducted for state income taxes each year. He has no other expenses that he can deduct for tax purposes. He has found a home that he likes that is on the market for $76,000. If he makes a down payment of 5%, his monthly payment of principal and interest will be $432.88 on a 6% mortgage with a thirty-year term.

Joe decides to purchase the home on January 1st of the year. The next year when he files his taxes, his deductible expenses are as follows:

State income taxes	$1,400
Property Taxes	$1,140
Mortgage Interest	$4,308
Total	$6,848

Because his deductible expenses exceed his standard deduction of $4,700, he can itemize them on his tax return. Joe is excited, because he had always heard that owning a home saves you a lot a money on your taxes. However, once he completes his tax return, his excitement begins to die down. If he had continued to rent his apartment, he would have gotten the standard deduction of $4,700, which would have saved him about $705 in taxes. Buying a home allowed him to itemize, but those itemized deductions only saved him an additional $322 in taxes. Exactly what did Joe spend to get that additional $322 in tax savings?:

Table 10-1

Renting vs. Owning

	Joe the Renter	Joe the Homeowner
Rent	$6,000	
Mortgage Payments		$6,096
Insurance*	$100	$300
Property Taxes		$1,140
Total	$6,100	$7,536

* Renter's Insurance vs. Homeowner's Insurance

Being a homeowner is going to start off costing Joe an extra $1,436 per year in out-of-pocket cash, which does not include the cost of maintenance. This figure could go up each year, as his expenses for property taxes, homeowner's insurance, and maintenance will likely rise through the years. Joe will initially save an additional $322 in taxes, which lowers his initial net out-of-pocket cash flow for becoming a homeowner to $1,114. However, he will still end up spending more money on being a homeowner than he will save on taxes. Nevertheless, Joe is happy he bought the house. He has much more room than he had in his apartment. He loves his neighborhood and his neighbors. But he now knows that buying a home just for the tax deduction is not a smart idea. Now you know it too!

Maybe you want to buy a house because it is a "can't lose" proposition. Don't home prices always go up? Unfortunately, the answer to this questions is no! Home prices are a function of supply and demand, as it is with all investments. While the supply of homes is somewhat limited, which helps home prices to generally rise over time, there are circumstances when home prices can decline.

In 1985, I bought my first home, which was a condominium. Unfortunately, I was not aware that there was a glut of condominiums in the city. Apparently, several builders wanted to cash in on the popularity of condos. As a result, there were many more condos for sale than there were condo buyers and prices started to fall. In the three or four years following my purchase, the value of my condo fell about 8%. It was not until around 1992 that the value of my condo was equal to what I originally paid for it. Thank goodness we didn't have to sell during that time, or we would have lost a lot of money.

Houston, TX was a fast growing city in the late 1970s and early 1980s. It was heavily dependent on the oil industry, and when that industry fell on hard times in the mid-1980s, so did Houston home prices. Prices in the city fell over 20% and took about seven years to recover. Many communities across the country have experienced similar real estate price declines at some point in their history.

There are many factors that can cause home prices to decline. Adverse changes in local industry, population shifts, and deterioration in environmental conditions are just a few. All of this just highlights the fact that home buying is by no means a risk-free endeavor.

How can you tell if buying a home will be a good investment? Well, as I like to tell my clients, let's crunch the numbers.

Do the Math

If you talk to any bonafide real estate professional, he or she will tell you that in order to calculate the return on investment (ROI) for a property, you have to examine the cash flows. What are cash flows? Cash flows are represented as dollars received or dollars paid. When you purchase a home as your primary residence, Table 10-2 shows a list of possible cash flows.

Once you have identified the cash flows, you are now ready to calculate the return on investment for your home purchase by using the Internal Rate of Return (IRR) method. IRR is the rate of return that makes the present value of all future cash flows, including the

Table 10-2

Cash Flows to Determine Return on Investment	
Inflows	**Outflows**
• Tax Benefits • Net proceeds from the future sale of the property	• Down payment • Closing Costs • Mortgage Payments • Homeowner's Insurance • Property Taxes • Maintenance & Repairs

final market value of the property, equal to the current market value of the property. To better understand this definition, let's look at an example.

Tom and Linda are buying a house that has a purchase price of $110,000. They are going to make a $22,000 down payment (20%), and finance the remaining $88,000 with a thirty-year mortgage that has a 6% interest rate. Their closing costs are 3% of the mortgage balance, which is $2,640. The payments on this mortgage are paid annually, so the payment of principal and interest amounts to $6,393. Their federal tax rate is 27%.

We will assume that the value of Tom and Linda's home will appreciate at a rate of 3% per year, and they will sell the home at the end of the ten-year period. The following annual expenses are calculated as a percentage of the home's value:

- Property taxes – 1.50%
- Property insurance – 0.35%
- Maintenance & upkeep – 1.00%

Each year's tax benefits are calculated by totaling the deductible real estate expenses (mortgage interest and property taxes) and multiplying them by the homeowner's tax rate. The net sales proceeds are calculated by assuming a 3% growth rate in the value of the property, less the mortgage balance at the time of the sale, and 6.50% in selling costs. There is no capital gains tax because they will have held the property for over two years and would get a $500,000 capital gains exemption on the sales proceeds. The cash outflows were calculated by totaling all out-of-pocket expenses associated with owning the property. This figure consists of the mortgage payment, property taxes, property insurance, and annual maintenance. Property taxes, property insurance, and annual maintenance increase at the same rate as increases in property values (3% per year). Table 10-3 provides a summary of the cash flows and the resulting IRR calculation:[5]

Table 10-3

Is Your Home a Good Investment?
An IRR Analysis of a Residential Home Purchase and Sale

Period	Cash Outflows	Tax Benefits	Net Sales Proceeds	Net Flows
Down Payment & Closing Costs				($ 24,640)
Year 1	$9,528	$1,871		($ 7,657)
Year 2	$9,622	$1,866		($ 7,756)
Year 3	$9,719	$1,861		($ 7,858)
Year 4	$9,819	$1,855		($ 7,964)
Year 5	$9,921	$1,848		($ 8,073)
Year 6	$10,027	$1,840		($ 8,187)
Year 7	$10,137	$1,832		($ 8,305)
Year 8	$10,249	$1,822		($ 8,427)
Year 9	$10,364	$1,811		($ 8,553)
Year 10	$10,484	$1,800	$64,893	$ 56,209
			IRR	-9.17%

In this example, the rate of return achieved for this home purchase is −9.17% per year when calculated using the IRR method. This hardly appears to be an attractive investment, but we should intuitively know this anyway. In order for your home purchase to have a positive rate of return, the rate of growth for the value of your home has to exceed your costs to acquire and maintain the home.

---

[5]The IRR calculations used in this table and elsewhere were calculated by using the IRR function in Microsoft® Excel.

Even when you adjust for tax benefits, the rate of appreciation in your home's value is rarely enough to significantly overcome your acquisition and maintenance costs. What if Tom and Linda held the property for 20 years? The IRR improves to –3.84%. What if they held it for 30 years? It gets better, but the IRR is still negative at –1.71%.

Many people find this hard to believe or accept for a variety of reasons. First, there are some who believe that the only out-of-pocket expense of buying a home is the down payment. This is not true because every mortgage payment that you make consists of principal and interest. The principal payments that you make are additional investments in the property. You are continually adding investment dollars to the property until you sell the property or payoff the mortgage loan.

Next, rates of appreciation for residential real estate usually range anywhere from 3% to 5% per year. Yes, there are exceptions. For example, if you purchase a home in an area that is being overbuilt, you may actually experience a negative rate of appreciation. This happens because the supply of homes is greater than the demand for those same homes. This causes prices to fall. There are also areas that are highly desirable or where demand far exceeds supply. In these cases, appreciation rates can be 8% to 10% per year, or higher. A good real estate agent can tell you what the appreciation rate has been for the area you're interested in. She can also tell you what she thinks the appreciation rate will be for that neighborhood over the next five years.

How can you improve your chances of generating a positive return on the purchase of a home as your primary residence? First, don't pay too much for the house. Buying a home is very exciting and there are many emotions that may come into play when you are making your purchase. Just don't let those emotions lead you to pay more for the property than what it is worth. Next, properly maintain your home. It is very easy to neglect routine maintenance. Unfortunately, this usually means that little repairs turn into big ones. Be very timely with maintenance and you'll reduce your overall cash outflow for that expense. Finally, reduce your mortgage expense.

Although there is a tax deduction for mortgage interest, there is still a net cost to carrying one. If you are only planning on being in the home for a few years, you won't benefit much by trying to accelerate any payments on your loan. But if you are going to be in the house for more than seven years, reducing your mortgage expense through payment acceleration will improve the investment return on the property. All of these things will help reduce your cash outflows associated with owning the property and therefore improve your IRR.

Another important term you should know in order to understand the rate of return on your home purchase is cost of capital. Cost of capital is basically the opportunity cost of using your money to buy a home instead of investing it elsewhere. Some people also refer to it as the required rate of return, because it is the rate that you must earn to match the average rate of return on your other investments. All that the IRR calculation does is find the rate of return that makes the cash flows (in and out) equal. Table 10-4 summarizes how changes in the IRR of your real estate purchase can affect your financial wealth:

Table 10-4

How Changes in IRR Affect Your Financial Wealth

Investment Rate of Return	Real Estate Investor's Wealth
Internal Rate of Return < Cost of Capital	Decrease
Internal Rate of Return = Cost of Capital	No Change
Internal Rate of Return > Cost of Capital	Increase

So, when is real estate an investment? Real estate can be an excellent investment when it generates an income. That is why rental real estate is often referred to as investment property. To further examine the investment potential of rental real estate, let's use the same information in the previous example. This time, instead of Tom and Linda purchasing the property for their own use, they are going to rent it out for $7,800 per year. Annual rents will increase by .5% per year. The cash outflows are the same as before. Since the property is being rented, property insurance and annual maintenance are included in the tax benefits calculation because they are now deductible expenses. Total deductible expenses are netted against rental income to calculate net tax benefits. Depreciation was not included in this example because it is a pay-me-now-or-pay-me-later expense. Taking depreciation on a rental property provides tax benefits now, but it lowers your cost basis in the property, which will cause you to pay higher capital gains taxes when you sell. If you don't take depreciation now, you're not getting the tax break, but your capital gains tax will be lower when you sell the property. Table 10-5 shows the IRR analysis of the property as a rental.

Table 10-5

How Rental Property Can Be Investment Property
An IRR Analysis of a Rental Real Estate Purchase

Year	Cash Outflows	Rental Income	Net Tax Benefits	Net Sales Proceeds	Net Flows
	Down Payment & Closing Costs				($24,640)
1	$9,528	$7,800	$166		($1,562)
2	$9,622	$7,839	$163		($1,620)
3	$9,719	$7,878	$159		($1,682)
4	$9,819	$7,918	$155		($1,746)
5	$9,922	$7,957	$151		($1,814)
6	$10,027	$7,997	$146		($1,884)
7	$10,136	$8,037	$141		($1,958)
8	$10,249	$8,077	$134		($2,038)
9	$10,364	$8,118	$128		($2,118)
10	$10,484	$8,158	$120	$55,159	$52,953
				IRR	3.21%

In this example, the rate of return achieved for this real estate purchase is 3.21% per year when calculated using the IRR method. This is a big improvement over the first example, and the improvement can be attributed primarily to the inclusion of rental income. However, the results of this analysis raise several other questions.

What if you can't rent the property at a high enough rent? What if you paid too much to buy the property? What if you borrowed too much money to buy the property? What if your tenant moves out unexpectedly, and leaves the property vacant for several months? What if your tenants are constantly damaging your property, causing your maintenance expense to be much higher than expected? All of these scenarios will negatively affect your IRR.

Very few individuals, whether buying real estate for personal use or as an investment, bother to calculate any type expected rate of return. Even after they have owned the property for several years, they still don't know whether the purchase was generating a positive or negative return. This strikes me as very strange because, especially in the case of investment real estate, most people buy property with the belief that they will make money. If you aren't calculating your rate of return using IRR or something similar to it, how can you know if the property is performing up to your expectations? You can't.

This leads me to comment on the many real estate books, audiotapes, and infomercials that seem to make real estate investing so easy. Here is a list of some their claims:

- Investing in real estate is easy
- You can make lots of money fast
- You can walk away with money at closing
- You can easily buy properties with no money down

To save you time, and hopefully some money, here is my opinion on each of those claims:

Investing in real estate is easy. No it isn't! In Chapter 7, I talked about how money that is ready to be invested will find the easiest path with the highest return in accordance to an acceptable level of risk. If successful investing in real estate were truly easy, it would attract too many investors, which would drive down the profitability of all subsequent real estate investment opportunities. Many of my clients and friends who are real estate investors all tell me the same thing: Investing in real estate requires a lot of work. I've heard too many stories about how being a landlord can be a real pain. I've had too many clients call me to request funds out of their account to pay for massive repairs to rental properties damaged by tenants. Oh, and by the way, those same tenants skipped out owing back rent. Don't be fooled. Successful investing in real estate is not easy!

You can make lots of money fast. Successful investing in real estate takes time. Lots of time. The very nature of investing in real estate requires time. It takes time to locate suitable properties. A good friend of mine who is a real estate investor spends months looking for prospective properties. Most of the ones that he finds turn out not to be good deals, or the negotiation process breaks down. It takes time to secure financing. It takes time to get appraisals done. The only way that you can get real estate deals done quickly is to pay for them in cash. Making lots of money fast in real estate investing is a rare occurrence.

You can walk away with money at closing. Now, I've actually seen people do this. There are many ways that some people pull this off, none of which I would recommend that you try. Additionally, many of these transactions require winks, nods, blind eyes, and deaf ears between some or all of the participants. Consider the following example (all names are fictitious). Sam Seller had a property he wanted to sell. The house had recently appraised for $50,000 and was in good shape. Bobby Buyer decided to buy the property, but he didn't have enough money to do the deal. Bobby convinced Sam to write up the sales contract for $62,500, but to include a seller's decorating and repair allowance of $12,500 (wink, wink). Lucy Lender then sent a request to Andy Appraiser to appraise the property. Andy's search for comparable sales within two miles of this property showed that several homes that were similar to this one recently sold for about $50,000. However, after conferring with Bobby and Sam, he agreed that the house was worth $62,500 and prepared his report to show that value (nod, nod). Lucy got the appraisal back and noticed that the sales contract showed seller concessions that represented 20% of the sales price. Seller concessions in excess of 3–4% of the sales price are supposed to reduce the maximum loan amount. Lucy called Bobby to tell him she couldn't loan him the full loan amount. But after some discussion, he convinced her to do the loan because of all of the future business he was going to do with her bank (blind eye). Finally, while Larry Lawyer was conducting the loan closing, he overheard Bobby telling Sam that he found a tenant for the property. He then asked Bobby to sign the standard bank form that required him to certify that he was buying the home as his primary residence. Mortgage rates are lower for primary residence financing, plus you are allowed to borrow more money against the property. Failure to certify is supposed to stop the loan closing. Larry allowed Bobby to sign the form certifying that he was going to live in the house as his primary residence. (deaf ear, wink, wink, nod, nod). Sam got a check for $50,000 ($62,500 - $12,500 allowance). The bank got a $62,500 loan on a property worth $50,000. Bobby owed $62,500 on a property worth $50,000. He also got a check for $12,500 to decorate and repair the property (which was in good shape and he had no intention to decorate). He spent $1,000 on minor repairs to the property, and spent $11,500 on trying to convince his friends that he was a big-time real estate investor. About a year later, the bank foreclosed on the property because Bobby couldn't make the payments (his tenants kept skipping out without paying rent). Bobby couldn't sell the property because he owed more on it than it was worth. Lucy was fired for approving a loan outside of normal guidelines. The moral of this story is that doing a deal to get money back at closing is very risky. Fortunately, most of the people involved in a real estate transaction wouldn't even think of doing something outside of guidelines. However, it does happen. Even if you don't consider the moral, ethical, and legal issues involved, getting money back at closing rarely makes sense because all you are doing is borrowing more money. The more you borrow to purchase an investment property, the more difficult it becomes to make a profit. Trying to make a profit is why you should decide to become a real estate investor.

You can easily buy properties with no money down. This isn't impossible to do, but it isn't easy either. More importantly, it rarely makes financial sense to do it. The ultimate profitability of a real estate transaction depends upon one thing: positive cash flow. To generate positive cash flow, you must receive more in rental income and/or capital gains than you pay out in expenses and/or mortgage payments. Trying to buy a property with no money down usually means that you are getting 100% financing or more. This increases your costs to acquire and carry the property, which can reduce profitability. Nothing-down purchases are also difficult to do because most lenders require minimum down payments of 20–30%. Your source of funds for the down payment must be verified before the loan closing and in most cases cannot come from the seller. Lenders know that properties where the borrower has very little equity are very risky and have high foreclosure rates. Borrowers who have little or no equity in the property are more willing to walk away if things go wrong. Also, when a property is foreclosed on, it usually sells at a discount to its appraised value. If a lender doesn't have a cushion in the form equity from the borrower, they are likely to suffer a big loss when the house is sold in foreclosure. Lenders want to make money too, so it is unrealistic to think that you will find one that is willing to take on all of the risk of the transaction. Buying properties with no money down is not easy, nor is it always advisable.

The real deal on real estate is that it is an investment like any other investment. Lower your fees and expenses, and you increase your chances for profit. Extremely high rates of return are the exception rather than the rule. Before you buy a piece of property, make sure the expected rate of return is sufficient to help you achieve your financial goals.

Why Do It?

Let me say that I firmly believe that becoming a homeowner is a good thing to do. You just need to make sure you want to buy a home for the right reasons. You should buy a home for personal use first and foremost because you need a place to live. Secondly, you buy a home because it is in a neighborhood that is conducive for you to live in a way that is most beneficial for you. Next, you buy a home because you want to control your housing costs instead of being subject to annual rent increases from your landlord. Finally, you buy a home because it may turn out to be a good investment.

How To Qualify For A Mortgage

Buying a home is one of the most significant financial transactions that you will encounter in your lifetime. In fact, you will probably go through it more than once.

After deciding which house to buy, you need to decide how you are going to pay for it. Unless you are going to pay cash for the house, you will probably need to borrow the money in the form of a mortgage loan. You can save yourself a lot of headache and possibly heartache by pre-qualifying yourself for the mortgage before you look for the home of your dreams or before you see your mortgage lender.

How can you pre-qualify yourself? If you can add, subtract, multiply, and divide, you can pre-qualify yourself for a mortgage. The rules are relatively standard throughout the industry. All you will need is a calculator and some time to determine just how much house you can afford.

What Kind Of Mortgage Do You Need?

There are basically three mortgage types: FHA, VA, and conventional.

An FHA mortgage is a mortgage guaranteed by the Federal Housing Administration (FHA) through the U.S. Department of Housing and Urban Development (HUD). These mortgages allow lower down payments and may also allow you to finance some of your closing costs, such as your mortgage insurance premium. This can help you to minimize the amount of money that you need for closing. If you are a first time home buyer, this type of mortgage may interest you.

A VA mortgage is similar to the FHA mortgage except that it is guaranteed by the Veterans Administration (VA). These mortgages may allow up to 100% financing based on the appraised value of the home being purchased and your level of entitlement to VA benefits. VA guidelines also allow the financing of certain closing costs. If you are a veteran, check with your real estate agent or local VA office for more information.

Conventional mortgages are those mortgage loans offered by lenders without any type of special guarantee from a government agency. The amount of financing available will vary from lender to lender.

Mortgage products come in two forms: fixed rate and adjustable rate. Fixed rate mortgages are those where the interest rate on the loan is fixed and will not change. An adjustable rate mortgage (ARM) is a mortgage where the rate can change during the life of the loan. The frequency of rate change depends on the type of ARM being offered. ARMs will also have some type of cap or limit as to how high your rate can go. There will also be a limit as to how much it can change within a set period of time. Usually, the rate on these loans is tied to an index.

Should you get a fixed or adjustable rate mortgage? It all depends on your particular situation. If you only plan on being in the house for a short period for time, you may want to go with the ARM. By the time your rate fully adjusts to a market rate from the low initial rate, you may be ready to sell or refinance. If you need a lower rate to qualify for a mortgage, the ARM may also be your best choice. If you prefer a stable payment or if the mere thought of a fluctuating interest rate will cause you to have sleepless nights, go with the fixed rate. Even though you may initially pay a higher rate than with the ARM, the peace of mind you receive by having a fixed rate loan may be worth it.

Playing The Rate Game

When you are shopping around, you will get many different rate quotes. Each lender that you call will quote you a rate, and tell you whether there are any points or if there is an origination fee. These fees affect the actual interest rate for your loan.

An origination fee is a fee that the lender may charge for originating or processing the mortgage. The purpose of this fee is to help the lender cover some of their initial expenses incurred in processing your application and servicing the loan. This fee will is normally around 1% of the loan amount. Some lenders may charge more than 1% and many charge less than 1% or no fee at all. A discount point is a form of prepaid interest that you pay to the lender in exchange for a lower rate. The more discount points you pay, the lower your rate. In order to compare apples to apples, you need to compare rates based on their annual percentage yield (APY). APY takes into account any points that you may pay to reduce your rate. Here is an example of how points can affect your rate:

Interest Rate	Points (Rebate)	APY
5.375%	2.0%	5.727%
5.625%	1.0%	5.887%
5.875%	0.0%	6.045%

You may now ask, "Why should I pay points?" Again, the answer depends on your particular circumstances. If you have plenty of cash for down payment and closing costs but need a lower rate to qualify, you may want to pay additional points to get that lower rate. Lenders like discount points because they get some of their interest upfront. That's why the base rate on a mortgage with points will be lower than that of a mortgage without them. Also, since you are pre-paying some of your interest costs by paying points, your total interest expense over the life of the mortgage may be lowered. Otherwise, if you want to lower your total closing costs, minimize or don't pay any discount points.

Basic Terms You Should Know

During your loan interview, here are a few basic terms that your loan interviewer should review with you:

Loan Prepayment – This option allows you to make additional payments to principal or pay the loan off early without penalty (Don't get a loan without it!).

Prepaid Interest – With most lenders, your monthly payments will consist of principal and accrued interest from the previous month. If you close on your mortgage and your first mortgage payment isn't due within the next 30 days, you most likely will have to pay prepaid interest. This will range anywhere from 1 to 31 days of daily interest depending on which month you close. Your prepaid interest will be lower if you close later in the month.

Private Mortgage Insurance (PMI) – This is required anytime your down payment is less than 20% of the purchase price. PMI protects the lender against loss should you default on the loan. Most loans that go into default are those that had a down payment of less than 20% of the purchase price. If PMI were not available, it would be very difficult to obtain financing if you wanted to have a down payment of less than 20%. In exchange for letting you have a lower down payment, lenders require you to purchase PMI to cover them in case you default. Mortgage insurance purchased for FHA and VA loans works the same way.

Annual Percentage Yield (APY) – This is the actual or effective interest rate for the loan. This rate tells you your true cost of borrowing and is affected by prepaid interest, other mandatory prepaids, origination fees, discount points, and the term of the loan. The lower the aforementioned items, the lower your APY.

Loan-To-Value Ratio (LTV) – This is the amount of money you wish to borrow divided by the purchase price or appraised value of the property, whichever is less. This ratio is important as it is used throughout the entire mortgage process.

The Secondary Market

Throughout the entire process, you may hear some reference to the term "secondary market." When someone uses this term, they are usually referring to Fannie Mae (FNMA – Federal National Mortgage Association) or Freddie Mac (FHLMC – Federal Home Loan Mortgage Corporation). These companies act as middlemen in the mortgage marketplace between mortgage lenders and investors.

The primary function of a secondary marketer is to purchase mortgage loans from lenders, assemble the loans into pools or mortgages, and package the pools as mortgage-backed securities for sale to investors. The ability of a lender to sell their loans on the secondary market gives them liquidity, which ultimately means that funds will be continually available to make future mortgage loans.

The Qualifying Ratios and What They Mean

Qualifying ratios are percentages that determine the recommended maximums that a person's new mortgage payment and total debt should represent of their gross monthly income. The two ratios used are called the housing ratio and the debt ratio. The housing ratio is based on your new mortgage payment consisting of principal, interest, taxes, insurance, and homeowner association dues (if required), divided by your gross monthly income. The debt ratio is based on your new mortgage payment plus all of your other monthly obligations, such as installment loans, credit cards, and lines of credit. These ratios are determined by the lender or a secondary marketer, such as Freddie Mac or Fannie Mae.

Most lenders use 28% for the housing ratio and 36% for the debt ratio. However, some lenders do use different ratios. If you are a first time home buyer or if you live in an area where housing costs are much higher than in other parts of the country, higher ratios may be used. Check with your local lender or real estate agent for more information.

The Qualifying Process

When you submit your application to the lender, they should review it for completeness. Additionally, they should make sure that they have all of the information that they initially need. While you are in the office, they may give you an idea as to how your application looks in terms of qualifying for the mortgage. Your lender will begin the process of verifying the information on your application. They will order a copy of your credit report and order an appraisal for the house you are trying to buy. Once this information has been returned to the lender and deemed satisfactory, you should receive final approval.

What If You Don't Qualify

This is not the end of the world! Ratios are guidelines for lenders to follow. It may be possible to have your loan approved if your application does not meet the standard qualifying guidelines. However, you should note that exceptions to normal qualifying ratios are allowed only if the lender feels there are other overriding or compensating factors involved in the application. Additionally, exceptions approved by the lender may require that you accept a mortgage with a higher interest rate.

If the information in your verifications or credit report causes you not to qualify, you may have to provide additional information or explanations. To avoid having problems late in the processing phase of your mortgage application, do some pre-qualifying on your own. Be open and honest with the lender about any potential pitfalls in your loan application

What if you don't have enough money for the down payment? You have several options. You can borrow the money for your down payment, as long as it is from a secured source. For example, if you have a car, certificate of deposit, stocks, bonds, or any other asset in which you have equity, you can borrow against it to generate the cash needed to cover your down payment. The only stipulation is that the payment on this loan must be included in your debt ratio.

You can also use money received from someone as a gift. If the gift is less than 20% of the purchase price, you will still be required to put in at least 5% of the purchase price on your own. If the gift is 20% or more of the purchase price, you don't have to put in anything.

There are also some programs available that provide down payment assistance (DPA). This assistance is usually in the form of a cash gift, credit for work completed (sweat equity), or a low-interest or interest-free loan. Most of these programs are offered by legitimate non-profit organizations and foundations. One of my favorite DPAs is the Individual Development Account or IDA.

IDAs are a type of asset accumulation account that began to gain in popularity during the 1990s. The IDA was designed to help low-income families purchase their first home, pay for higher education expenses, or start a small business. Participants in the program are usually required to successfully complete a financial literacy training program and commit to saving a certain amount (usually $1,000) over a set time period. When completed, they can receive a dollar for dollar match, and in some cases, as much as six for one. The funds are yours to use for the designated purpose, and do not have to be repaid. Non-profit organizations or private foundations usually fund an IDA program, although some major corporations fund such programs for their employees.

IDA programs are available in just about every state, but usually in just a few select counties. Availability is expanding all the time, so make sure that you check with your local public housing authority or community development corporation for more information. For general information about the program, contact the Corporation for Enterprise Development at 202-408-9788, or on the Internet go to www.idanetwork.org.

In recent years there has been a proliferation of DPA programs available from what some people call gifting organizations. These companies are usually set up as non-profit organizations. Their pitch is that they can help you buy the home of your dreams with little or no money down. However, it is my opinion that potential homeowners face several risks when they purchase a home through these programs. Here's how they work.

These organizations provide gift money to homebuyers. There are usually no income restrictions, and the purchase price of the home can't exceed the limits imposed by program guidelines. These guidelines vary from program to program, and city to city.

In order to participate, you must purchase a home from a builder or seller who is enrolled in the DPA program of the gifting organization. This is the first red flag. In most other DPA programs, you can buy a home from whomever you want, without them having to have an affiliation with the program. The fact that there are only certain builders or sellers who you can buy from indicates that there is a special relationship between them and the gifting organization.

When a builder or seller signs up with one of these DPA programs, he agrees to pay the gifting organization a service fee. Part of the fee goes into a pool of funds from which gifts are made. The other part of the fee goes to the gifting organization to cover operating expenses. This service fee is usually in the range of 2% to 6% of the purchase price of the home, which brings us to red flag number two. All builders have a certain amount of profit that they want to make on the sale of their home. All sellers have a certain amount of equity (or profit) that they want to get out of the sale of their home. If you know you are going to incur an additional cost to sell the home, then you usually mark up the price so that you still end up netting the same amount of equity or profit that you were expecting.

For example, let's assume Mr. Builder has a home he wants to sell that lists for $100,000. He knows he won't get $100,000 for the house because most potential homebuyers make offers to buy that are less than the list price. The typical reduction in list price in his area is 5%. The standard real estate sales commission is 6% of the final sales price. The typical seller's closing costs run about 1% of the final sales price.

A representative of a gifting organization has contacted Mr. Builder about joining their program. He tells Mr. Builder that a gifting program can help him sell his home faster because more people will be able to afford his home. He also tells Mr. Builder that he might even make more money because homes sold under their program aren't discounted. The service fee for their program is 4% of the final sales price. Mr. Builder tells the representative that he'll think about it. He then goes back to his office and puts together an analysis, which is shown in Table 10-6.

Table 10-6

How Participation in DPA Programs Affect Builder Profits

	Normal Sale	Normal Sale w/DPA	Adjusted Sale w/DPA
List Price	$100,000	$100,000	$100,000
Avg. Reduction In List Price	5%	5%	0%
Final Sales Price	$95,000	$95,000	$100,000
Sales Commission	$5,700	$5,700	$6,000
Seller's Closing Costs	$950	$950	$1,000
DPA Service Fee	$0	$3,800	$4,000
Sub-Total	$88,350	$84,550	$89,000
Builder's Cost of Home	$78,850	$78,850	$78,850
Net Profit	$9,500	$5,700	$10,150
Net Profit Margin (%)	10%	6%	10.15%

There are several things that come to Mr. Builder's attention after he runs the numbers. Participation in the gifting organization's DPA program under normal market conditions will cause his net profit to decline by 40% ($5,700 vs. $9,500). But if the price of the home can be marked up to cover the service fee, he can maintain his net profit margin, and in the case of this example, actually make a little more money. Since the selling price of a home purchased through one of these programs is usually non-negotiable, it looks like a win-win situation for everyone involved.

The truth of the matter is that there are several substantial risks to you when you purchase a home in this manner. What a home is worth is what someone else is willing to pay for it. In the above example, the home sold through the gifting organization's DPA program had a higher selling price only because it had to be marked up to cover the service fee. This has the effect of artificially boosting home prices.

Next, this type of transaction is nothing more than a back door means of obtaining 100% financing for the purchase of your home. This puts you at risk because you will have little or no equity in the home in the early years of the mortgage. Should you have to sell the home during these early years, you might end up owing more money on the house than it is worth. Additionally, if you weren't able to save enough money for a down payment because you had poor spending habits, buying a home is the last thing you need to do.

In fact, it is my opinion that this type of DPA program is a lot like going to a 50% off sale at your favorite department store, only to find out that they doubled the original price before you got there. You still end up paying full price! While I am sure that some people may benefit from this type of program, the risks far outweigh the benefits.

Buying a home is a big step in your financial life. If you can't qualify to buy a home because you don't have enough money for the down payment, you may just need to wait until you can save the money on your own. However, if you still feel the time is right for you to become a homeowner, look for a DPA program that doesn't put you at risk.

Other Helpful Information

The following are some helpful tips that may help you along in the processing phase of your mortgage application. All of these tips may not apply due to varying degrees of compliance by lenders to secondary market guidelines or independent lender policy and procedure:

- Average and current balances for all checking, savings, and investment accounts that are being verified should be the same for the last three to four months prior to a loan application. If there is a significant difference between the average and current balance (i.e., current balance greater than average balance), be prepared to provide copies of statements to show the source of any large deposits that were recently made into the account.
- Proceeds from unsecured loans cannot be used to cover your down payment. Proceeds from secured loans can be used for down payment, but the monthly payment for that loan will be included in your debt ratio. If there is no stated payment, one may be computed by your lender for qualification purposes.
- If receiving a cash gift from a relative for down payment and/or closing costs, and the gift is less than 20% of the purchase price of the home, you will still have to provide 5% of the purchase price in your own funds for down payment. If the gift is greater than 20% of the purchase price, this rule does not apply. FHA and VA mortgages do not require minimum contributions by the borrower when gifts are involved.
- Earnest money is money that you give to the real estate agent to show that you are serious about buying that house. It is also considered to be part of your down payment. Be sure to provide a copy of your earnest money check at the time of loan application, especially if your earnest money exceeds 2% of the purchase price.

195

- If you are currently separated or divorced, be prepared to provide copies of your divorce decree or separation agreement. If you are paying alimony and/or child support, copies of those documents will be required. If you are receiving alimony and/or child support and want to use it as income for qualification purposes, copies of those documents will be required. Also, you may be asked to provide proof that you have received it for the last twelve months (i.e., canceled checks, bank statements, etc.).

- Be prepared to provide copies of tax returns for the last two years if using dividends, interest, commissions, or rental income to qualify.

- If you are self-employed, you may be required to provide copies of tax returns for the last two years. You may also be asked to provide copies of a current balance sheet and year-to-date profit and loss statement. You must have been in business for at least two years in order for self-employment income to be used.

- You should have a good credit history. In the event there are some adverse items showing on your credit report, be prepared to provide a written explanation as to what circumstances may have caused the adverse ratings to occur. In general, your credit history should be clean with no late payments for at least the last twelve months. This is especially true for your current mortgage or rental payment history. If not, you may run into problems getting your applications approved.

- You should have had relatively stable or continuous employment for the last two years or more. Provide written explanations for any frequent job changes or gaps in employment.

Mortgage lending is as much of an art as it is a science. Earlier in the book, I mentioned that there is a trade-off between risk and return. The more risk an investor is asked to assume, the more return he is going to require. Mortgage lenders are investors. The more risk that you, the mortgage applicant, ask them to assume in approving your mortgage, the more return they will require in the form of higher interest rates.

When you sign a contract to purchase a home, you are under legal obligation to meet the terms of that contract within a set period of time. Failure to do so can result in you losing the home you wish to purchase and possibly any earnest money you may have paid. The more preparation that you do, the smoother your mortgage application process will be. Again, your real estate agent can be valuable in helping you with some of the legwork that may be required on your part to process your application.

Managing Your Real Estate Debt

Once you have made the decision to obtain a mortgage, then you must try to manage it in a prudent manner. Here are some strategies that you can adopt to help you accelerate the liquidation of the debt.

One of the ways that you can accelerate the liquidation of your mortgage is to increase the frequency of payments. Most mortgage payments are made on a monthly basis. However, you can save a lot on interest and pay your mortgage off early if you are able to make biweekly payments instead. To do this, you must first have a mortgage that does not have a pre-payment penalty. Next, you must have a lender that will accept biweekly payments. Here's an example of how it would work.

Suppose you took out a 30-year mortgage for $100,000, at an interest rate of 6.50%. Your monthly payments would be $632.07 per month. If you paid on the mortgage for the full thirty-year term, the total amount of interest paid would be $127,544.49. If you were able to make biweekly payments of $316.03, you would pay the mortgage off in about 24 years and pay $98,170.54 in interest. This represents a six-year reduction in your term and interest savings of $29,373.95.

There are two reasons why this works. First, on the day that you close on your mortgage, the interest clock starts ticking. Interest is added to your mortgage everyday. Every payment that you make on the mortgage should pay the interest that has been added on since the last payment, plus some of the principal. Since payments of principal reduce your mortgage balance, the amount of interest that is added on should be less than the previous period, since the balance that it is being calculated on is now less. By making more frequent payments, you give the interest less time to build up, therefore allowing more of your payment to go towards the principal. This is one of the reasons your balance is going down faster than normal. The other reason is that when you cut your monthly payment in half and start paying that amount every two weeks, you are making the equivalent of one extra monthly payment each year.

Now if you aren't able to make biweekly payments, you can just pay extra on the mortgage. Using the above example, suppose you immediately started paying an extra $100 per month on your monthly payment of $632.07. You would then pay the mortgage off in a little less than 21 years and pay $82,505.14. This represents a nine-year reduction in your term and interest savings of $45,039.35.

As I said earlier, these are mortgage reduction strategies that are fairly easy to implement. However, before you try any of them, there are some important factors that you should consider:

- How long will you own the property?
- What is the tax impact?
- Is this the best use of your extra dollars?

If you plan on owning the property for seven years or less, accelerated balance reduction strategies probably won't help you that much. There will not have been enough time to elapse to make that much of a difference. You also have to look at the tax impact. Accelerated balance reduction strategies are like a double-edged sword. The more money you save on interest, the lower your mortgage interest deduction will be. The lower your mortgage interest deduction, the higher your tax liability (if you itemize). Finally, you must consider whether or not accelerated mortgage reduction is the best use of your extra dollars. Would you be better off using your extra dollars to liquidate high interest rate credit cards? Would you be better off investing those extra dollars? If the after-tax return on an investment is more than the tax savings of the mortgage, it will make more sense to invest rather than reduce the mortgage.

Refinancing

Refinancing your current mortgage is also a good technique to help you properly manage your mortgage debt. When you refinance a mortgage, you are essentially replacing your current mortgage with another. The primary reason you refinance is to get better terms than what you already have. This may come in the form of a lower interest rate or a shorter term. Either of these can save you on interest charges and help you to pay your home off sooner.

When you refinance, you should be in a better position after the transaction than before. To achieve this, your new rate should be less than the rate on the previous mortgage. Also, your new mortgage term should be equal to or less than the number of payments you had remaining on the original mortgage. Let's look at an example.

Suppose you purchased a new home ten years ago and financed it with a mortgage of $100,000. Your interest rate was 8%, the term of the mortgage was 30 years, and your monthly payment of principal and interest was $733.76. Now, interest rates have come down and you can refinance your mortgage with a rate of 6%. You call up your current mortgage holder and find out that your current balance is $87,724.70.

You grab a pencil, a piece of paper, and a calculator so that you figure out some other numbers that you will need in order to make a good decision. The first thing that you do is figure out how much principal you have paid on the mortgage. This is easy. You just subtract your current balance of $87,724.70 from the original mortgage amount of $100,000, and the result of $12,275.30 is the amount of principal paid. Now you want to figure out how much interest you have paid.

This calculation is easy too. You know that you've been paying on the mortgage for ten years. So you multiply 10 years by 12 payments per year and come up with a total of 120 payments. Then you multiply 120 payments by the monthly payment (principal and interest only) amount of $733.76, and the result is $88,051.20. Subtracting the $12,275.30 you paid in principal from this number, you now know that you have paid $75,775.90 in mortgage interest.

You are now ready to call a mortgage lender to get some additional information. So you call up your local mortgage loan officer and she tells you that the going rate for a mortgage over 15 years is 6%. This is great news because you have twenty years remaining on your existing mortgage. Your mortgage loan officer then proceeds to tell you that your new mortgage payment will be $628.49. This represents a monthly savings of $105.27. Your mortgage loan officer then informs you that you could save even more per month if you were to refinance for thirty years instead of twenty. She tells you the payment for a thirty-year refinance would be $525.95. This means your monthly savings will be $207.81. You tell her that you will think about it and call her back later. Now you are ready to study all of your options.

Your first option is to do nothing and just keep your current mortgage. To consider this option, you need to figure out how much interest you will pay on your existing mortgage if you pay on it for the full term of thirty years. First you multiply 30 years by 12 payments per year, for a total of 360 payments. Then you multiply 360 payments by the monthly payment of $733.76. This gives you a total amount paid of $264,153.60. Subtracting the original loan amount of $100,000, you now know that your existing mortgage will cost you $164,153.60 in interest.

Your next option is to refinance your current balance for twenty years, which is exactly how much time you have left on your current mortgage. You multiply 20 years by 12 payments per year, for a total of 240 payments. Then you multiply 240 payments by the new payment of $628.49. This gives you a total amount paid of $150,837.60. Subtracting the refinanced loan amount of $87,724.70, you now know that this new mortgage will cost you $63,112.90 in mortgage interest. Adding the $75,775.90 of mortgage interest you paid on the original mortgage up until the point you refinanced, your total cost for mortgage financing over the thirty–year period is

$138,888.80. This represents a savings of $25,264.80 in mortgage interest. Clearly, refinancing for twenty years at an interest rate of 6% makes a lot of sense.

But wait! Didn't the mortgage loan officer say that you could save even more if you refinanced for 30 years? You proceed to find out by multiplying 360 payments by the payment amount of $525.95, with a result of $189,342. Subtracting the refinanced loan amount of $87,724.70, you now know that this mortgage will cost you $101,617.30. Adding the $75,775.90 of mortgage interest you paid on the original mortgage up until the point you refinanced, your total cost for mortgage financing over the forty-year period is $177,393.20. This represents an increased cost of $13,239.60. Your total financing cost went up because you extended the terms. You quickly decide that this is not an option you want to pursue.

From this example, you can see there are several factors you must consider before you refinance. First, you should always make sure the refinance is going to improve your situation. Next, if you are strug-gling to pay your bills and you could use a lower mortgage payment to improve your cash flow, then refinancing your mortgage with extended terms may not be a bad idea. However, you should also be aware that if your credit has deteriorated since you first got your mortgage, the rate you are offered when you refinance may be higher that what you already have. This could make your refinance very costly over time. Finally, should you decide to stay in the property over the long term, make sure you take advantage of the accelerated debt reduction strategies discussed earlier.

When refinancing your home, you can sometimes do what is called a cash-out refinance. With this transaction, you can usually borrow enough to payoff your existing mortgage and receive addi-tional funds to use for other purposes such as home improvement, educational expenses, or debt consolidation. With this type of refi-nance, you should think carefully before you proceed.

Cash-out refinancing can work because the interest rate is usually less than what you would pay for a personal loan or unsecured line of credit. However, most personal or consumer debt is typically financed for no more than five years. Transferring that type of debt to a mortgage with a term of 15 years or longer can mean higher total interest costs. Even worse, it may mean that you are still paying for things long after they have been used or thrown away. If you are considering a cash-out refinance, make sure you look at the bottom line cost of this type of refinance.

Part III

Pathways to Success

Chapter 11
Have You Worked Your Garden?

Some think that when you reach a state of financial independence or material comfort, all you need to do is sit back, relax, and enjoy. But the following Scriptures in Genesis 2:10–15 highlight the assignment that God has given to all of us with respect to this garden called Earth:

> 10 And a river went out of Eden to water the garden; and from thence it was parted, and became into four heads.
> 11 The name of the first *is* Pison: that *is* it which compasseth the whole land of Havilah, where *there is* gold;
> 12 And the gold of that land *is* good: there *is* bdellium and the onyx stone.
> 13 And the name of the second river *is* Gihon: the same *is* it that compasseth the whole land of Ethiopia.
> 14 And the name of the third river *is* Hiddekel: that *is* it which goeth toward the east of Assyria. And the fourth river *is* Euphrates.
> 15 And the LORD God took the man, and put him into the garden of Eden to dress it and to keep it.

In verse 15, we read that God put man in the garden "to dress it and to keep it." The word "dress" is translated from the Hebrew word *abad*. Its primary meaning is "to serve." The word "keep" is translated from the Hebrew word *shamar*. Its primary meaning is "to keep, guard, or observe." Your assignment from God is to be a servant or worker, and keep, guard, and watch over all that He has placed in your care.

The very nature of a garden requires you to work. The soil must be prepared or tilled before seeds are planted. Once the seeds are planted, they must be watered. Once the seeds start to grow, you must continually work the garden to get rid of weeds so it will be as fruitful as possible. The one thing you cannot do is sit back and do nothing.

A river serves many purposes in the ecosystem. It helps to feed and nourish the land around it. It provides water for man to drink. Water evaporates from the river to help form clouds that rain on the dry lands. God gave Adam four rivers to sustain himself and other life in the garden. If one of the rivers were to go dry, he would still have the others available to him.

A river also changes the land through which it runs. It can overflow, develop tributaries, branches, or even other rivers. Such actions can bring new life to areas that were previously dry or without life. The river was the most important part of the Garden of Eden because it was its life force. Adam had to take great care to keep the river clean and pure.

But Satan hated what was going on in the garden. He knew that all rivers have a source. The source of the river in the Garden of Eden was the heart of God. If Adam continued to keep the garden as God instructed him, the garden might begin to spread beyond its existing boundaries. This was a threat to Satan.

Throughout the Bible, sinfulness and evil are often identified as being dry places. The Garden of Eden was a lush place that was full of life. Outside of the garden, the world was dry, harsh, and desolate. This was Satan's domain. Because of this, we may now understand why he hated what was going on in the garden. If a river that flowed from the heart of God was allowed to overflow, or develop tributaries, branches, or other rivers, it would surely bring life to those parts of the world. If Satan could cutoff the rivers, his world of sin and evil could remain.

So he entered the garden, took the form of a serpent, and eventually got Eve and Adam to give in to sin. The purity of God cannot coexist with sin. The sin committed by Adam and Eve polluted the rivers of the garden and threatened to choke out its growth. To make the garden pure again, God cast out Adam and Eve. Now, they were cutoff from the very garden that allowed them to prosper and live well. They failed at their assignment. They failed to keep sin out of the garden!

Because of the fall of Adam and Eve, we are all born into a world that is spiritually dry, harsh, and desolate. Nevertheless, each of us can make it back to Eden. How? By accepting Jesus Christ as our personal Saviour. Eden is no longer a place here on earth, but is now the Kingdom of God. When we accept Jesus, the Kingdom of God will reside in our hearts (see Luke 17:21). Like Adam, we will be charged with the responsibility to "dress it and keep it."

But just as he did with Adam, Satan will hate the work in your garden as well. He knows that God is the source of the rivers that flow in the hearts of the born-again. He knows that the Blood of Jesus is the water that runs in your rivers. Satan will try his best to choke the rivers in your garden with sin.

Genesis 2:10–14 tells us the names of the rivers, but take a look at the meaning of each name. Pison means "increase." Gihon means "bursting forth." Hiddekel means "rapid." Euphrates means "fruitfulness." The name of each river was a clue to the blessings that awaited Adam if only he would have remained obedient. But, we can learn from Adam's mistakes. God has given us more than one river as well. Just like Adam, these rivers will provide a bounty of blessings, if we are obedient to His Word.

From a financial standpoint, many of you have only discovered one of your rivers. Maybe that river is the job that you go to every day. It is your primary source for sustaining yourself and your family. Your job is your life. But what if your job is taken away from you? What if you get laid off? Your river (job) has dried up. This can be devastating if you haven't discovered your other rivers.

Where are your other rivers? They're already in your personal garden. You just have to find them. An investment portfolio can be a river. Owning your own business can be a river. Owning rental real estate can be a river. All of these can help sustain you and your family if one of your other rivers should dry up. More importantly, these rivers can **increase, rapidly bursting forth** to bring **fruitfulness** in your life and the lives of others. Like the rivers in the Garden of Eden, they can be resources to help you fulfill your assignment. But you just can't sit there and do nothing.

You are required to work (keep) the garden. Additionally, you should remember that you are here to serve (dress) the garden. You work for the garden; the garden doesn't work for you. Your life should be based on service to others. Financial resources will be the tools to help you fulfill your assignment of service.

Chapter 12
The WOW Factor!

If you are really serious about building wealth, there is a lifelong formula for success that you must adhere to:

Work + Obedience + Wisdom = True Wealth

To make this formula easy to remember, I often refer to it as the WOW Factor. Let's take a closer look at each part of the formula:

Work

The first component of your lifelong formula for success is Work. We've all heard the saying "God helps those who help themselves." The hand of God is always working in our lives. But some of us try to work Him too hard. We're constantly praying to God to bail us out of one situation after another. However, in most cases, God has already given us the tools to solve the problem. We just have to get busy and put the tools to work.

In Proverbs 13:11, Solomon tells us that "Wealth gotten by vanity shall be diminished: but he that gathereth by labour shall increase." When you gain wealth at the expense of others through selfish means, such as theft, fraud, or deception, it will be diminished. When Solomon speaks of wealth being diminished, he means that you will lose it due to a lack of wisdom (bad decisions or investments), or by the same means through which you gained it (theft, fraud, etc.). Also, this type of wealth will be diminished in the eyes of God. But when you gain wealth through hard work, it shall increase.

God hates laziness. He does not like for His resources to be wasted, as revealed through Solomon in the following verse from Proverbs 18:9:

He also that is slothful in his work is brother to him that is a great waster.

I once had a conversation with one of my clients where I was strongly encouraging her to try to handle her finances better. She first told me that she was going to just leave it in God's hands. I told her that was a good idea, but she needed to use her own hands as well. She acknowledged my point by saying, "Yeah, I know. God don't bless no mess!"

As I stated in Chapter 1, if you want something to happen in your life, three things must occur. First, it must be part of God's will for you. Next, you must be complete in your faith and obedience to Him. Finally, you must do everything that is physically and mentally required of you to make it happen. In others words, you've got to work, and work hard! Nothing will happen unless you put forth the effort.

Not long after I decided to become an independent financial advisor, I had one of those days. You know, one of those days where nothing goes right. After I got home from work, my wife asked me to go to the store with her. I agreed to go, but I was so tired from my day at the office, I asked her to drive. As we drove to the store, she was talking, but I wasn't really listening. I was reflecting on what had happened that day, and wondering if I made the right decision to go into business for myself. Just then, my eyes began to focus on the flight of a bird in the sky.

There were other birds flying nearby, but this bird seemed to be smaller, so it must have been younger. The thing that caught my eye was that this bird was flapping its wings like crazy just to keep up! The very minute it stopped flapping its wings to glide, it began to lose altitude. But, as soon as it started flapping its wings again, it was flying just as high as the other birds. Right then, although my wife couldn't see it because I was staring out of my window, I began to smile. Why? Because, I knew right then that just like a teacher illustrates the answer to a problem on a chalkboard, God had just given me a live illustration as an answer to my problem.

You see, I was really getting frustrated that things weren't going as well as planned. I was working very hard, doing all of things that were necessary for me to succeed, but the business had not measured up to my expectations. But God showed me that I was that little bird. To keep up, I was going to have to work hard and "flap my wings." The very minute that I would try to take it easy and "glide," I would lose altitude just like the little bird in the sky.

From that point on, and even to this very day, I have this message on my computer that reminds me to ask: Have you flapped your wings today? It is a subtle but powerful reminder of the task at hand. A bird will never fly, unless it flaps its wings. You will never reach the heights of spiritual and financial success unless you "flap your wings." When you first start out, just like the little bird, you're going to have to flap your wings like crazy too! However, as you mature and grow, you will be able to fly with much less effort, and glide (take it easy) for much longer periods of time without losing much altitude.

God is a God of action. He is active in your life every day. However, you must sometimes take action if you want to gain access to His blessings. I am often dismayed when ministers preach that your "financial breakthrough" is on the way, but they don't tell you how to "break" your bad financial habits so that you can finally get "through" the mess that you are in. They tell you that *all* you need to do is pray and believe. Yes, you should pray and believe that God will help you. But I'm here to tell you that in most cases, there will be no lightning bolt to zap your overdue bills, nor will there be a burning bush to burn up your bad credit report. In addition to praying to God for help, and believing that He will help you, you've got to do your part. Learn all you can about handling your finances better. Seek wise counsel to help you make good financial decisions. And, don't forget to "flap your wings!" It's the only way that you will see a change.

Obedience

The next component of the formula is Obedience. I believe there are three aspects to spiritual obedience. They are faith, stewardship, and giving. Each one is a key that is required to unlock the rewards of obedience, as discussed in Chapter 3. If you don't have all three keys, you cannot gain access to all that God has planned for you.

Faith

The first spiritual key is faith. Above all else, you must have faith. But, how much do you need? The Scriptures tell us that all you need is faith the size of a mustard seed. The mustard seed is one of the tiniest seeds in the garden. However, a mustard tree can grow to be very large. There were many instances where Jesus scolded the disciples and others for their lack of faith. Despite the fact that Jesus often told them that all they needed to do was "believe," they continually fell short. The analogy of the mustard seed is significant for one main reason. If great things can be achieved with just a little bit of faith, then think of what a lot of faith can do.

Faith is a power that resides in all of us. But, like electricity, we only see the results of faith when we use it. We all have many devices in our homes that need electricity to function. These devices will not work until you connect them to a source of power. Then, you must press the "on" button to make them work. Faith works exactly the same way.

First, we must connect to the power source of our faith, and that's Jesus Christ. In Luke 8:43–48, we read the following story:

43 And a woman having an issue of blood twelve years, which had spent all her living upon physicians, neither could be healed of any,

44 Came behind him, and touched the border of his garment: and immediately her issue of blood stanched.

45 And Jesus said, Who touched me? When all denied, Peter and they that were with him said, Master, the multitude throng thee and press thee, and sayest thou, Who touched me?

46 And Jesus said, Somebody hath touched me: for I perceive that virtue is gone out of me.

47 And when the woman saw that she was not hid, she came
trembling, and falling down before him, she declared
unto him before all the people for what cause she had
touched him, and how she was healed immediately.

48 And he said unto her, Daughter, be of good comfort: thy
faith hath made thee whole; go in peace.

In this particular passage, Jesus is on His way to the home of
Jairus. Jairus begged Jesus to come and see his daughter because he
thought she was dying. As Jesus made His way to the home of Jairus,
a large crowd had gathered around Him. In this crowd was a woman
who had a twelve-year bleeding problem (a hemophiliac?), and she
made her way through the crowd to touch Jesus. This woman had
been sick for twelve years, and no one had been able to heal her. She
could have very easily given up, but instead "turned on" her faith. It
was her faith that led her to believe that if she could just touch the
hem of Jesus' garment, she could be healed. Because Jesus was
making His way through a crowd, it is most likely that many people
were touching Him. Why is it that this woman was the only one
who drew virtue (power) from Jesus?

It was faith. Her faith connected her to the source of all power,
Jesus Christ, through which all things are possible. In fact, even
though the woman told the crowd why she touched Him and how
she had instantly been healed, Jesus told her that it was her faith that
had healed her. Like the woman in this story, the ability to fix your
financial problems, as well as any other problem, already resides in
you. All you have to do is plug into the source, Jesus Christ, and
press the "on" button called faith.

Stewardship

Stewardship is the process through which we serve as administra-
tors or caretakers of what God has blessed us with. Stewardship is
very important to achieving financial success. God uses us as channels to not only help ourselves, but to help others as well. Therefore,
financial increase must be placed in the hands of those who will use

it wisely. If you want more financially, you must prove that you can be a good steward with what you have been given already.

God places resources where they will be most profitable for Him, not you. This is not profit in a purely financial sense, but where the resources will yield the best results. Stewardship allows you to prove to God that you can be trusted to handle to the best of your ability all that He may place in your care.

Giving

Giving plays a major part in building a life of true wealth. For some, giving seems to be the opposite of wealth building. There are those who feel that since they had to work so hard to get their financial wealth, it makes no sense to give any of it away. This line of thinking is wrong on two fronts. First, it assumes that the wealth that we have obtained belongs to us. It does not. Everything that we have belongs to God. Next, it incorrectly assumes that any financial wealth that we obtain is to be used primarily for our selfish desires. While financial blessings are gifts that should be enjoyed, we must always be aware of the unmet needs of others. In Luke 12:48, we read the following:

> "...For unto whomsoever much is given, of him shall be much required: and to whom men have committed much, of him they will ask the more."

Whatever God has abundantly blessed you with in your life, whether it is wealth, wisdom, knowledge, or health, He requires that you not only use these gifts for the maintenance and upbuilding of His kingdom, but that you also exercise excellent stewardship with these gifts as well. Because much has been given to you, you will be asked to do more simply because you have a greater capacity to do so. Now let's examine some forms of giving.

Alms and Offerings. An offering is a gift to God. Offerings in today's world are general gifts to the church that are usually made in the form of money. In the Bible, offerings usually consisted of animals (dead or alive), grains, fruits, or money. Burnt offerings and sacrifices were the main types of offerings made under Mosaic Law. These types of offerings were made to atone for your sins. In the Old Testament, the word "offering" or "offerings" is found 973 times. However, in the New Testament, it is only mentioned 16 times. The difference in the frequency of mentions of the word offering in the New Testament versus the Old Testament can be attributed to one thing: the crucifixion of Jesus.

God offered His Son Jesus as the ultimate sacrifice. Once the blood of Jesus was offered upon the cross as atonement for the sins of the world, burnt offerings and sacrifices were deemed unnecessary and insufficient, hence their diminished mentions in the New Testament. From that point on, offerings to God and His church were primarily in the form of money, and are considered to be general gifts.

Alms are another form of giving, and are defined as donations to the poor or needy. Although the concept is present in the Old Testament, we do not actually find the word "alms" until we read the New Testament. Alms in the modern world would be the equivalent of donating to the various churches, charities, or nonprofit organizations that support the poor and needy. In some cases, a more effective means of giving alms is when you give directly to those in need. The benefits of this type of giving are twofold in that the person receiving your gift gets full use of it, and it also allows you to make a direct connection with the recipient.

Christians should have a natural desire to give to those in need. It is an important part of God's ministry on Earth. You should give not for recognition or because you need the tax deduction, but primarily because you genuinely care. It doesn't matter what others think of your generosity. Only God can measure the true intent of the heart. He will ultimately hold you accountable.

Tithing. Another form of giving is tithing. To tithe means to pay a tenth. What is the purpose of a tithe? The purpose of a tithe is to provide support for the worship of God, the maintenance of those employed by the business of support for the worship of God, relief of the poor, and the support of any service or activity embarked upon for the glory of God.

Is tithing a law (commandment) or a principle? What is the difference between a law and a principle? A law is defined as a rule of conduct or procedure established by custom, agreement, or authority. A law can also be defined as a body of principles or precepts (rule or principle) held to express the divine will of God, especially as revealed in the Bible. A principle is defined as a basic truth, law, or assumption; a rule or standard; the collectivity of moral or ethical standards or judgments.

Looking at the definitions of a law and principle, they are very similar. However, I will make a contrast between them based on God's reaction to following or not following either. When you disobey God's laws or commandments, you will be punished. When you don't follow His principles, you may not be punished, but things just won't work out as best as they could. Obeying God's laws and commandments pleases Him and leads to a blessed and abundant life. Scripture says if you are good in His sight, He will provide you with wisdom, knowledge, and joy (Ecclesiastes 2:26). Following God's principles, which are based on true wisdom and His perfect knowledge, helps determine your level of blessing and abundance. To help us determine whether tithing is principle or law, let's look at the history of tithing in the Bible.

When did the practice of tithing begin? No one is really sure. There is a debate as to when the practice of tithing started because it was a part of Christian and heathen societies. However, the first appearance of tithing in the Bible appears in the 14th chapter of Genesis.

In this chapter, Abram finds out that his nephew Lot has been abducted and Lot's goods have been stolen. Abram assembled an army of 318 of his best-trained men to do battle, and they conducted a night raid to bring back Lot and all of the stolen goods. The attack was very successful, and Abram was able to liberate Lot and the other men and women who had been captured.

After his return, Abram was greeted by Melchizedek, the king of Salem and a priest, not of any other deities, but of the true and living God. In Genesis 14:18–20, we read the following:

18 And Melchizedek king of Salem brought forth bread and wine: and he was the priest of the most high God.

19 And he blessed him, and said, Blessed be Abram of the most high God, possessor of heaven and earth:

20 And blessed be the most high God, which hath delivered thine enemies into thy hand. And he gave him tithes of all.

The bread and wine offered by Melchizedek was an offering to help refresh Abram and his battle-weary troops. He also blessed Abram and blessed God for delivering Lot's captors into the hand of Abram and his army. As was probably customary, Abram offered a tithe of the recovered goods to Melchizedek (verse 20; also see Hebrews 7:4). It is important to note that the tithe was not to God.

Next, we read the following in Genesis 28:22:

And this stone, which I have set for a pillar, shall be God's house: and of all that thou shalt give me I will surely give the tenth unto thee.

This verse is the voice of Jacob, the son of Isaac and Rebekah, twin brother to Esau, and grandson of Abraham. Leading up to this verse, Jacob had led a very interesting life. First, he tricked his twin brother out of his birthright (Genesis 25:31–33). He then deceived his father Isaac in order to claim the birthright (Genesis 27:18–29). Next, he paid the price for his sins because he had to flee to Haran (a city located in Mesopotamia) to stay with Rebekah's brother Laban, because Esau was planning to kill him for what he did. Jacob was in a world of trouble.

Before he reached Haran, he stopped for the night and placed a stone under his head to use as a pillow. After he fell asleep, God appeared to him in a dream. In the dream, God told Jacob how He would take care of him. He told Jacob He would not leave him until He had done what He promised. When Jacob woke up, he knew that he had been in the presence of the Lord. Better yet, he knew that everything was going to be alright. He then made a promise to God that if God got him out of this trouble, took care of his basic needs (food and clothing), and one day allowed him to go home to his father's house in peace, he would wholeheartedly claim the Lord as his God.

In Genesis 28:22, Jacob pledges to build an altar, at which he will worship God and recognize it to be the House of God. The word "shalt" in this verse is very important because it takes on the future tense. Jacob knows that God has been so good to him and answered him in his day of distress (Genesis 35:3), that of all that he will receive from God, he will "surely give a tenth (tithe) unto thee." This is the first reference of a tithe to be given to the glory of God.

In Leviticus and Deuteronomy, the two books of law in the Bible, we find the first references of the act of tithing as a matter of law:

Leviticus 27:30–33

30 And all the tithe of the land, whether of the seed of the land, or of the fruit of the tree, is the LORD'S: it is holy unto the LORD.

31 And if a man will at all redeem ought of his tithes, he shall add thereto the fifth part thereof.

32 And concerning the tithe of the herd, or of the flock, even of whatsoever passeth under the rod, the tenth shall be holy unto the LORD.

33 He shall not search whether it be good or bad, neither shall he change it: and if he change it at all, then both it and the change thereof shall be holy; it shall not be redeemed.

Deuteronomy 14:22–23

22 Thou shalt truly tithe all the increase of thy seed, that the field bringeth forth year by year.

23 And thou shalt eat before the LORD thy God, in the place which he shall choose to place his name there, the tithe of thy corn, of thy wine, and of thine oil, and the firstlings of thy herds and of thy flocks; that thou mayest learn to fear the LORD thy God always.

The law of tithing was commanded to the children of Israel by the Levites. The Levites were of the tribe of Levi, the third son of Jacob by Leah, and were set aside by God for His service. The Levites gave up everything to be in complete service to God. In return for this pledge of servitude to God, the Israelites were to tithe of their increase to the Levites. This tithe allowed the Levites to be independent, comfortable, and able to do God's work without distraction.

How did it come that the Levites were to be the beneficiary of the tithes of the Israelites? It was by holy order from God, as it is written in Numbers 18:20–32:

20 And the LORD spake unto Aaron, Thou shalt have no inheritance in their land, neither shalt thou have any part among them: I am thy part and thine inheritance among the children of Israel.

21 And, behold, I have given the children of Levi all the tenth in Israel for an inheritance, for their service which they serve, even the service of the tabernacle of the congregation.

22 Neither must the children of Israel henceforth come nigh the tabernacle of the congregation, lest they bear sin, and die.

23 But the Levites shall do the service of the tabernacle of the congregation, and they shall bear their iniquity: it shall be a statute for ever throughout your generations, that among the children of Israel they have no inheritance.

24 But the tithes of the children of Israel, which they offer as an heave offering unto the LORD, I have given to the Levites to inherit: therefore I have said unto them, Among the children of Israel they shall have no inheritance.

25 And the LORD spake unto Moses, saying,

26 Thus speak unto the Levites, and say unto them, When ye take of the children of Israel the tithes which I have given you from them for your inheritance, then ye shall

offer up an heave offering of it for the LORD, even a
tenth part of the tithe.

27 And this your heave offering shall be reckoned unto you,
as though it were the corn of the threshingfloor, and as
the fulness of the winepress.

28 Thus ye also shall offer an heave offering unto the LORD
of all your tithes, which ye receive of the children of
Israel; and ye shall give thereof the LORD'S heave
offering to Aaron the priest.

29 Out of all your gifts ye shall offer every heave offering of
the LORD, of all the best thereof, even the hallowed part
thereof out of it.

30 Therefore thou shalt say unto them, When ye have
heaved the best thereof from it, then it shall be counted
unto the Levites as the increase of the threshingfloor, and
as the increase of the winepress.

31 And ye shall eat it in every place, ye and your house
holds: for it is your reward for your service in the
tabernacle of the congregation.

32 And ye shall bear no sin by reason of it, when ye have
heaved from it the best of it: neither shall ye pollute the
holy things of the children of Israel, lest ye die.

Aaron was the brother of Moses. He was a Levite and a high
priest. God told him that he and the rest of the Levites have no
inheritance in the land of the Israelites, but that Aaron shouldn't
worry because He, God Almighty, is their inheritance (verse 20). The
sole function of a Levite was to be of service for God. In addition to
other things, they were responsible for guarding the tabernacle and
making sure that no unclean persons entered it or stole anything
from it. They were also responsible for assisting the priests during
worship services and carrying the vessels of the sanctuary when
required. These were tasks for the Levites and the Levites alone. If
they did not fulfill their duties as they should, they would take the
blame and suffer for it (bear their iniquity). This life of Godly service
was a statute throughout the Levite generations. If you were born a

Levite, you knew what your profession would be (verse 23).

So the children of Israel were to offer a "heave offering," meaning "not burdensome," to God. God then instructed them to tithe and give the tithe to the Levites as their inheritance from Him (verse 24). Then God spoke to Moses and told him to tell the Levites that they shall offer up a heave offering as a tithe (verse 26). God then directed the Levites to take the offering that they were to give to Him, and give it to Aaron.

So let's recap. God told the children of Israel to give a tithe to the Levites. Then God told the Levites to give a tenth of the tithe to Aaron, the high priest. To relate this passage to today, think of the Levites as today's church and its many ministries. Your tithes go to support the church and its ministries for its service to God. The second tithe is from the church and would be given to its modern-day high priest, the pastor. This would be the equivalent of the pastor's salary and total compensation.

Now that we understand what tithes are to be used for, let's continue to examine the practice of tithing as we move through time in the Bible.

In the Old Testament, tithing was treated as law. However, there is evidence that the Israelites did not always adhere to the law of tithing or freely give:

Nehemiah 13:10-11
10 And I perceived that the portions of the Levites had not been given them: for the Levites and the singers, that did the work, were fled every one to his field.
11 Then contended I with the rulers, and said, Why is the house of God forsaken? And I gathered them together, and set them in their place.

Here, the Levites were forced to abandon their work in sacred service because people weren't tithing as they should. Things were so bad that they had to go to their fields to farm so they could sustain themselves. Nehemiah chastised the rulers (high priests) for allowing the house of God to be forsaken, via the diminished care and maintenance of the Levites.

Next in Malachi, we read of another instance where tithing, as a part of the Mosaic Law, is not being followed. Malachi, the prophet, spoke to the high priest and all of Judah:

> *Malachi 3:8–10*
> 8 Will a man rob God? Yet ye have robbed me. But ye say,
>   Wherein have we robbed thee? In tithes and offerings.
> 9 Ye are cursed with a curse: for ye have robbed me, even
>   this whole nation.
> 10 Bring ye all the tithes into the storehouse, that there may
>   be meat in mine house, and prove me now herewith,
>   saith the LORD of hosts, if I will not open you the
>   windows of heaven, and pour you out a blessing, that
>   there shall not be room enough to receive it.

It appears that the tithes are not coming in as they should because Malachi begins verse 10 by saying, "Bring ye all...." This implies that the tithes are either being deliberately withheld or mis-represented as a full tithe. Nevertheless, Malachi instructs them to bring all of the tithes to the storehouse. The storehouse was a place like a vault where they kept the monetary tithes, or like a cellar or storage room where they kept the animal or agricultural tithes. The phrase "...that there may be meat in mine house" refers to food or resources taken from the storehouse for the Levites and priests to live on. Contrary to popular belief, the storehouse and the church are not the same thing. The storehouse was usually near the church so that the Levites could get what they needed for themselves and also for the poor and the needy.

The phrase "...and prove me now herewith, saith the LORD of hosts" is a very important phrase in this passage. God has told us that He will keep His promise and that He will take care of us. God is challenging us to try Him; conduct an experiment. See what happens when you bring your tithes with a glad heart. The results of the experiment are already known and given in the last part of the verse where it says "...if I will not open you the windows of heaven, and pour you out a blessing, that there shall not be room enough to receive it."

The assumption here is that the "windows of heaven" have been shut because you have been an unfaithful giver. Give as you should and God's grace will fall down like rain from the sky and shine on you like the sun. To receive such is truly a blessing. Rain and sun are needed in order to have a bountiful harvest. God's grace and mercy are needed for you to have a bountiful life. By bringing all of your tithes into the storehouse, God's blessings will pour down on you in such a way that you will not have enough room in your life to receive them.

I have often met individuals who misinterpret this verse to mean that the blessings that you will receive are primarily financial. While a financial blessing is possible, it is not specifically mentioned or implied. In fact, it is this type of approach to tithing that leads to a slot machine mentality with respect to God. People like this give only because they think the big payoff is coming. They behave as if to say, "Come on Jesus!! I've been dropping money in this ministry slot machine for a long time. My payoff should be coming any minute now." When the expected financial payoff doesn't come, they often become frustrated and disillusioned because they think that they have been faithful, but somehow have not received their proper payoff.

First of all, you can't buy a blessing. Next, God does not operate on our time. When He decides to bless us, it will be on His schedule and not ours. It will also be at the very best time for us to receive it. By focusing primarily on financial blessings, you are placing your faith in money, and not God, because you feel that money is the answer to your problems. God is always the answer to your problems. There are so many ways that He can bless us, including financially. Open your heart to appreciate all of God's blessings, big and small. You will see that abundance has been yours all the while, you just never saw it.

Additionally, there are some people who are only concerned with the act of tithing and the perception it leaves when it becomes known to others. Jesus offers the following criticism in Matthew

23:23:

> Woe unto you, scribes and Pharisees, hypocrites! for ye pay tithe of mint and anise and cummin, and have omitted the weightier matters of the law, judgment, mercy, and faith: these ought ye to have done, and not to leave the other undone.

The Pharisees were known for being overly concerned with ritual and outward appearances. Because of this, their motives were always suspicious. To maintain an appearance of piety, the Pharisees insisted on adhering to Mosaic Law, which said that the people should tithe of the fruits of the earth. Their interpretation of fruits of the earth was to pay tithes of mint, anise, and cumin. Ordinarily, you would not consider this a very big deal except for one thing: mint, anise, and cumin were considered to be commodity herbs of little value, whose main purpose was to make things taste or smell good. Remember, the purpose of a tithe was to support the Levites and the high priest. While I am sure that the Levites and others appreciated the aromatic qualities of these three herbs, I doubt that they had much use for them.

This was the hypocrisy of the Pharisees. The Pharisees were caught up in the act of tithing, and they made sure everyone knew that they were tithers according to their "strict" interpretation of the Law. But they were in effect robbing God, not giving Him what He was due because they were tithing things that were of little use to the Levites. Additionally, they should have been more concerned with the important aspects of the Mosaic Law that embraced the matters of judgement, mercy, and faith.

This is not to say that tithing was not important. In fact, in Matthew 23:23, Jesus tells the Pharisees that they should tithe (...these ought ye to have done...). However, there are other things that are more important (...weightier matters of the law). I believe this speaks to a basic tenet of our relationship with God: free will.

Tithing is like the planting of seeds. Plant the seeds of tithing in fertile ground and God's ministry can grow in fruitful abundance.

The Apostle Paul speaks to us in 2 Corinthians 9:6–8 with regard to sowing the seeds of giving:

6 But this I say, He which soweth sparingly shall reap also sparingly; and he which soweth bountifully shall reap also bountifully.

7 Every man according as he purposeth in his heart, so let him give; not grudgingly, or of necessity: for God loveth a cheerful giver.

8 And God is able to make all grace abound toward you; that ye, always having all sufficiency in all things, may abound to every good work:

Here, we see tithing being treated as a principle rather than a law. Verse 6 describes the old saying, "You reap what you sow." Verse 7 has several key parts in it. First, the phrase "Every man according as he purposeth in his heart" seems to indicate that it is not important as to how much you give, but more so why you give. The next phrase, "...so let him give; not grudgingly, or of necessity: for God loveth a cheerful giver," implies that the giver has a choice. He is not compelled, as a matter of law to give, but because of his own desire to do so. The giver should not give grudgingly or out of some sense of obligation or undue influence, but more so out of the gladness of his heart because God loves a cheerful giver. Finally, in verse 8 we see confirmation of the old spiritual, "You Can't Beat God's Giving (No Matter How You Try)." God is able to make all grace abound toward you. So you should take comfort in knowing that when you give in gladness and love, it will not result in you having less. When you give in this manner, God's giving in return will be more, such that you will be satisfied and content in all aspects of your life. This state of sufficiency frees you from the pursuit of things you want, allowing you to focus on doing more good works.

There once was a man who wanted to be a very successful farmer. Being a Christian man, he faithfully prayed for God to bless him with a bountiful harvest. As the planting season began, he watched with glee as the sun would shine and the fields received good rain.

He awoke each day and ran out to see how much his fields had grown. But strangely, nothing was growing. Nevertheless, he continued to pray to God for a bountiful harvest.

Many days began to pass and there was still no growth in the fields. Sensing something was wrong, he began to ask God why He had forsaken him. The farmer prayed and prayed for a bountiful harvest. Sadly, the fields remained barren. Disappointed and disillusioned, he never attempted farming again and died many years later a bitter man.

As he faced God on Judgement Day, he told Him of his plans to become a great farmer. The farmer told God of how his great harvest would have helped to feed the world. He would have put many people to work on his farm. The lives of so many people would have benefited from his harvest, if only God had done His part. "Instead," the farmer said, "all that You gave me were barren fields."

God responded, "Your fields were not barren. They grew nothing because you never planted any seeds." God then told the farmer, "Had you planted any seeds, you would have indeed fed the world. Instead, many went hungry. Had you planted any seeds, you would have employed thousands. Instead, many struggled because they could find no other work. Yes, the lives of many would have been changed. If only you had planted the seeds I had already given you. But you never took the time to use the seeds I had already given you, which would have brought forth the bountiful harvest that was awaiting you. All that you asked for was waiting for you. If only you had taken the first step of planting the seeds I gave you. Instead, the blessings that were yours were given to someone else."

Don't forsake a bountiful harvest that awaits you. Invest in God's ministry by planting the seeds of tithe and giving. Tithing and giving are good things to do. Fertilize those seeds with love and gladness. By giving God His due, you will not end up with less. As He said, test Him and allow Him to prove it to you. He will truly pour you blessings that the barns of your life cannot hold.

So is tithing a matter of law or principle? Consider this: in the United States, we have this set of rules and regulations called the Internal Revenue Code. If according to these rules and regulations it is determined that you owe taxes, you are required to pay them. If you don't pay your taxes, you may be subject to financial penalties, sent to jail, or both. Most of the people that I know do not like paying taxes and spend a considerable amount of time, energy, and resources trying to reduce the amount of taxes that they must pay. In fact, I have never met anyone who so loves to pay taxes that they actually try to send more than is due. Nevertheless, most people grudgingly pay their taxes rather than face the punishment for not doing so.

It is my belief that tithing is more a principle than a law, or commandment. God wants us to tithe because it is the right thing to do, not because we are compelled to. He wants us to tithe because of love, not fear. He wants us to tithe because we see the benefits of investing in His Kingdom.

Anyone who approaches tithing as a matter of law is engaged in something called legalism. Legalism, within the context of Christianity, asserts that adherence to the Law atones for one's sin. However, if you believe that you are bound to tithe as a matter of Law, then you are also bound to keep the hundreds of other commandments of Law that are outlined in the Old Testament. Scripture clearly tells us that if you keep one Law, you have to keep them all:

Galatians 3:10
For as many as are of the works of the law are under the curse: for it is written, Cursed is every one that continueth not in all things which are written in the book of the law to do them.

The Law can be divided into two categories. First, you have the moral Law, or what is commonly known as the Ten Commandments. This part of the Law is a reflection of God. It is from His heart, so it speaks of what is morally pure and holy. It is a blueprint of how we should live. The other part of the law is what we refer to as the Law of Moses (Mosaic Law). These laws are guidelines for human conduct, and were specifically designed to direct the Jews with regard to the civil, judicial, criminal, and ceremonial aspects of their lives. It was believed that adhering to the Law developed righteousness and love.

Mosaic Law was not final when it was first rendered, as parts of it were later explained, clarified, and amended by some of the prophets (see Ezekiel, chapter 18). In fact, it is believed by some that the distinction between Mosaic Law and the moral Law of God is clearly denoted by their placement with the Ark of the Covenant. The Ten Commandments were placed inside the Ark (see Exodus 25:16; 40:20). The Book of Mosaic Law was placed on the side of the Ark (see Deuteronomy 31:24–26). Some of the more modern Bible translations state that it was placed "beside" the Ark.

The problem with Mosaic Law is that it reveals the sinful nature of man. Because we are not perfect, anyone who tries to live by the law is doomed to a life of condemnation. As Galatians 3:10 says, you will be cursed if you don't do all things according to the Law.

Jesus came to fulfill the law, as He tells us in Matthew 5:17:

> Think not that I am come to destroy the law, or the prophets: I am not come to destroy, but to fulfil.

Jesus' death on the cross was the ultimate atonement for human sin. Therefore, we are no longer bound by the Law: Consider the following verse, Romans 10:4:

> For Christ *is* the end of the law for righteousness to every one that believeth.

Only Jesus Christ can give salvation. No amount of adherence to the Law, including tithing, ever will. We are now justified by our faith in the Gospel of Jesus Christ, as shown in Romans 5:1–2:

> 1 Therefore being justified by faith, we have peace with God through our Lord Jesus Christ:
> 2 By whom also we have access by faith into this grace wherein we stand, and rejoice in hope of the glory of God.

Additionally, we are told in Galatians 5:18 the following:

But if ye be led of the Spirit, ye are not under the law.

Finally, the Apostle Paul gives us the best advice, as we are told the following in Titus 3:9:

But avoid foolish questions, and genealogies, and conten-
tions, and strivings about the law; for they are unprofitable
and vain.

Forget all of the crazy formulas and rules for tithing that arise out of people trying to reduce it to a science. Give because you want to give. Give according to what your heart tells you to give. Most importantly, do not limit your giving to a tithe, especially if your heart leads you to do so and you have the financial capacity to make it happen. It is the only standard by which you will be measured on Judgement Day.

Giving is an investment in God's ministry that provides you with a variety of returns. Consider the following verses in 2 Corinthians 9:9–15:

9 (As it is written, He hath dispersed abroad; he hath given
to the poor: his righteousness remaineth for ever.

10 Now he that ministereth seed to the sower both minister
bread for *your* food, and multiply your seed sown, and
increase the fruits of your righteousness;)

11 Being enriched in every thing to all bountifulness, which
causeth through us thanksgiving to God.

12 For the administration of this service not only supplieth
the want of the saints, but is abundant also by many
thanksgivings unto God;

13 Whiles by the experiment of this ministration they
glorify God for your professed subjection unto the gospel
of Christ, and for *your* liberal distribution unto them,
and unto all *men*;

14 And by their prayer for you, which long after you for the
exceeding grace of God in you.

15 Thanks *be* unto God for his unspeakable gift.

These verses are a continuation of when the Apostle Paul was speaking to the church of Corinth. As previously discussed, verses 6–8 in this same chapter address the true nature of giving. Verse 9 extols the virtues of giving to the poor and the benefits thereof by paraphrasing Psalms 112:9 (He hath dispersed, he hath given to the poor; his righteousness endureth for ever; his horn shall be exalted with honour).

In verse 10, Paul tells us that God is the source of all fruitfulness. It is God who provides you with seed to sow. It is God who provides bread for you to eat. It is God who causes your seed to multiply, bearing fruits of righteousness and helping you to build up your treasure in Heaven. As a result, you will be blessed in all phases of your life. The abundance you receive from God will bless you with many opportunities to be generous to others. Your commitment to giving not only meets the needs of God's people, but it is a gift that keeps on giving. The kindness and care that you show to the less fortunate can inspire them to help others as well. You will become a vessel of God, through which praises and thanks to Him will flow (verses 11 and 12).

Your commitment to meeting the needs of the poor allows others to see the Light of God in you. Others will praise God for His help through you and offer prayer for you, because of the grace and blessings He has bestowed upon you (verses 13 and 14). Finally, verse 15 sums it up: Thanks be to God for his unspeakable gift. You know that God gave us the ultimate gift—His son, Jesus Christ. More specifically, when you accept this gift of unconditional love from God, your life should become an example of Jesus' ministry while He was here on earth. To show love, care, and compassion toward your fellow man is truly a gift.

I can't emphasize enough how important giving is. But, I must say that there needs to be a radical change in how the general leadership of churches and ministries approaches the subject. When I speak to church groups, I get more questions about tithing than anything else. The reasons for this are many, ranging from outright false teaching to a lack of stewardship training.

Regardless of the reason, there needs to be a new approach to teaching Christians about tithing, and giving in general. Consider the following:

> In 2000, the average person gave 2.64% of his income to the church. This is down from 3.10% of income given in 1968.[6]

In general, churchgoers in America do not give as much as they should. I find it disturbing that the rate of giving has been so low for so long. However, I find it more disturbing that the collective leadership of the Christian church has not found any constructive ways to deal with the issue.

I can tell you from experience that there are many people who do not fully understand what is scripturally expected of them with respect to giving. In these circumstances, stewardship training programs can be very effective in helping to raise giving levels. Other churches just seem to be in a mode of constant begging. Members of these congregations often grow weary of the constant appeals, tuning them out or ignoring them altogether. Even worse are the church leaders who are constantly beating their congregations over the head with the Cross, telling them they are destined for Hell if they don't give. Scaring people into giving doesn't work. It never has.

Monetary gifts to churches and ministries are often characterized as being financial seeds. Staying with this line of thinking, I would like to suggest that in order for your financial seed to be pleasing to God, it must meet three criteria:

- It must given cheerfully
- It must not be given out of compulsion
- It must be sown into good ground

---

[6] Source: empty tomb, inc. annual series, The State of Church Giving through 2000 (2002 edition). Figures are based on disposable (after-tax) personal income.

The first two items are self-explanatory, and I have discussed them in detail throughout the book. However, the third item bears further discussion because I think it is the one that may best explain the current level of giving in this country.

Any church or ministry that accepts financial gifts to help meet the needs of others, according to God's mandate, must strive to do so in an effective and efficient manner. It must possess the highest levels of accountability. It must become "good ground." How can you know whether the churches or ministries that you support are "good ground?" You will know by the fruit they bear.

I can usually tell what is important to a person by looking at the entries in his or her checkbook. Where they spend their money and how much they spend tells me a lot about their priorities. Churches and ministries are no different. How much is being spent on administration? How much is being spent on overhead? How much is being spent on meeting the needs of the congregation or ministry patrons? Is more money being spent on attending conferences and conventions than is being spent on educational scholarships? Is the mission of the church or ministry being fulfilled? People like to see results. If you can't tell where your financial gifts or contributions are going, or how effectively they are being used, it is your duty to redirect them to a better place. If you were carrying a bucket filled with water to give drink to the thirsty, would you continue to use that bucket if it had a hole in it? No, you would either fix the hole or get a new bucket. Ineffective and inefficient churches and ministries are buckets with holes. As a giver, you should try to help fix the hole or find a new bucket. This is part of your stewardship duties.

This is sometimes difficult to do because financial information from a church or ministry can be difficult to obtain. Many of them do not have the ability or procedures in place to generate good financial statements. In some cases, the leadership is afraid to release all financial information because they feel that it causes dissension among its members or supporters. However, this is a weak excuse because if the affairs of the church or ministry are being handled as they should be, there can be no valid challenge to their appropriateness.

Non-profit organizations with $25,000 or more in revenue are required to file Form 990 with the Internal Revenue Service. This form details how much money they took in, how it was spent, how much was paid to its officers, and other relevant information. This form is an excellent report card of how well the organization is using the resources being placed in its care. However, churches, and any organizations that are either controlled by or directly affiliated with a church, are exempt from having to file a Form 990.

If your church or ministry solicits donors for financial support, it should be able to provide full financial disclosure to anyone who asks. The benefits of such openness are many. If there are questions as to the organization's effectiveness or efficiency, they can be quickly laid to rest because the financial disclosures will tell the true story. When rumors and questions are allowed to go unanswered, they take on a life of their own and can sabotage the organization's goals and objectives. Additionally, when potential and existing donors see that the church or ministry is being a good steward of the resources being placed in its care, they may be willing to increase their level of support. Full disclosure is a good thing and should be embraced. It is a sign that the church or ministry is "good ground," and worthy of your financial seeds.

Anything that is truly of the Spirit of God can withstand any scrutiny from man. A refusal to release such information is either a sign that financial improprieties may actually exist, or that the organization has no faith that God will be their defender against unjust persecution. When churches and ministries don't manage financial resources as they should, they become fertile ground for excuses (weeds). Church members or ministry supporters begin to withhold or redirect their contributions because they feel that they won't be used as they should. There will always be people who make excuses not to give. However, churches and ministries must make exceptional efforts to make sure that the efficiency and effectiveness of their organization is not one of them.

The whole beauty of the story of Ananias and Sapphira was not the fact that they dropped dead because they lied about their giving. The wonderful thing about that story is that they, and others, were led to give because they were filled with the Holy Spirit. Proper education on the subject of giving, combined with the Spirit of God, is a powerful mix that can solve a lot of the problems of the world. All that a church or ministry needs to do is to focus on providing Spirit-based results. If it can do that, the money will take care of itself.

☙❧❧❧

So, there you have it: the three aspects of obedience that unlock the doors to God's blessings. *Faith* gives you access to God's mercy and grace. *Stewardship* gives you access to God's resources in accordance to your ability to properly manage them. *Giving* gives you access to God's heart.

Wisdom

The third component of the formula for success is Wisdom. We are told in Ecclesiastes 2:26 that God will give you wisdom, knowledge, and joy when you are obedient to His Word. These three things go hand in hand. However, wisdom is the most important of the three.

I have often heard people say that knowledge is power. I disagree. Knowledge is a thing (a noun), so it cannot do anything by itself. It needs a verb. Therefore, it is my belief that knowledge is not power, but the use of knowledge is. Now, wisdom is the moral and ethical application of knowledge. Therefore, when God blesses you with wisdom and knowledge, the wisdom you receive will allow you to use the knowledge that you have received in a way that is pleasing to God and beneficial to you. When use of knowledge is not accompanied by wisdom, bad things can happen.

For example, in 2002, we were hit with two of the largest corporate scandals in U.S. history: Enron and Worldcom. In both cases, individuals were accused and convicted of manipulating financial records for direct or indirect financial gain. Meanwhile, investors in these two companies lost over $200 billion.

The individuals involved in these tragedies were generally

regarded as smart people. They possessed a significant amount of financial knowledge. Unfortunately, they used it to devise schemes to defraud investors. However, I would argue that they also lacked wisdom, because wisdom would have shown them that such a scheme was wrong, many people could get hurt, and they would most likely get caught.

When you wrap wisdom around your knowledge, good things will happen to you. These good things will bring you joy. When you collectively use wisdom, knowledge, and joy, you possess true power. This power is a gift that comes from God. You can only receive this gift if you are obedient to His Word.

༄ༀ༄

So let's review the formula again:

Work + Obedience + Wisdom = True Wealth

The beauty of this formula is that it will help you build wealth in all areas of your life. It will help you build financial wealth, but more importantly it will help you build wealth of a heavenly nature. Study the WOW Factor and learn it well. Success awaits you if you do.

Chapter 13
Managing the Wealth-Building Process

Maintaining good physical and spiritual health is a process that you have to actively manage. Building financial wealth is no different. You've learned a lot about the nuts and bolts of building wealth, but what else do you need?

Here are some other things you should know to help you manage the wealth-building process.

Patience and Commitment

A lot of people talk about wanting to be financially successful. Unfortunately, many of them are missing the two ingredients necessary to make it happen: patience and commitment. The oak tree is the perfect example of an investment that requires patience. The timber of the oak tree is desired when strength and hardness are important. The bark of the oak tree is also used in tanning and dyeing applications as well. However, to reap the benefits of this wonderful tree, be prepared to wait. It typically takes 50 to 60 years before the tree will bear its well-known fruit, the acorn. Its timber will not be ready to be felled until it is between 150 and 200 years of age. If you are planning on being an oak tree farmer, you will either have to reap the harvest of someone else's efforts, or sow the seeds for someone's future benefit.

Oak continues to be a premium wood because very few people have the patience needed to reap the benefits of being an oak tree farmer. Most people want to see the benefits of their efforts sooner rather than later. It's no different in the world of investing and financial planning.

Many people start with good intentions when they choose a financial goal. As long as they can see improving results, they are happy and satisfied. But if progress on the goal begins to stall, they become nervous and fidgety. Like children on a long vacation drive, they want to know "Are we there yet?"

Patience is a wonderful gift from God. We all have it. We just have to learn how to develop it. The world of investing will give you many opportunities to learn how to be patient. But, you cannot experience the benefits of patience unless you possess one more attribute: commitment. When it comes to financial planning, it is great to have a financial goal. What is more important is to have a commitment to that goal. The best of financial plans will be laid to waste without commitment.

Dalbar, Inc. is one of the nation's leading financial services research firms. They conduct an annual study entitled "Quantitative Analysis of Investor Behavior" (QAIB), which examines real investor returns based on actual cash flows into and out of equity, fixed income, and money market mutual funds. QAIB is updated annually, and the following results are from the January 1984–December 2002 study:

- The average fixed income investor realized an annualized return of 4.24%, compared to 11.70% for the long-term government bond index for the same period.
- The average equity fund investor realized an annualized return of 2.57%, compared to a 3.14% rate of inflation, and 12.22% for the S&P 500 Index during the same period.

Why is it that so many individual investors grossly underperformed the market? It all boils down to two reasons: behavior and timing.

Individual investors often engage in behaviors that prohibit them from receiving all of the gains that the market can give them. Kathleen Gurney, PhD is a psychologist with more than 20 years of experience specializing in the psychodynamics of money management and investing. Her work has uncovered certain relationships that we must understand before we can achieve consistent success in the world of investing:

- The majority of investment losses result not from poor trading decisions, but more so from emotional and attitudinal causes.
- Few investors have the self-knowledge, emotional stamina, or self-control to make rational, intelligent, and profitable decisions, particularly in times of stress.

Gurney also says that the field of behavioral finance has given us several insights into the emotional miscues that negatively impact investors' returns, which the Dalbar study so strongly illustrates.

One of these emotions is the fear of losing money. We hate to lose money. Psychologically, we give greater weight to a previous investment loss than we do to a potential gain. The drive to avoid financial losses often sabotages future investment gains or opportunities. Additionally, the fear of losing money can be so strong that some people will psych themselves out of investing altogether.

The other emotion that negatively impacts our investment decision making is worry. Worry is a natural emotion, but investors often worry about the wrong risks. Investors worry more about things they cannot control instead of things they can control. Current crises are often exaggerated into end-of-the-world scenarios. None of us knows how much we can ultimately make on an investment, but we all know how much we can lose. Because the risk of losing all of your money is one of the few risks that you can clearly identify, it is the one to which you can pay the most attention. Investors will often ignore information that may clearly indicate a wiser course of action in order to cling to the belief that there is something in their control that they can do to avoid financial disaster.

Based on her research into the attitudes and feelings that drive money management and investment behavior, Gurney offers the following solutions:

- If investors can gain control of their emotions and act on facts instead of feelings, they can increase their chances of being successful.
- Successful investment behaviors can be learned. By

becoming self-aware, self-confident, self-motivated, and responsible, you will develop good behaviors that will help you minimize investment mistakes.

I often tell my clients that successful investing is achieved with patience and brilliance, and patience is 90% of the formula. Time heals most wounds and portfolios. Sometimes, investors make the mistake of trying to be "too smart." They overanalyze the situation and try to find mathematical formulas or trading strategies to elimi- nate the uncertainties of investing. While some people can make good use of such brilliance, most of us won't because we don't have enough control over our emotions.

Have you ever been standing in line at your grocery store and your line is moving slowly? You look across at the other checkout lines, and everyone else seems to be checking out quickly. After a few more seconds of observing everyone else's seemingly good fortune, you just can't stand it anymore, and you get out of your line into another one that you think will get you checked out faster. But, as luck would have it, the very second you get into the new line, it starts to move even more slowly than the other lines. Frustrated, you look over at the line you were in originally, and it is now zipping along. Had you stayed where you were, you would have been checked out and on your way. Now you're stuck in another slow-moving line. These grocery store behaviors are very similar to how individuals manage their investments.

Poor investment behaviors can cause you to make poor invest- ment decisions. To get close to the return of the S&P 500 during the period covered by Dalbar's QAIB Study, all an investor would have had to do was to invest in a security (mutual fund, ETF, etc.) based on the index beginning in January 1984, and remain invested through December 2002 (remember, you can't invest directly in an index, but you can invest in a security based on the index).

Something had to happen to cause investors to alter the timing of their cash flows during this time period. Here's a partial list of events that could have affected their investment decisions:

- 1984 - AT&T divestiture
- 1986 - Oil prices collapsed
- 1987 - Stock market crashed
- 1989 - Berlin Wall opened
- 1990 - Iraq invaded Kuwait
- 1991 - Soviet Union collapsed
- 1993 - U.S. Congress passed NAFTA
- 1994 - Rapidly rising interest rates
- 1997 - Hong Kong returned to China
- 1998 - Asian economic crisis
- 1999 - Fear of Y2K computer problems
- 2000 - Nasdaq began to collapse
- 2001 - Terrorists attack World Trade Center and Pentagon
- 2002 - War looms with Iraq

Looking at the list, it is no wonder that investors would have been worried. I am sure that some of the investors in the QAIB study thought they could get out "when things got bad," and get back in when "things get better." If so, to meet or beat the market's return, they would have had to make two perfect decisions: The best time to get out and the best time to get back in. The problem with this line of thinking is that while you may miss some of the really bad days, you will most likely miss some of the good days too. Miss just a few of the good days, and you will never catch up to the market. Most of the investors examined in the QAIB study were not successful because they lacked the patience to wait through market downturns, and they were not committed enough to their financial goals.

Embrace patience and commitment. They are wonderful companions to have on your investment journey. They will serve you well.

Be an Investor

There is a difference between a consumer, a saver, and an investor. A consumer spends his money now. From a financial planning perspective, an overly active consumer mentality works to the detriment of any goal to build wealth. A saver is someone who puts money away with a fear of what happened in the past. Maybe he grew up poor. Maybe he invested before and lost a lot of money. Whatever the situation, the saver never wants to go back to that unpleasant experience he had before. Therefore, he tends to put his money in the safest things possible so he won't lose any money. An investor is someone who has faith in the future. The investor knows that there are investments that have prospered during good times and bad. More importantly, he believes that there will be investments that will do the same in the future. Investors know that the only way to participate in the prosperity of these companies is to own their securities, such as stocks or bonds. Be an investor!

Spring Into Action

Once you have decided to improve your financial situation, there is one more thing you must remember: You can't be a financial eagle if you keep hanging around chickens! It will be difficult for you to reach the heights of financial success, spiritual development, and stewardship if the people who are closest to you aren't reaching for the same.

While it is important to reach out and help others in need, you must be careful not to become a crutch for someone else who is more than capable of walking on their own. In 2 Thessalonians 3:10–13, the Apostle Paul reiterates this point of view:

10 For even when we were with you, this we commanded you, that if any would not work, neither should he eat.

11 For we hear that there are some which walk among you disorderly, working not at all, but are busybodies.

12 Now them that are such we command and exhort by our Lord Jesus Christ, that with quietness they work, and eat their own bread.

13 But ye, brethren, be not weary in well doing.

Some people will never get their act together if they feel that they can always count on you to bail them out. More importantly, if you should ever come to a point where you need help, some of these same people who you have helped and sacrificed your financial well being for will not be there to help you. Sometimes you have to learn how to say no today, so that you can be in a better position to say yes tomorrow.

I do not have a green thumb. My wife takes care of watering and caring for the plants in our home. However, there was one plant that my wife must have forgotten about because it was really sickly looking. I decided to take it upon myself to try to bring this plant back to health. I watered it, and a few days later, I checked on it and it didn't look any better. I watered it again and made a note to myself to check on it again in a few days.

Several days later, it still didn't look any better. Upon closer examination, I noticed that it had a lot of dead stems and leaves attached to it. Sensing that this might be part of the problem, I began to cut away all of the dead leaves and stems. A few weeks later, I checked on the plant and was very surprised to see that it was looking better. In fact, it had even begun to sprout new growth. It wasn't until some time later that I found out why.

I happened to be reading an article somewhere that talked about the importance of pruning. It said that if a plant has any stems attached to it that are dead, it uses a lot of its energy trying to regenerate them or bring them back to health. If the dead stems aren't removed, the plant becomes weak and possibly dies.

In the Book of John, chapter 15, verses 1–2, Jesus uses an example to describe our relationship with God that is very similar to what I experienced with my house plants:

1 I am the true vine, and my Father is the husbandman.
2 Every branch in me that beareth not fruit he taketh away: and every *branch* that beareth fruit, he purgeth it, that it may bring forth more fruit.

In verse 1, Jesus tells us that He is the true vine, and God is like the farmer who planted the vine, and now tends to it. In verse 2, He tells us that if there are things in our lives that do not bear witness to

His Word, He will prune or cut them away. Also, in order to help us grow more spiritually, He will prune us further so that we will become even more fruitful in our daily lives.

That's when I thought about the plant. If plants could talk, I'm sure that they would tell us that pruning does not feel good. However, every plant knows that it is a necessary process for growth and development. My plant was thriving because all of the dead stems and leaves had been cut away. Energy that was wasted on trying to bring back that which was already dead was now available to be used by the plant to generate new growth. Then I thought about it from a financial planning perspective. How many people are unable to reach their financial goals because they have too many dead stems in their life?

Most pruning should be done in the winter or early spring while the plants are still dormant. If the financial success that awaits you is still lying dormant, now is the time to spring into action. Spring is the season of new growth and renewal. Make the decision now to remove all dead stems from your life. Bad spending habits are dead stems. Cut them away. Excessive debt is a dead stem. Cut it away. Individuals who do not share your desire to either improve their own situation or help you improve yours are dead stems. Cut them away. Doing so will allow God's blessings to bear fruit in all areas of your life.

Doing It Yourself versus Getting Help

There is nothing mystical about managing money. As I have said before, if you can add, subtract, multiply, and divide, you can do it. The decision to do it yourself or get someone to help you boils down to three factors:

- Do you have the time?
- Do you have the desire?
- Do you have the ability?

To help you decide which way is best for you, let's look at some of the pros and cons of managing your money yourself versus getting someone to help you.

Doing It Yourself

The main reason to manage your own money is that it allows you to lower your cost of investing. The more you save on investment costs, the more you have to invest. The more you have to invest, the bigger the opportunity to grow your investment portfolio.

If you are going to manage your money, you need time. As your investments grow in size or complexity, you will need even more time to properly manage them. Therefore, you should carefully consider exactly how much time you have available to manage your money.

If you are just getting started, you will spend most of your time learning about the investment process. A good place to start is your local library. There, you will find a variety of books, written at various levels of sophistication. Your librarian can provide some insight as to which books would be appropriate for your level of interest. You should also visit the periodicals section of the library. There, you can review the many magazines and newspapers that cover personal finance and investment topics. Should you decide to purchase any books, or subscribe to any magazines or newspapers, you will have a good idea as to which ones will best meet your needs.

You can also get a lot of information from the Internet. The Internet is also where you should exercise the most caution as well. I think that the Internet is one of the greatest things that has ever happened to individual investors. The primary benefit of the Internet is that it helped to increase the transparency of the investment world. Before the Internet, the world of investing was like the Land of Oz. If you wanted to learn about investing, or if you wanted to find a good investment, you had to go see the Wizard, otherwise known as your broker. Once you made your request to the Wizard, and after a lot of thunder, fire, and smoke, the Wizard would decide if you were worthy of your request. The Internet changed all that. The Internet allowed you to see that the Wizard was not this all-powerful, all-knowing being, but just a little person pulling a bunch of levers. Like Dorothy, the Lion, the Scarecrow, and the Tin Man, the Internet has allowed the individual investor to find out that much of the investment information he thought he had to get from someone else was already available to him. Now, you can find out how other brokerage firms rate a stock. You can find out what other firms charge to execute a trade. You can find out how well a firm's investment recommendations have performed. Yes, Dorothy, you can go back to Kansas. Somewhere, over the rainbow, investment dreams can come true!

Again, the Internet can be a dangerous place. While there are many websites that provide very useful information, there are probably more that contain inaccurate, out-of-date, or downright fraudulent information. Chat rooms and message boards can sometimes provide useful information as well, but are more likely used to disseminate false or misleading information. Criminals can use the Internet to make lies look legitimate. Spend some time trying to locate good, reliable sites and stick with those.

Once you figure out how you will spend your time learning about investing, the next thing you need to do is figure out how much your time is worth. Why do this? Because the value of your time is a key factor in determining the true cost of managing your own money. Let's look at an example.

Ima N. Vestor is new to investing and has decided that she is going to manage her investments. She is the office manager for a local construction firm and makes about $30,000 a year. She has just enrolled in her company's 401(k) plan, has some money in a bank savings account, and is looking to start investing $50 per month in the stock of a local company through its dividend reinvestment plan. Ima is married, has two children, and is active in her church and community.

Ima normally works a 40-hour week. If she ever has to work overtime, her employer pays her time and a half. Because she places a premium on her personal time, she figures that since her employer pays her time and a half for extra hours worked, her personal time should be worth double her hourly wage. She makes $14.42 per hour, so the rate for her personal time is twice that or $28.84. After careful consideration, she figures that she can devote an average of 30 minutes per week to monitoring her investments and reading various articles and publications to keep her investment knowledge up-to-date. She has decided to spend $50 this year to buy two books on personal finance, and she will also spend $25 on a personal finance magazine subscription. Ima calculates her annual cost to manage her investments as follows:

> 0.5 hours (30 minutes) x 52 weeks = 26 hours
> 26 hours x $28.84 per hour = $749.84
> Book purchases = $50.00
> Magazine subscriptions = $25.00
> Total annual costs to manage her money = $824.84
> Average cost per month = $68.74

Now Ima has all the information she needs to determine if she made a good decision to manage her own money. If she can find a financial advisor who would charge her less than $68.74 per month to manage her money, then it will be worth her while to let him or her do it. Since she has not been able to find anybody yet, she feels that managing her own investments is the best option for now.

Some of you might disagree! She didn't actually charge herself to manage her investments, so her out-of-pocket cost of investing should be much less. Such an observation is absolutely correct. However, the point of this example is to get you to realize that we make decisions like this all the time. How many times do you eat at a restaurant each week? Why do you go to a restaurant instead of preparing your own food? Growing up, I can probably count on one hand the times that all five of my family members dined together at a restaurant. Why? Because my mom could not see "spending all that money on restaurant food" that didn't taste as good as her own. My mom was a great cook, and I certainly would not argue that any restaurant's food tasted better than hers. Even if I ever found such a restaurant, I would never have had the nerve to tell her that such a place existed. But what about the convenience? What about the time saved? In my mom's mind, the cost of buying a meal at a restaurant was never less than her cost to prepare that same meal for her family.

I take my car to one of those quick-lube shops to get the oil changed. I have friends who change the oil in their own cars. They do it to save money, and they always tell me how easy it is. I have even watched them do it, and it seems to be a fairly simple procedure. Nevertheless, I still take my car to the quick–lube shop. I am a very busy person, and because I am so busy, some of life's little tasks tend to get postponed. For example, my wife won't let me build a storage shed in my backyard because she knows that the materials to build the shed will sit in my backyard for six months, and it will take another six months for me to get around to building it. If I decided to start changing the oil in my car, it would probably get the same treatment. Eventually, the money saved on oil changes would be overshadowed by the cost of replacing engines due to overdue oil changes. For $25 and thirty minutes of my time, I can avoid the ulti-mate consequences of trying to do it myself.

If you are going to manage your own money, you should have an honest discussion with yourself. Are you really going to set aside an adequate amount of time to do it? Your time does have value. How much of it are you going to give up to manage your own money? Many investors make major mistakes in managing their money simply because they don't have the time. Do you really have a desire to do it? Do you have a genuine interest in the process of money management? Do you have the basic skills needed to do it? Are you willing to acquire the skills to do it? If you answered yes to these questions, then I am confident that you will be very successful in managing your money.

Getting Help

Working with an advisor can be an important step in managing your money. However, there are several steps you should take to ensure that you are working with someone who has your best inter-ests at heart.

Why might you need a financial advisor in the first place? In

Proverbs 11:14, Solomon writes, "Where no counsel is, the people fall: but in the multitude of counselors there is safety." Additionally, he writes in Proverbs 15:22 that "Without counsel purposes are disappointed: but in the multitude of counsellors they are established." Remember, all wisdom and knowledge comes from God. It is very unrealistic to think that you and I, or anyone else, have all of the answers. Therefore, it is important to seek counsel or advice from others, which helps to achieve two things. First, it helps to confirm whether you are right or wrong in your approach to your situation. Next, once the right approach to your situation has been confirmed, you can now go about it with confidence and good spirit.

How do you separate the good financial advisors from the bad? Solomon also writes in Proverbs 13:20, "He that walketh with wise men shall be wise: but a companion of fools shall be destroyed." A wise man fears the Lord, and it is this fear that is the beginning of knowledge (Proverbs 1:7). Therefore, a good financial advisor should possess the following: Christian values and financial knowledge. The more you "walk with" or listen to wise people, the more knowledge and wisdom you will retain.

There are plenty of non-Christians who offer financial advice. However, if that person is using standards other than God's laws and principles, then the results of your decisions based on that advice would not be the best. There are also many people who claim to be Christians who are not qualified to offer financial advice. Notice I used the word "claim" because a Christian person would not offer advice in an area in which he was not qualified. Additionally, there are many people who claim to be Christians who offer bad financial advice. These people are not wise and, as stated in the Scripture, if you listen to them you will be ruined and destroyed, or become like them. Therefore, how can you guard against falling into this trap?

Ask God to lead you in your search for good financial counsel. Then ask people whose judgement you trust for referrals. Chances are that if the advisor has worked well for them, he may be a good fit for you. Interview the prospective advisor so that you can get a feel for whether or not you will be able to work together.

Consider all information and pray. It is written in Proverbs

14:15 that "the simple believeth every word: but the prudent man looketh well to his going." When man follows sin, he is sometimes characterized as being foolish, weak, silly, or even "simple." Sinners tend to believe almost anything they hear, no matter how absurd or contrary to God's Word it may be. There will be those who are good with words (smooth talkers) and make dramatic presentations as to why their way is the right way. They may even have a list of people who can vouch for their "success." But, even the wicked have witnesses; therefore, you must exercise due care. Proverbs 14:15 simply says to consider all information so that you can make a good decision. Seek God's guidance. Seek the advice of others you trust. If it sounds too good to be true, it probably is. If you do a good job of checking things out, you will have a less likely chance of working with someone who will give you poor advice.

Next, you should understand how advisors get paid. Financial advisors can be paid by commissions, fees, or both. When an advisor is paid by commission, there usually is no separate financial planning fee. The advisor will deliver advisory services with the expectation that he will be compensated through the purchase or sale of investments. Some call this a transaction-based relationship because the advisor doesn't make any money unless you buy or sell something. It is the transactional nature of this type of relationship that can cause problems.

The reason this type of advisor compensation is often criticized is because of something called churning. Churning is where an advisor executes excessive trades in your account for the sole purpose of generating commissions. Critics point to such activities as proof that commissions put the goals of the advisor ahead of those of his clients.

But there are many financial advisors who are compensated by commissions, who do an excellent job for their clients, and do it at a fair price. Especially if you are a buy-and-hold investor, paying by commission can be the most cost-effective way to invest.

When you are working with a fee-based advisor, you can pay the advisory fees in several different ways:

- As a percentage of assets

- As an hourly fee
- As an annual retainer

It seems that more and more people are touting the benefits of fee-based advisory. The common benefit offered is that it puts the advisor and the client on the same side of the table, or to put it another way, the advisor doesn't make more money unless the client makes more money. However, there are several criticisms of the fee-based model that bear consideration.

First, it has been my experience that if you are an active trader, or you are an investor who has a lot of planning issues that need frequent attention, fee-based advisory can work out to be a good deal. If you are a buy-and-hold investor, or if you have a fairly simple financial situation, you will probably overpay for service under a fee-based advisory agreement, especially if you are paying a fee based on assets under management.

Next, an indication that fee-based advisory agreements aren't always in an investor's best interest is in the way they are pitched to advisors. When I was considering opening my own financial services firm, I talked with several broker dealers. There were a few who were fee-only platforms. They all made fairly convincing arguments that I should consider going fee-only because that's what clients were demanding. Nearly every one of them also made the following statement: Don't you want to annuitize your business?

As I explained earlier in this book, an annuity is a guaranteed series of payments. A fee-based advisory is often pitched to advisors as a way to earn more money or smooth out their income streams. This can sometimes cause advisors to get lazy because they know they will get paid whether they have actually delivered any service or not. Most advisors who are fee-based are diligent professionals who work very hard for their clients, and do it at a fair price. But you should be aware that the opportunity for abuse does exist.

A lot of advisors switched their clients to fee-based arrangements during the bull market of the 1990s. Because portfolio values were rising, fee-based incomes rose as well. However, during the market declines of 2000–2002, many fee-based advisors saw their incomes go down as much as 50% because total assets under management declined with the market. For some, the answer to this dilemma was to switch to annual retainer fees. A retainer fee is a set fee paid for services to be rendered independent of assets under management. Now, the fee is totally separated from the client's portfolio value. For some investors, this arrangement will work well.

The bottom line to all of this is that the price you should pay for advice and service should be equal to or less than the value you assign to it. The fact that you're paying for it via commissions or fees is secondary. If an advisor is going to rip you off under a commission-based advisory agreement, I can assure you he would find a way to do the same under a fee-based advisory agreement. Take the time to understand how your advisor is paid, compare the costs between several compensation arrangements, and choose the one that works best for you.

Why would anybody hire a financial advisor? Tiger Woods is widely recognized as one of the greatest golfers ever in the history of the game. There probably aren't many people who know more about the technical side of golf than him. Yet he still consults his caddy on almost every hole because he knows his caddy might make a suggestion that saves him a stroke, and golf is a game where it takes only one stroke to win.

You may possess the basic skills needed to manage your own money, but a good financial advisor can be like a good caddy. She can suggest some things for your financial plan that you didn't think about, or didn't have the time to think about, which can make the difference between success and failure.

Chapter 14
Final Thoughts

It Doesn't Take Much

People often tell me that they don't have any money to invest. There are others who think that it takes a lot of money to invest. The truth is that it doesn't take much to invest at all. Almost anyone can build a very nice nest egg for himself without having to set aside large amounts of money.

A Dollar a Day

Many of us waste at least a dollar a day. We spend it at the vending machines buying chips, candy, or soda. Or maybe you spend an extra dollar or more buying that value meal at the fast food restaurant. Some of you may even use that dollar to buy that chance-of-a-lifetime lottery ticket. But what if I showed you how anyone could become a millionaire just by investing a dollar a day?

Yes, it's true. You can become a millionaire just by committing to invest a dollar a day. First, you'll need a little help. Let's assume that on the day you were born, your loving parents decided that they would open an account for you and add to it $1 every day (for those of you who get paid monthly, that works out to be $30.42 per month, which is what these calculation are based on). Let's also assume that this account will earn an average of 10% per year. At the age of ten, the account would have grown to $6,231. The actual amount of money that your parents would have invested is $3,650. At the age of 18, the account would have grown to $18,269 and the actual amount invested is only $6,571.

Now you're 18 years old, and your parents sit you down and explain what they have done. They are going to turn the account over to you under one condition: you must continue to invest a dollar a day into this account. Being the grateful child that you are, you cheerfully agree and diligently continue to add a dollar a day to the account. At age 30, the account now totals $68,764. At age 40, the account has grown to $192,379. At age 50, your account balance is $527,008. And at age 57, your account balance totals $1,061,869! Congratulations! You are now a millionaire! Even more amazing is that all you and your parents had to invest over this 57-year period was $20,807. (This is a hypothetical example and not indicative of any security's performance. Future performance cannot be guaranteed, and actual investment yields will fluctuate with market conditions.)

The lesson from all of this is that some of us spend a certain amount of money each day and can't remember where it went. We always seem to find ways to pay for the things we want such as expensive cars, clothes, and big-screen TVs, but we resist investing because we think we can't afford it. If you're not investing now, I am sure that you could invest a dollar a day or more and would never miss it. Winning a million dollars surely would be nice, but just in case it never happens, you should be working hard to invest and accumulate it on your own. You can build wealth over time if you stay committed.

Think about what a wonderful head start you could give your children by investing a dollar a day while they are young. Educating your children as to the value of investing will serve them well throughout their lifetime. What if you are age 50 or older? It's never too late to start! No matter how old you are, getting started with an investment of a dollar a day or more can help you build a portfolio that can help take care of you, your family, and others. There are many investments such as stock dividend reinvestment plans (DRIPs) and mutual funds that will let you invest as little as $25 per month. Do your homework to find out what's available or seek out an investment professional to help you get started.

It's Never Too Late

When is the best time to start investing for your future and developing a financial plan? Obviously, the earlier you start, the better. You should also take comfort in the fact that it is never too late to get started.

No matter what state your personal finances are in, you can make a positive change by following God's word. God is a God of change. He can take what may seem to be hopeless and impossible and make it true and certain. Even though you may feel like you won't accomplish much, doing something is better than doing nothing. Consider the following story.

One day, I received a call from a lady who had just read a newspaper article I wrote based on the dollar-a-day concept described in the previous section. She told me that the article really spoke to her and she wanted to find out more about investing. I scheduled an appointment for her to come in the following week.

When we met, I spent some time trying to find out more about her financial and personal life. She had retired several years earlier from a local hosiery manufacturer. She had no personal or retirement savings because she spent most of it helping her children and other family members. Her only source of income was her Social Security benefit and income from a part-time job.

Because she knew very little about investing, I took some time to explain what some of her investment options were. We talked about stocks, bonds, CDs, money market funds, and mutual funds. I explained how each one worked, and we also discussed the investment risks of each. She then asked me a question that I hear quite often: "Do you think I'm too old to invest?" I emphatically replied that she would never be too old to invest. I told her that she may not know how long she will live, but for however many years she is blessed to live, a good investment plan could help her to accumulate assets that could add to the quality of her life. She then said something that really warmed my heart. She said, "I don't expect to use this for myself. I would really like to build this up so that I can have something to pass on to my children or grandchildren." It occurred to me at that point that she was an oak tree farmer. She was planting the seeds for something that she wanted to benefit others beyond her lifetime. But I also emphasized that should she need some of it or all of it, it would be available. I then asked her how much could she realistically afford to invest on a monthly basis without putting a strain on her budget. She told me that she could afford to invest $50 per month.

I recommended that we take $25 each month and put it into a money market fund. The money market fund is relatively safe and stable, and would serve as an emergency fund. The other $25 each month would go into a growth and income stock mutual fund to provide growth for the portfolio.

I am proud to say that it has been a couple of years since we started the program, and she has stuck with it. She has made only one withdrawal, and the account is still growing quite nicely. She is even thinking about adding extra money to the account and increasing her monthly contribution. Since she opened the account, she has asked questions so that she can learn even more about investing. She has seen how the stock market goes up and down. She has learned how to be patient. She has become an investor.

You can become one too. It's never too late!

Take Up Thy Bed

If it's not one thing going wrong, it's another. Every time you turn around, something or someone is adversely affecting your plans to get your financial life together. Before you know it, 20 or 30 years has passed and you're no better off than when you first started on your own.

There are many of us who have issues that affect us for a long time. We know that there is an answer to our problem somewhere, but we just can't seem to find it. Frustrated, we sometimes give up and wait on someone to solve our problems for us. In the Book of John, there is a story about a man who had issues for a long time. The solution to his problem came in the form of a question:

> *John 5:2–9*
> 2 Now there is at Jerusalem by the sheep *market* a pool,
>   which is called in the Hebrew tongue Bethesda, having
>   five porches.
> 3 In these lay a great multitude of impotent folk, of blind,

halt, withered, waiting for the moving of the water.

4 For an angel went down at a certain season into the pool, and troubled the water: whosoever then first after the troubling of the water stepped in was made whole of whatsoever disease he had.

5 And a certain man was there, which had an infirmity thirty and eight years.

6 When Jesus saw him lie, and knew that he had been now a long time *in that case*, he saith unto him, Wilt thou be made whole?

7 The impotent man answered him, Sir, I have no man, when the water is troubled, to put me into the pool: but while I am coming, another steppeth down before me.

8 Jesus saith unto him, Rise, take up thy bed, and walk.

9 And immediately the man was made whole, and took up his bed, and walked: and on the same day was the sabbath.

At the pool of Bethesda, it was known that during a certain time of the year, God would send an angel to stir (trouble) the water. Whoever stepped into the water first would be cured of whatever disease or affliction they had (verse 4). Apparently, many people knew of this miraculous occurrence because verse 3 tells us that there was "a great multitude of impotent folk, of blind, halt, withered, waiting for the moving of the water."

One aspect of this story that makes me sad is the fact that these people are waiting. They are waiting, watching, and listening for any clue that the water is about to stir. I'm sure that there were a lot of false starts. Maybe the wind would blow, or the earth would tremble, and the water would stir. Immediately, there was a mad dash by the people to be the first in the water, only to have their expectations fade because it was not the real thing. Some probably emerged from the pool and assumed their waiting position again. Others left in total frustration, never to return.

Another aspect of this story that makes me sad is that for you to be successful in your quest to healed, you had to be able to run faster than everybody else, or have someone to carry you who could be faster than everyone else. For those who were blind or crippled, this was a task that was probably next to impossible to successfully complete.

But there was a man at the pool who had been there for a long time. He had a sickness that had lasted 38 years (verse 5). Jesus saw him lying there and *knew* he had been there a long time. Because of this, Jesus asked him a very simple question: "Wilt thou be made whole?"(verse 6).

To me, that seemed like a very simple question that required a yes or no answer. But what did the man do? He started giving excuses (verse 7). He had no one to carry him, and someone always beat him to the pool before he could get there. Before he could spout any more excuses, Jesus very simply told him, "Rise, take up thy bed, and walk."(verse 8).

This was a turning point in this man's life. If he continued to do what he had always done, he would probably be on the banks of the pool of Bethesda for another 38 years. To have a different outcome, he had to do something *different*. He had to *rise*! Now, the realities of the physical world would tell you that if you have been crippled for 38 years, you just couldn't get up and walk. But through the omnipotent power of God as manifested through Jesus Christ, you should know that through Him all things are possible. All this man had to do was to have faith in what Jesus told him to do, and do it.

In that same directive, Jesus gave two other instructions. He told him to take up his bed and walk. The bed was a symbol of his affliction. It supported him and gave him some comfort while he waited to be healed. Now, he had the bed tucked under *his* arm. It no longer defined who he was. The only thing remaining to complete the change was the last instruction. He had to walk.

After completing the first instruction to rise, the man had experienced a major change. But, he was still standing in the same spot where he was waiting to be healed. Jesus told him to walk for several reasons. First, when Jesus gives you a set of instructions, He wants you to do them all. Next, walking was the final proof of the miracle. To all who knew this man as a cripple, to see him walking was an immediate verification that something extraordinary had happened to him. Finally, he needed to be able to walk so that he could go and tell others of his good news. Jesus told him to walk so that he could be a witness.

Some of you have had a financial affliction for a long time. Some of you have also had an idea of what it would take to cure it. But like the man at the pool of Bethesda, you have been waiting for someone to solve your problems for you. I hope that as you have read this book, you have realized that Jesus knows what your problems are. Just like the man at the pool, Jesus poses the question to you: Wilt thou be made whole?

Are you willing to own up to your own shortcomings? Are you willing to recognize that financial wealth might have held too much prominence in your life? Are you willing to fix the problem? Are you willing to have faith and believe that God has already provided a solution? This book has given you a lot information that I am sure will help you to rise above your problems, take up your bed, and walk in a life full of contentment and prosperity. Now, the only thing left for you to do, is to just do it.

The Last Word

Exactly what does God require of us? For however long we are blessed to live on this Earth, what is it that He really wants us to do? Does He want us to make lots of money? Does He want us to drive the most expensive car that is made? Does He want us to build big palatial churches in His honor? The answer is in Micah 6:1–8:

1 Hear ye now what the LORD saith; Arise, contend thou before the mountains, and let the hills hear thy voice.

2 Hear ye, O mountains, the LORD'S controversy, and ye strong foundations of the earth: for the LORD hath a controversy with his people, and he will plead with Israel.

3 O my people, what have I done unto thee? and wherein have I wearied thee? testify against me.

4 For I brought thee up out of the land of Egypt, and redeemed thee out of the house of servants; and I sent

before thee Moses, Aaron, and Miriam.

5 O my people, remember now what Balak king of Moab consulted, and what Balaam the son of Beor answered him from Shittim unto Gilgal; that ye may know the righteousness of the LORD.

6 Wherewith shall I come before the LORD, *and* bow myself before the high God? shall I come before him with burnt offerings, with calves of a year old?

7 Will the LORD be pleased with thousands of rams, *or* with ten thousands of rivers of oil? shall I give my first born *for* my transgression, the fruit of my body *for* the sin of my soul?

8 He hath shewed thee, O man, what is good; and what doth the LORD require of thee, but to do justly, and to love mercy, and to walk humbly with thy God?

In fact, in Micah 6:6–8, God tells us what is really important. In these verses, God is angry because the Israelites continue to disobey Him, despite all that He has done for them. In their fear, they nervously ask what must they do to please Him? Does God want them to give Him burnt offerings? Does He want thousands of rams? Maybe He wants thousands of rivers of oil or even their first-born child? Micah answers these questions in verse 8, where he says "He hath shewed thee, O man, what is good; and what doth the LORD require of thee, but to do justly, and to love mercy, and to walk humbly with thy God?"

Micah 6:8 is one of my favorite verses in the Bible and it is considered by many to be the basis of true religion. All that God wants us to do is to be just, love mercy, and humbly walk with Him.

This seems simple enough to understand, but it has been all too easy for many of us to overlook. In today's modern society, there has been a separation of the personality of God, as manifested by His Son Jesus, and the principles and laws of God as dictated by the Bible. But I'm here to tell you that you cannot have one without the other.

Many pastors tell their congregations that God loves them and will take care of them. They tell them that God is a problem solver and a healer. When we are down and out, these are all good things to hear and they are all true. However, some of these same pastors are often reluctant to talk about the principles of God and about being accountable to them because doing so can be uncomfortable. We need to hear both.

What does it mean to "act justly"? To act justly means to treat others fairly. A good starting point to acting justly would be the Ten Commandments as listed in Exodus 20:3–17. The Bible also offers many other examples of how we should treat our fellow man. Study the Bible and study it well. There can be justice for all only if all of us embrace it. As it is stated in James 1:22, "But be ye doers of the word, and not hearers only, deceiving your own selves." Learn to act justly. It is what God requires of us.

What does it mean to "love mercy"? God shows His faithfulness to us each day through His mercy and grace. To truly love mercy, you must be as willing to grant it as you are willing to receive it. The very nature of human beings makes it difficult for us to embrace mercy. Pride makes it hard for some people to say "I'm sorry" or "I forgive you." Mercy is so important that Jesus made it part of the Lord's Prayer, where He says "...and forgive us our trespasses as we forgive those who trespass against us." We must learn to love mercy. It is what God requires of us.

Finally, what does it mean to "walk humbly with your God?" To humble yourself means to be submissive. However, when we find ourselves struggling in our relationship with God, it is usually because we are not willing to completely submit to Him. Are you willing to follow God? Are you willing to do His will? When you pray, do you ask God to give you what you want, or are you willing to receive what God wants for you?

To humble yourself, you must strip away all that gets in the way of you having a true relationship with God. If you don't, God will strip those things away for you. On the Highway of Life, you will encounter many bumps, potholes, and roadblocks. However, you can safely complete your journey with faith and humility unto God. Give your hand to God. Let Him lead you. Learn to walk humbly with God. It is what He requires of us.

Wealth is a multifaceted jewel. There are many aspects of wealth beyond mere financial definitions. Embrace God's laws and principles. Empty yourself of worldly desires so that you can be filled with the Spirit of God. Be just to others, love mercy, and walk humbly with God. That, my friend, is how you Build Wealth through Spiritual Health.

Bible Outline

This outline is from the Bible Statistics section of the Abundant Bible website located at www.abundantbible.org. Abundant Bible is a mega-site of Bible, Christian, and religious information. This website is an excellent resource, and I thank Bible Desk of St. Petersburg, FL, the publisher of the website, for their permission to use their Bible statistics and information in this appendix.

The Old Testament

⚜⚜ Book 1 ⚜⚜

BOOK NAME: Genesis. Origin; generation; source; begetting the first book of Moses.
THEME:
BY: Moses
DATE WRITTEN: 1450 B.C.-1400 B.C.
DATES COVERED: The beginning to 1620 B.C.; Chapter 12 to the end—1921 B.C.-1689 B.C.
FOR/TO: A general record
WHERE WRITTEN: In the wilderness
STATISTICS: 50 chapters, 1533 verses, 38,267 words
MISC: From the Creation to Joseph

⚜⚜ Book 2 ⚜⚜

BOOK NAME: Exodus. Departure, going out; the second book of Moses.
THEME: Deliverance from Egypt
BY: Moses
DATE WRITTEN: 1450 B.C.-1400 B.C., 1580 B.C.-1230 B.C.
DATES COVERED: 1677 B.C.-1461 B.C., 1530 B.C.-1450 B.C.
FOR/TO: The Israelites
WHERE WRITTEN: In the wilderness
STATISTICS: 40 chapters, 1213 verses, 32,692 words
MISC: Joseph through the descendants of Jacob
The Exodus
Moses: 40 years thinking he was somebody
40 years learning he was nobody
40 years discovering what God can do with a nobody.

☙☙ *Book 3* ☙☙

BOOK NAME: Leviticus. He called; pertaining to the Levite, of the Levites; the book of atonement, the book of laws; the third book of Moses.

THEME: Genesis-man ruined; Exodus-man redeemed; Leviticus-man worshipping

BY: Moses (Ezra 6:18 refers to the book of Moses)

DATE WRITTEN: 1450 B.C.-1400 B.C.

DATES COVERED: 1462 B.C.-1461 B.C.

FOR/TO: The Israelites

WHERE WRITTEN: In the wilderness, Mt Sinai region

STATISTICS: 27 chapters, 859 verses, 24,546 words

MISC: Without Leviticus, the powerful message of the cross is more difficult to understand—Holiness, sacrifice, atonement, and dedication.

☙☙ *Book 4* ☙☙

BOOK NAME: Numbers. In the wilderness; the book of the march; the fourth book of Moses.

THEME: Walk, worship, service

BY: Moses named as the author more than 80 times

DATE WRITTEN: 1450 B.C.-1400 B.C.

DATES COVERED: 1461 B.C.-1423 B.C.

FOR/TO: The Israelites

WHERE WRITTEN: In the wilderness, Mt. Sinai

STATISTICS: 36 chapters, 1288 verses, 32,902 or 32,092 words

MISC: Chapters 1-21 wilderness years; 26-36 new generation, covers about 39 years.

☙☙ *Book 5* ☙☙

BOOK NAME: Deuteronomy. These are the words; a copy of the Law; this second law; the second law giving; repetition of the Law; the fifth book of Moses.

THEME: Renewal of the Covenant; God is One

BY: Moses (Deuteronomy 31:9, 24); also describes his death—34:5-12.

DATE WRITTEN: 1450 B.C.-1400 B.C.

DATES COVERED: 1423 B.C.-1422 B.C.

FOR/TO: The Israelites

WHERE WRITTEN: In the wilderness, on the banks of Jordan

STATISTICS: 34 chapters, 959 verses, 28,461 words

MISC: More than 80 references to this book in the New Testament.

❧❧ Book 6 ❧❧

BOOK NAME: Joshua. Jehovah is salvation
THEME: Conquering the Land
BY: Joshua, or perhaps Phinehas, Eleazar, Samuel, or Jeremiah
DATE WRITTEN: 1370 B.C.-1330 B.C., before 1200 B.C., 1235 B.C., 1410 B.C.-1390 B.C.
DATES COVERED: 1422 B.C.-1362 B.C.
FOR/TO: The Israelites
WHERE WRITTEN: Canaan
STATISTICS: 24 chapters, 685 verses, 18,858 words
MISC:

❧❧ Book 7 ❧❧

BOOK NAME: Judges
THEME: Compromise and confusion
BY: Unknown, a contemporary of Samuel, Samuel, Phinehas, Hezekiah, Jeremiah, Ezekiel, Ezra
DATE WRITTEN: 1050 B.C.-1000 B.C., 1390 B.C.-1350 B.C., 1300 B.C.-1050 B.C.
DATES COVERED: 1416 B.C.-1065 B.C.
FOR/TO: The Israelites
WHERE WRITTEN: Canaan
STATISTICS: 21 chapters, 618 verses, 18,976 words
MISC:

❧❧ Book 8 ❧❧

BOOK NAME Ruth
THEME: God working through the joys and tragedies of life, famine, death, loneliness, etc., to fulfill the purpose of God—the birth of Christ of which Ruth had part in the lineage; love, kinsman, redeemer.
BY: Unknown, Samuel by tradition, Hezekiah, Ezra
DATE WRITTEN: Unknown, 10th century B.C. to 400 B.C., 399 B.C.-300 B.C., 1100 B.C., about the time of David
DATES COVERED: 1261 B.C.-1251 B.C.
FOR/TO: The Israelites
WHERE WRITTEN: Unknown
STATISTICS: 4 chapters, 85 verses, 2,578 words
MISC: Ruth was a Moabitess.

❧❧ Book 9 ❧❧

BOOK NAME: First Samuel
THEME: Samuel, Saul, and David

BY: Uncertain, Samuel and Abiathar, a son of the prophets, or possibly others
DATE WRITTEN: 1000 B.C.-950 B.C., 11th century B.C., 1070 B.C.-1011 B.C., 1000 B.C.-850 B.C.
DATES COVERED: 1126 B.C.-1025 B.C.
FOR/TO: The Israelites
WHERE WRITTEN: Unknown
STATISTICS: 31 chapters, 810 verses, 25,061 words
MISC: Parts occurred after Samuel's death. First and Second Samuel were one book. Sometimes they were entitled First and Second Kings; and First and Second Kings were Third and Fourth Kings.

✑✑ *Book 10* ✑✑

BOOK NAME: Second Samuel
THEME: Begins with the death of Saul and follows David's reign
BY: Uncertain, Samuel and Abiathar, a son of the prophets, or possibly others
DATE WRITTEN: 10th century B.C., 1011 B.C.-975 B.C., 1000 B.C.-850B.C.
DATES COVERED: 1025 B.C.-988 B.C.
FOR/TO: The leaders of Israel
WHERE WRITTEN: Unknown
STATISTICS: 24 chapters, 695 verses, 20,612 words
MISC: First and Second Samuel were one book. Sometimes they were entitled First and Second Kings; and First and Second Kings was Third and Fourth Kings.

✑✑ *Book 11* ✑✑

BOOK NAME: First Kings
THEME: A kingdom united, then divided
BY: Unknown, perhaps a Jewish captive; Jeremiah by tradition
DATE WRITTEN: 562 B.C.-536 B.C., over a period ending by the 6th century B.C., 971 B.C.-850 B.C.
DATES COVERED: 1025 B.C.-864 B.C.
FOR/TO: The people of Israel
WHERE WRITTEN: Unknown, perhaps in the area of Babylon
STATISTICS: 22 chapters, 816 verses, 24,524 words
MISC: First and Second Kings originally known as Third and Fourth Kings. Some think Jeremiah wrote it, as Jeremiah 52 and 2 Kings 24, 25 nearly identical.

🎜🎜 *Book 12* 🎜🎜

BOOK NAME: Second Kings
THEME: Exploits of the kings of Judah and Israel
BY: Unknown, perhaps a Jewish captive; Jeremiah by tradition; probably the same person that wrote 1st Kings
DATE WRITTEN: 562 B.C.-536 B.C., over a period ending by the 6th century B.C., 971 B.C.-850 B.C., 852 B.C.-586 B.C.
DATES COVERED: 870 B.C.-561 B.C.
FOR/TO: The people of Israel
WHERE WRITTEN: Unknown, perhaps in the area of Babylon
STATISTICS: 25 chapters, 719 verses, 23,532 words
MISC: First and Second Kings originally known as Third and Fourth Kings. Some think Jeremiah wrote it, as Jeremiah 52 and 2 Kings 24, 25 nearly identical.

🎜🎜 *Book 13* 🎜🎜

BOOK NAME: First Chronicles. The affairs of the days
THEME: Genealogy and history of Israel
BY: Ezra by tradition
DATE WRITTEN: 500 B.C.-450 B.C., written about 100 years after Kings, 5th century B.C., 360 B.C.
DATES COVERED: 1699 B.C.-444 B.C.
FOR/TO: The people of Israel
WHERE WRITTEN: Unknown
STATISTICS: 29 chapters, 942 verses, 20,369 words
MISC: First and Second Chronicles were once one. First and Second Chronicles and Ezra perhaps one history.

🎜🎜 *Book 14* 🎜🎜

BOOK NAME: Second Chronicles
THEME: The greatness of Judah
BY: Ezra by tradition
DATE WRITTEN: 500 B.C.-450 B.C., written about 100 years after Kings, 5th century B.C., 330 B.C., 971 B.C.-609 B.C.
DATES COVERED: 1015 B.C.-539 B.C.
FOR/TO: The people of Israel
WHERE WRITTEN: Unknown
STATISTICS: 36 chapters, 822 verses, 26,074 words
MISC: First and Second Chronicles were once one. First and Second Chronicles and Ezra perhaps one history.

❧❧ *Book 15* ❧❧

BOOK NAME: Ezra
THEME: The return and rebuilding
BY: Probably Ezra
DATE WRITTEN: 456 B.C.-444 B.C., 444 B.C.-398 B.C., 538 B.C.-457 B.C.
DATES COVERED: 1723 B.C.-457 B.C.
FOR/TO: The people of Israel
WHERE WRITTEN: Unknown, perhaps Jerusalem
STATISTICS: 10 chapters, 280 verses, 7,441 words
MISC: Spans about 80 years, beginning about 538 B.C. Nehemiah, First and Second Chronicles, and Ezra considered a literary work (called Priestly History of Israel).

❧❧ *Book 16* ❧❧

BOOK NAME: Nehemiah. Also called Second Ezra
THEME: Rebuilding Jerusalem's walls and problems
BY: Nehemiah and later scribes
DATE WRITTEN: 420 B.C., 445 B.C.-432 B.C.
DATES COVERED: 536 B..C-432 B.C., 445 B.C.-425 B.C., about 20 years
FOR/TO: The people of Israel
WHERE WRITTEN: Unknown, perhaps Jerusalem
STATISTICS: 13 chapters, 406 verses, 10,483 words
MISC: Artaxerxes I, whom Nehemiah served as cupbearer, was the son of Ahasuerus (Xerxes), who took Esther to be his queen.

❧❧ *Book 17* ❧❧

BOOK NAME: Esther. The volume of Esther
THEME: Divine providence of God.
BY: Unknown, a Jew who lived in Persia; not Mordecai-10:2,3
DATE WRITTEN: After 456 B.C., 5th century B.C., 486 B.C.-465 B.C.
DATES COVERED: 598 B.C.-473 B.C., 485 B.C.-473 B.C., 10 years
FOR/TO: The people of Israel
WHERE WRITTEN: Unknown
STATISTICS: 10 chapters, 167 verses, 5637 words
MISC: Esther, a person whose name meant star, her Hebrew name was Hadassah-2:7. Jerusalem, the temple of God, and the name of God are omitted. This book fits in between the 6th and 7th chapters of Ezra. The deuterocanon adds 6 chapters to

Esther that most Protestant Bibles do not contain.

✄✄ *Book 18* ✄✄

BOOK NAME: Job
THEME: Suffering and service
BY: Unknown, perhaps Job, Moses, Elihu, Solomon, or Isaiah
DATE WRITTEN: Unknown, perhaps during Solomon's time, 900 B.C.
DATES COVERED: 1997 B.C.-1827 B.C., 2000 B.C., unknown
FOR/TO: No specific people
WHERE WRITTEN: Unknown
STATISTICS: 42 chapters, 1070 verses, 10,102 words
MISC: Poetical, wisdom books—Job, Proverbs, Psalms, Ecclesiastes, Lamentations, Song of Solomon. Uz—perhaps in the area of Idumaea, unknown, perhaps southern Lebanon. Some consider this to be the oldest book in the Bible. Mentioned by Ezekiel 14:14,20. Job pleads for death, then mercy, but no response. He wishes someone to resolve the quarrel between them; then finally faces problems with courage and asks God to bring him through painful trials (16:18-17:3) (19:25-27).

✄✄ *Book 19* ✄✄

BOOK NAME: Psalms. To the collection; praises; book of praises
THEME: Conquest of fear by faith, praise, and trust
Book 1, 1-41 Reflect Genesis
Book 2, 41-72 Israel's cry for deliverance to Israel's king
Book 3, 73-89 Sanctuary—dominant note, parallel Leviticus
Book 4, 90-106 Corresponds to Numbers, the fourth book of Moses
Book 5, 107-150 Linked with Deuteronomy, God's Word Selah—meaning unknown, many opinions —pause in the music accompanying a psalm or prayer; suspension (of music) as a pause.
BY: 72 credited to David, but he may not be the author of some. 12 to Asaph, 12 to sons of Korah, 2 to Solomon (72 and 127), 1 to Ethan, and 1 to Moses. All, but 34, bear some title as a superscription; about 50 anonymous. Titles based on traditions.
DATE WRITTEN: Unknown, some contain elements varying by more than a thousand years
DATES COVERED: 1423 B.C.-444 B.C., unknown

FOR/TO: The Jewish people
WHERE WRITTEN: Many places
STATISTICS: 150 chapters, 2461 verses, 43,743 words
MISC:

✠✠ Book 20 ✠✠

BOOK NAME: Proverbs
THEME: Moral and ethical principles; wisdom; the fear of the Lord is the beginning of wisdom-Pv 9:10
BY: Solomon—1 to 22:16; Agur and mother of King Lemuel latter portions of Pv 30, 31? Solomon also credited with 25 to 29; author unknown—22:17 to 24:34 and 30:1 to 31:31
DATE WRITTEN: 10th century B.C., 970 B.C.-930 B.C., 900 B.C.
DATES COVERED: 982 B.C.-961 B.C.
FOR/TO: Young people
WHERE WRITTEN: Jerusalem
STATISTICS: 31 chapters, 915 verses, 15,043 words
MISC: Chapters: 1-9 Contrasts good and evil; wisdom calls the simple to forsake sin; the harlot calls him to indulgence. 10:1-22:16 Treatment; through chapter 15 by contrast "but;" wisdom and folly; fool, scorner, slothful, froward. 22:17-24:22 24:23-24:34 25:1-29:27 30:1-31:31
Other breakdowns:
   1-10 Counsel for young men
   11-20 Counsel for all men
   21-31 Counsel for kings and rulers
   31 Women's rights (also called)

✠✠ Book 21 ✠✠

BOOK NAME: Ecclesiastes. Assembly; one who assembles; one who collects; one who addresses an assembly; preacher; member of the assembly
THEME: Earthly goals lead to emptiness; happiness through science, philosophy, pleasure, mirth, drinking, building, possessions, wealth, music, materialism—all are empty. He tried fatalism, natural religion, wealth, morality—all are empty.
BY: Unknown. Solomon by tradition; however, many believe it was someone else.
DATE WRITTEN: Tenth century B.C., 962-922 B.C.
DATES COVERED: 947 B.C.
FOR/TO: Young people

WHERE WRITTEN: Jerusalem
STATISTICS: 12 chapters, 222 verses, 5,584 words
MISC: Solomon used as the central character. Vanity—emptiness or meaningless. "Under the sun" may mean without God in the world. Remembering the Creator, means a young person must come to the recognition that he is not the Creator or the master of his own life. "Under the sun" occurs about 29 times. God gives meaning to life—all else is vanity and meaningless.

♫♫ Book 22 ♫♫

BOOK NAME: Song of Solomon. Song of songs; best of the songs
THEME: God's love
BY: Perhaps Solomon by tradition
DATE WRITTEN: Tenth century B.C., 962 B.C.-922 B.C., 1014 B.C.
DATES COVERED: 962 B.C.
FOR/TO: To the bride
WHERE WRITTEN: Jerusalem
STATISTICS: 8 chapters, 117 verses, 2661 words
MISC: The Jews regarded it as a song expressing the love relationship between God and His chosen people. Also regarded as between Solomon and his wife. Typical—Christ and the church, plus other views.

♫♫ Book 23 ♫♫

BOOK NAME: Isaiah. Jehovah is salvation
THEME: Messiah
BY: Isaiah
DATE WRITTEN: 740 B.C.-698 B.C., 8th century B.C., 750 B.C.-680 B.C.
DATES COVERED: From Lucifer fallen to 539 B.C.
FOR/TO: Judah and the Jewish nation
WHERE WRITTEN: Unknown, perhaps Jerusalem
STATISTICS: 66 chapters, 1292 verses, 37,044 words
MISC: He was martyred by being sawn asunder-ref Heb 11:37, tradition says by King Manasseh.

♫♫ Book 24 ♫♫

BOOK NAME: Jeremiah. The appointed one of the Lord
THEME: Judgment is at hand
BY: Jeremiah, recorded by his scribe Baruch

270

DATE WRITTEN: 640 B.C.-577 B.C.
DATES COVERED: From the earth without form and void to 539 B.C.,
7th century B.C.
FOR/TO: Mainly Jews in Judah
WHERE WRITTEN: Perhaps Jerusalem
STATISTICS: 52 chapters, 1364 verses, 42,659 words
MISC: Some believe Jeremiah died in Egypt. Tradition
says that Jewish refugees stoned him to death in
Egypt.

❧❧ Book 25 ❧❧

BOOK NAME: Lamentations. Ah, howl, alas, cry aloud, or lament
THEME: Mourning for Jerusalem shows there comes a time
when prayers will not be answered, and
whatsoever a man sows, he shall reap.
BY: Jeremiah-2 Chronicles 35:25
DATE WRITTEN: Perhaps 640 B.C.-586 B.C., about 586 B.C.
DATES COVERED: 586 B.C.
FOR/TO: Exiles in Babylon
WHERE WRITTEN: Jerusalem
STATISTICS: 5 chapters, 154 verses, 3415 words
MISC: Five poems—one for each chapter. The first four
each have 22 stanzas. The fifth also has 22, but
not alphabetical as the first 4. The fifth one is
more of a prayer.

❧❧ Book 26 ❧❧

BOOK NAME: Ezekiel. God strengthens
THEME: Judgment and glory
BY: Ezekiel
DATE WRITTEN: 6th century B.C., 593 B.C.-570 B.C.
DATES COVERED: Thou hast been in Eden to 571 B.C.
FOR/TO: Exiles in Babylon
WHERE WRITTEN: Babylon
STATISTICS: 48 chapters, 1273 verses, 39,407 words
MISC:

❧❧ Book 27 ❧❧

BOOK NAME: Daniel
THEME: Rise and fall of kingdoms
BY: Daniel
DATE WRITTEN: Perhaps 605 B.C.-536 B.C., 6th century B.C.
DATES COVERED: 605 B.C.-537 B.C.

FOR/TO: Exiles in Babylon
WHERE WRITTEN: Babylon
STATISTICS: 12 chapters, 357 verses, 11,606 words
MISC: Daniel lived under three rulers:
    1. Nebuchadnezzar-Babylon
    2. Darius the Mede (Median)
    3. Cyrus (Persian)

✐✐ Book 28 ✐✐

BOOK NAME: Hosea
THEME: Redeeming love
BY: Hosea
DATE WRITTEN: 755–715 B.C., about 760 B.C.
DATES COVERED: 770 B.C.-723 B.C.
FOR/TO: Northern ten tribes
WHERE WRITTEN: Northern kingdom of Israel
STATISTICS: 14 chapters, 197 verses, 5175 words
MISC: Prophesied to the northern kingdom about the time of Isaiah. Hosea called the prophet with the broken heart—Hosea's marriage. Likewise, Israel's unfaithfulness to the Lord is depicted as a wife who has turned her back on a faithful husband in order to follow evil lovers.

✐✐ Book 29 ✐✐

BOOK NAME: Joel. Jehovah is God
THEME: The day of the Lord is coming. The attitude of a man's heart and life before the Lord will determine his reaction to that day.
BY: Joel
DATE WRITTEN: About 837 B.C.-795 B.C., about 400 B.C.
DATES COVERED: Unable to determine accurately, perhaps 836 B.C.-828 B.C.
FOR/TO: Two southern tribes
WHERE WRITTEN: Southern kingdom
STATISTICS: 3 chapters, 73 verses, 2034 words
MISC: Scholars disagree when Joel lived. Some believe he lived around 830 B.C., others believe about 400 B.C.

✐✐ Book 30 ✐✐

BOOK NAME: Amos. Burden-bearer
THEME: Judgment on sin
BY: Amos

DATE WRITTEN: Middle of the 8th century B.C., 765–750 B.C.
DATES COVERED: 764 B.C.
FOR/TO: Israel
WHERE WRITTEN: New Jerusalem
STATISTICS: 9 chapters, 146 verses, 4217 words
MISC: Prophesied in the northern kingdom and aroused antagonism. He returned to Judah. Because Israel will not repent, there is nothing left but destruction. The prophet of God often comes into conflict with the religious institutions of his day. Man's understanding of God and His purpose will always be distorted by his own sin and selfish interests. People do not recognize just how sinful and self-centered one really is and how deceitful the heart can be.

৸৹ৎ Book 31 ৸৹ৎ

BOOK NAME: Obadiah. Servant of the Lord; worshipper of the Lord
THEME: The doom of Edom
BY: Obadiah
DATE WRITTEN: About 586 B.C., 6th century B.C., 848 B.C.-841 B.C.
DATES COVERED: 864 B.C.
FOR/TO: The Edomites
WHERE WRITTEN: Judah
STATISTICS: 1 chapter, 21 verses, 670 words
MISC: Shortest Old Testament book

৸৹ৎ Book 32 ৸৹ৎ

BOOK NAME: Jonah
THEME: The mercy of God
BY: Jonah (2 Ki 14:25) (Mt 12:39-42)
DATE WRITTEN: 8th century B.C., 790 B.C.-749 B.C.
DATES COVERED: 767 B.C.
FOR/TO: Israel
WHERE WRITTEN: Israel
STATISTICS: 4 chapters, 48 verses, 1321 words
MISC:

৸৹ৎ Book 33 ৸৹ৎ

BOOK NAME: Micah. Who is like Yahweh?
THEME: Judgment and pardon

BY: Micah
DATE WRITTEN: 740 B.C.-687 B.C., 8th century B.C.
DATES COVERED: 744 B.C.-704 B.C.
FOR/TO: Judah and Israel
WHERE WRITTEN: Judah
STATISTICS: 7 chapters, 105 verses, 3153 words
MISC: Lived and prophesied in the southern kingdom. He condemned the sins of the northern kingdom. One of the greatest passages in the Bible is Micah's summary of true religion: Micah 6:8-What doth the LORD require of thee, but to do justly, and to love mercy, and to walk humbly with thy God?

❧❧ Book 34 ❧❧

BOOK NAME: Nahum. Consolation; consoler; burden
THEME: The burden of Nineveh
BY: Nahum
DATE WRITTEN: Before 612 B.C., 630 B.C.
DATES COVERED: 635 B.C.
FOR/TO: Nineveh
WHERE WRITTEN: Possibly Judah
STATISTICS: 3 chapters, 47 verses, 1285 words
MISC:

❧❧ Book 35 ❧❧

BOOK NAME: Habakkuk. To embrace; the embracer; one who embraces
THEME: The righteous shall live by faith
BY: Habakkuk
DATE WRITTEN: Unknown, perhaps 640 B.C. to 598 B.C.
DATES COVERED: Uncertain, possibly 606 B.C.
FOR/TO: Judah
WHERE WRITTEN: Judah
STATISTICS: 3 chapters, 56 verses, 1474 words
MISC: Faith is: repentance and humble trust in God. It is faithfulness, steadfast obedience to God. Faith is a whole way of life, a daily dependence upon God. When everything has gone wrong, and all possessions have been lost, and there is not anything to eat, faith will still rejoice in the God of his salvation. Faith says that God alone is enough.

✂❧ Book 36 ❧✂

BOOK NAME: Zephaniah. The Lord hides; whom Jehovah hides
or shelters
THEME: The day of the Lord
BY: Zephaniah
DATE WRITTEN: App 627 B.C.-607 B.C.
DATES COVERED: 624 B.C.
FOR/TO: Judah
WHERE WRITTEN: Judah
STATISTICS: 3 chapters, 53 verses, 1617 words
MISC:

✂❧ Book 37 ❧✂

BOOK NAME: Haggai
THEME: Rebuilding the temple
BY: Haggai
DATE WRITTEN: 520 B.C.
DATES COVERED: 521 B.C.
FOR/TO: Restored Israel
WHERE WRITTEN: Jerusalem
STATISTICS: 2 chapters, 38 verses, 1131 words
MISC:

✂❧ Book 38 ❧✂

BOOK NAME: Zechariah. The Lord remembers
THEME: The coming of Messiah
BY: Zechariah
DATE WRITTEN: 520 B.C.-487 B.C.
DATES COVERED: 521 B.C.-494 B.C.
FOR/TO: Restored Israel
WHERE WRITTEN: Jerusalem
STATISTICS: 14 chapters, 211 verses, 6444 words
MISC: 1-8 Call to repentance
9-14 The future of Israel and God's people
(8 visions of Zechariah)

✂❧ Book 39 ❧✂

BOOK NAME: Malachi. The messenger of Jehovah; the
messenger of the Lord
THEME: Rebuke
BY: Malachi
DATE WRITTEN: Unknown, perhaps 433 B.C.-400 B.C.
DATES COVERED: Unknown
FOR/TO: Israel

275

Building Wealth through Spiritual Health

WHERE WRITTEN: Judah
STATISTICS: 4 chapters, 55 verses, 1782 words
MISC:

The New Testament

✎✎ Book 40 ✎✎
BOOK NAME: Matthew. Gift of God
THEME: Emphasis seems to be on the fact that Jesus is Israel's promised Messiah—the One that would establish the Kingdom. Emphasis placed on the fact that He is the Son of David—of royal descent.
BY: The apostle Matthew (a tax collector)
DATE WRITTEN: Approximately A.D. 37 to 50
DATES COVERED: From Abraham to just before Jesus ascended to Heaven
FOR/TO:
WHERE WRITTEN: Perhaps written in Judea, perhaps Jerusalem
STATISTICS: 28 chapters, 1071 verses, 23,684 words
MISC: There are approximately 93 Old Testament quotes or allusions

✎✎ Book 41 ✎✎
BOOK NAME: Mark
THEME: Emphasis seems to be on Jesus being the Son of God and discipleship. Jesus is revealed as the Son of God and suffering, obedient servant of God the Father, Who gave up His life as a ransom for the sin of others in submission to God's will.
BY: Mark. The name of Yochanan (John) is the original Hebrew name. The name of Mark (the Latin name) (or Roman prefix which was later added) means "Polite Shining". He is believed to be the same one mentioned in the New Testament in Acts 12:12, 25; 13:5, 13; 15:37, 39; Col 4:10; 2 Tim 4:11; Phile. 24; 1 Peter 5:13. He was a Jewish believer, and his home was in Jerusalem. He was the son of Mary who lived in Jerusalem, whose house Peter came to after he was delivered from prison. He was a travel companion of Peter, Paul, and Barnabas.
DATE WRITTEN: Approximately A.D. 65 to 70. Some believe A.D. 60.

276

DATES COVERED: From John the Baptist to after the ascension of
Jesus into Heaven
FOR/TO:
WHERE WRITTEN: Unknown
STATISTICS: 16 chapters, 678 verses, 15,171 words
MISC: Approximately 49 Old Testament quotes

✁✁ *Book 42* ✁✁

BOOK NAME: Luke
THEME: Emphasis seems to be on the humanity of Christ.
He is the Son of Man that had been rejected by
Israel. As a result, Jesus was preached to the
Gentiles also. Jesus is presented as the universal
Savior—the Savior of the poor and rich, male and
female, Jew and Gentile, slave and free.
BY: Luke (the physician). At a later time, he also wrote
Acts as a sequel to the Gospel of Luke.
DATE WRITTEN: Approximately A.D. 58 to 60
DATES COVERED: From Adam to after Jesus ascended to Heaven
FOR/TO: Addressed to Theophilus, perhaps a community
leader, or government or Roman official.
WHERE WRITTEN: Unknown, some believe possibly Caesarea or
Rome
STATISTICS: 24 chapters, 1151 verses, 25,944 words
MISC: Approximately 80 quotes from the Old Testament

✁✁ *Book 43* ✁✁

BOOK NAME: John
THEME: Emphasis seems to be on showing the full deity of
Jesus. Jesus is revealed as the Word that was
made flesh in chapter one. Near the end of the
Gospel in 20:28, Thomas said, "My Lord and my
God." Jesus is clearly presented as the Christ (or
Messiah), the Son of God through many miracles.
BY: The apostle John
DATE WRITTEN: Approximately A.D. 85-90
DATES COVERED: From "In the beginning" to just prior to Jesus
ascending to be with His Father
FOR/TO:
WHERE WRITTEN: Probably at Ephesus
STATISTICS: 21 chapters, 878 verses, 19,099 words
MISC: Approximately 30 quotes from the Old Testament.
To record Jesus' signs (20:30,31) so readers
would believe in Jesus-ref 20:31.

⚮ *Book 44* ⚮

BOOK NAME: Acts of the Apostles
THEME: Primarily the acts of Peter and Paul
BY: Luke (the physician). He also wrote the Gospel of Luke at an earlier time.
DATE WRITTEN: About A.D. 62
DATES COVERED:
FOR/TO: Theophilus (a Gentile convert)
WHERE WRITTEN: Unknown
STATISTICS: 28 chapters, 1007 verses, 24,250 words
MISC: Luke and Acts are as 2 volumes of the same work.

⚮ *Book 45* ⚮

BOOK NAME: Romans
THEME:
BY: Paul
DATE WRITTEN: A.D. 55-59
DATES COVERED:
FOR/TO: To the believers in Rome
WHERE WRITTEN: On 3rd missionary trip, Corinth in Greece, or Philippi in Greece
STATISTICS: 16 chapters, 433 verses, 9447 words
MISC:

⚮ *Book 46* ⚮

BOOK NAME: First Corinthians
THEME:
BY: Paul
DATE WRITTEN: A.D. 53-56
DATES COVERED:
FOR/TO: The Corinthian church
WHERE WRITTEN: Ephesus-1 Corinthians 16:8; some say Philippi
STATISTICS: 16 chapters, 437 verses, 9489 words
MISC: Much opposition to Paul's preaching

⚮ *Book 47* ⚮

BOOK NAME: Second Corinthians
THEME:
BY: Paul
DATE WRITTEN: A.D. 54-57; about 1 year after First Corinthians
DATES COVERED:
FOR/TO: The Corinthian church
WHERE WRITTEN: Probably Philippi or Macedonia
STATISTICS: 13 chapters, 257 verses, 6092 words

MISC: Much about Paul in this epistle. Paul thought he
would meet Titus at Troas. He was troubled Titus
was not there. He went to Macedonia and found
him.

❧❧ *Book 48* ❧❧

BOOK NAME: Galatians
THEME:
BY: Paul
DATE WRITTEN: Various opinions ranging from as early as A.D. 48
to as late as A.D. 62, with perhaps A.D. 53 to 56
the most probable.
DATES COVERED:
FOR/TO: The Galatians
WHERE WRITTEN: Ephesus or Macedonia; alternate views are
Antioch, Rome, or Corinth
STATISTICS: 6 chapters, 149 verses, 3098 words
MISC: Paul upset about certain Jewish believers trying to
impose circumcision and the Mosaic law on the
Galatians.

❧❧ *Book 49* ❧❧

BOOK NAME: Ephesians
THEME:
BY: Paul
DATE WRITTEN: A.D. 60-62
DATES COVERED:
FOR/TO: The church at Ephesus
WHERE WRITTEN: From Rome
STATISTICS: 6 chapters, 155 verses, 3039 words
MISC: Colossians, Philemon, and Philippians called
prison epistles. Ephesians, Colossians, Philemon
believed to be all dispatched at the same time.
Eph 1-3 tells believers what they are in Christ, 4-6
what they should do because they are in Christ.
Some consider Ephesians offers the greatest
insight in all the Bible.

❧❧ *Book 50* ❧❧

BOOK NAME: Philippians
THEME:
BY: Paul
DATE WRITTEN: Between A.D. 54 to 62
DATES COVERED:

FOR/TO: The saints at Philippi
WHERE WRITTEN: Probably in prison at Rome, but others think in prison in Ephesus
STATISTICS: 4 chapters, 104 verses, 2002 words
MISC:

ᘒᘓᘒ *Book 51* ᘒᘓᘒ

BOOK NAME: Colossians
THEME:
BY: Paul
DATE WRITTEN: Between A.D. 55 to 63
DATES COVERED:
FOR/TO: The saints at Colosse
WHERE WRITTEN: From prison at Rome
STATISTICS: 4 chapters, 95 verses, 1998 words
MISC:

ᘒᘓᘒ *Book 52* ᘒᘓᘒ

BOOK NAME: First Thessalonians
THEME:
BY: Paul
DATE WRITTEN: A.D. 50-52
DATES COVERED:
FOR/TO: The church of the Thessalonians
WHERE WRITTEN: Corinth (Athens, Greece)
STATISTICS: 5 chapters, 89 verses, 1857 words
MISC:

ᘒᘓᘒ *Book 53* ᘒᘓᘒ

BOOK NAME: Second Thessalonians
THEME:
BY: Paul
DATE WRITTEN: A.D. 50-52; a few months after First Thessalonians
DATES COVERED:
FOR/TO: The church of the Thessalonians
WHERE WRITTEN: Corinth (Athens, Greece)
STATISTICS: 3 chapters, 47 verses, 1042 words
MISC:

ᘒᘓᘒ *Book 54* ᘒᘓᘒ

BOOK NAME: First Timothy
THEME:
BY: Paul
DATE WRITTEN: A.D. 61-65

DATES COVERED:
       FOR/TO: Timothy
WHERE WRITTEN: Rome or during travels; some say from Laodicea, the chief city of Phrygia
    STATISTICS: 6 chapters, 113 verses, 2269 words
         MISC:

✣✣ Book 55 ✣✣

BOOK NAME: Second Timothy
     THEME:
          BY: Paul
DATE WRITTEN: Considered to be the last epistle he wrote before his death, perhaps A.D. 64-68
DATES COVERED:
       FOR/TO: Timothy
WHERE WRITTEN: Rome during imprisonment
    STATISTICS: 4 chapters, 83 verses, 1703 words
         MISC:

✣✣ Book 56 ✣✣

BOOK NAME: Titus
     THEME:
          BY: Paul
DATE WRITTEN: A.D. 61-65
DATES COVERED:
       FOR/TO: Titus
WHERE WRITTEN: In Rome during imprisonment; alternate view is Macedonia
    STATISTICS: 3 chapters, 46 verses, 921 words
         MISC:

✣✣ Book 57 ✣✣

BOOK NAME: Philemon
     THEME:
          BY: Paul
DATE WRITTEN: Views range from A.D. 55 to 63
DATES COVERED:
       FOR/TO: Philemon, Apphia, Archippus, and the church in thy house
WHERE WRITTEN: Several views including prison at Rome, prison at Caesarea, or prison at Ephesus
    STATISTICS: 1 chapter, 25 verses, 445 words
         MISC: Four prison epistles: Colossians, Ephesians, Philippians, Philemon

≈≈ *Book 58* ≈≈

BOOK NAME: Hebrews
THEME:
BY: Unknown, possibly Paul, Apollos, Barnabas, Luke, Timothy, Aquila and Priscilla, Silas, Aristion, or Philip
DATE WRITTEN: From A.D. 65-80
DATES COVERED:
FOR/TO: Jewish believers
WHERE WRITTEN: Unknown; some think from Italy by Timothy
STATISTICS: 12 chapters, 303 verses, 6913 words
MISC: Some Jewish believers were in danger of going back from Christ to Moses (from Grace to the Law). This was an immediate danger-2:1, based on unbelief-3:12, conduct-5:13,14, neglect of public worship-10:25, weakness in prayer-12:12, instability in doctrine-13:9, refusal to teach others-5:12 and neglect of the Scriptures-2:1. Thought(?)—if following Christ brought persecution and Jewish practice did not, why not return to Judaism and be free from persecution?

≈≈ *Book 59* ≈≈

BOOK NAME: James
THEME:
BY: James, the brother of Christ (unlikely to be James, the son of Zebedee, as was martyred about A.D. 44)
DATE WRITTEN: Dates vary from A.D. 45-62
DATES COVERED:
FOR/TO: Jewish believers throughout the Roman Empire
WHERE WRITTEN: Unknown
STATISTICS: 5 chapters, 108 verses, 2309 words
MISC:

≈≈ *Book 60* ≈≈

BOOK NAME: First Peter
THEME:
BY: Peter
DATE WRITTEN: A.D. 64-66
DATES COVERED:
FOR/TO: Jewish believers scattered throughout Asia Minor
WHERE WRITTEN: Babylon, perhaps Rome
STATISTICS: 5 chapters, 105 verses, 2482 words

MISC:

✑✑ Book 61 ✑✑

BOOK NAME: Second Peter
THEME:
BY: Peter
DATE WRITTEN: A.D. 66
DATES COVERED:
FOR/TO: To all Christians
WHERE WRITTEN: Perhaps Rome
STATISTICS: 3 chapters, 61 verses, 1559 words
MISC:

✑✑ Book 62 ✑✑

BOOK NAME: First John
THEME:
BY: John the apostle
DATE WRITTEN: A.D. 85-95
DATES COVERED:
FOR/TO: Churches in Asia Minor
WHERE WRITTEN: Ephesus
STATISTICS: 5 chapters, 105 verses, 2523 words
MISC:

✑✑ Book 63 ✑✑

BOOK NAME: Second John
THEME:
BY: John the apostle
DATE WRITTEN: Unknown, perhaps A.D. 96-97
DATES COVERED:
FOR/TO: The elect lady and her children
WHERE WRITTEN: Unknown, perhaps Ephesus
STATISTICS: 1 chapter, 13 verses, 303 words
MISC:

✑✑ Book 64 ✑✑

BOOK NAME: Third John
THEME:
BY: John the apostle
DATE WRITTEN: Unknown, perhaps A.D. 97
DATES COVERED:
FOR/TO: Gaius of Derby, Acts 20:4; Gaius mentioned
several times in the New Testament
WHERE WRITTEN: Unknown

STATISTICS: 1 chapter, 14 verses, 299 words
MISC:

✣✣ *Book 65* ✣✣

BOOK NAME: Jude
THEME:
BY: Jude, the brother of James and Jesus, Mt 13:55;
Mk 6:3 Judas (or Jude) and James
DATE WRITTEN: Latter part of the first century. Estimates range
from as early as A.D. 67 to as late as 125
DATES COVERED:
FOR/TO: To the saints
WHERE WRITTEN: Unknown
STATISTICS: 1 chapter, 25 verses, 613 words
MISC:

✣✣ *Book 66* ✣✣

BOOK NAME: The Revelation
THEME: Prophecy
BY: John the apostle
DATE WRITTEN: A.D. 95-96
DATES COVERED: From the first church to New Jerusalem
FOR/TO: To the seven churches, all saints
WHERE WRITTEN: Island of Patmos
STATISTICS: 22 chapters, 404 verses, and 12,000 words
MISC: The grace of our Lord Jesus Christ be with you all.
Amen -Rev 22:21.

Bibliographical References

The Holy Bible. King James Version. Cambridge University Press, 1769

Blinson, Rick. Contentment: The Antithesis of Prosperity Teaching. www.kneeprints.org/Downloads/contentment.PDF

Brinson, Gary P; Hood, L. Randolph; Beebower, Gilbert L; "Determinants of Portfolio Performance", Financial Analyst Journal; Jan/Feb 1995, pg. 133-138

U.S. Census Bureau, The Big Payoff: Educational Attainment and Synthetic Estimates of Work-Life Earnings, July 2002, page 3

Trends in Student Aid 2002, The College Board, www.collegeboard.com

empty tomb, inc. annual series, The State of Church Giving through 2000 (2002 edition)

Index

1

12b-1 fee, 124

5

529 plans
  prepaid, 142
  savings, 142

8

80:20 Rule, 130

A

abad, 201
Abram, 211
alms, 210
Ananias, 10, 11, 227
annual percentage yield, 185
annualized return, 132
annuity
  deferred, 118
  fixed, 118
  immediate, 118
  variable, 118
APY. *See* annual percentage yield
ARM. *See* mortgage(s), types of,
  adjustable rate
asset allocation defined, 108

B

Bankruptcy
  Chapter 13, 94
  Chapter 7, 94
  defined, 93
basis of true religion, 253
Beatitudes, 4
behavioral finance, 232
Bethesda, pool of, 250

Blinson, Rick, 46
blue chip stocks, 120
bonds
  book entry, 116
  corporate bonds, 117
  coupon rate of a, 116
  credit ratings of, 118
  government bonds, 116
  municipal, 118
  savings bonds, 116
  secondary market, 115
Brinson, Hood, and Beebower,
  study by, 110

C

capitalism, 23
cash balance plans, 149–51
cash-out refinance, 197
churning, 243
Compound interest, 75
Corporation for Enterprise
  Development, 188
Coverdell Education Savings
  Account, 140
cubit, 45
custodial accounts, 139

D

Dalbar, Inc, 231
debt
  how to get out of, 92
  installment, 74
  mortgage, 75
  re-age, 88
  revolving, 75
  secured, 74
  unsecured, 74
debt management programs, 86
debt ratio, 186
deed, 169

deferred sales charge. *See* load, back-end
defined benefit plan, 148
defined contribution plan, 152
defined contribution plans
    after-tax contributions, 153
    pre-tax contributions, 152
distribution fee. *See* 12b-1 fee
diversification, 111
    defined, 109
Dividend Reinvestment Plan, 121
dividends, 120
down payment assistance, 187
DPA. *See* down payment assistance
DRIP. *See* Dividend Reinvestment Plan

E

Economic Growth and Tax Relief Act of 2001, 159
Economic Security Act. *See* Social Security Act of 1935
Economics, 101
Eden, Garden of
    four rivers
        Euphrates, 203
        Gihon, 203
        Hiddekel, 203
        Pison, 203
Education Bond Program, 139
Education IRA. See Coverdell Education Savings Account
EGTRA. See Economic Growth and Tax Relief Act of 2001
Employee Retirement Income Security Act, 154
Enron, 228
ERISA. *See* Employee Retirement Income Security Act
ERISA Section 404(c), 154
ERISA section 409(a), 156
ETF. *See* exchange-traded fund
exchange-traded fund, 123

F

fair share, 86
FDIC. *See* Federal Deposit Insurance Corporation
Federal Deposit Insurance Corporation, 112
Federal Housing Administration, 182
FHA. *See* Federal Housing Administration
FICO® credit score, 96
fiduciary, 139
financial planning
    software, 57
    stewardship, 66
    why people fail at, 57
Form 1099-C, 85
Form 990, 227

G

gifting organizations, 188
giving, as a percentage of income, 225
grants, 136
growth investing, 60
Gurney, Kathleen PhD, 231

H

Hope Scholarship Tax Credit, 144
housing ratio, 186
HUD. *See* U.S. Department of Housing and Urban Development

I

IDA. *See* Individual Development Account
Individual Development Account, 188
Individual Retirement Account, 156
    Brokerage IRA, 157
    Deposit IRA, 157

Roth IRA, 158
self-directed IRA, 157
SEP IRA, 159
SIMPLE IRA, 158
Spousal IRA, 158
Traditional IRA, 157
inflation risk, 162
insurance
disability, 64
long-term care, 65
term, 64
universal life, 64
variable, 64
whole life, 64
Internal Rate of Return, 172
Internet fraud, 105
Investment Policy Statement, 155
investments, types of
annuities, 118
bonds, 115
certificates of deposits, 112
money market funds, 114
mutual funds, 121
savings accounts, 112
stocks, 119
IPS. *See* Investment Policy Statement
IRA. *See* Individual Retirement Account
IRR. *See* Internal Rate of Return

J

Jacob, 212
Job, story of, 50–52

L

laws of finance, 8
legalism, 221
Lifetime Learning Credit, 144
load
back-end, 123
front-end, 123
loan prepayment, 184
loan-to-value ratio, 185

Lot, 211
LTV. *See* loan-to-value ratio

M

management fee, 124
market capitalization
classifications, 60
defined, 60
marketing fee. *See* 12b-1 fee
Melchizedek, 211
Monte Carlo simulation, 165
Morningstar Principia, 130
mortgage interest, 169
mortgage(s)
refinancing, 195
types of
adjustable rate, 183
conventional, 183
FHA, 182
fixed, 183
VA, 183
multilevel marketing, 106
Murray, Nick, 110
mutual funds
actively managed, 128
closed-end, 122
load, 123
no-load, 123
open-end, 122
passively managed, 128

N

NAV. *See* net asset value
net asset value, 122

O

offerings, 209

P

Pareto Principle, 130
Pareto, Vilfredo, 130

PBGC. See Pension Benefit Guaranty Corporation
Pension Benefit Guaranty Corporation, 150
pension payment options, 149
PMI. *See* private mortgage insurance
preferred stocks, 120
prepaid interest, 185
private mortgage insurance, 185
prosper
translated, 37
providence
defined, 40
Prudent Man Rule, 139
pyramid schemes, 106

Q

QAIB. *See* Quantitative Analysis of Investor Behavior
qualified retirement plan, 147
qualifying ratios, 186
Quantitative Analysis of Investor Behavior, 231

R

risk
fraud, 104
loss of opportunity, 103
loss of principal, 103
systematic, 102
unsystematic, 102
Rule of 72, 71

S

Sadducees, 9
sales charge. See load
Sapphira, 10, 11, 227
Savings Incentive Match Plan for Employees. *See* Individual Retirement Account, SIMPLE IRA

scams
how they happen, 104–5
types of, 105–7
scholarships, 136
Scriptures
1 Corinthians 10 verse 13, 24
1 John 5 verses 14–15, 16
1 Peter 1 verses 6–7, 25
1 Peter 5 verse 2, 33
1 Peter 5 verse 8, 30
1 Timothy 3 verse 3, 33
1 Timothy 3 verse 8, 33
1 Timothy 6 verses 17–19, 52
1 Timothy 6 verses 6–8, 14
1 Timothy 6 verses 9–10, 100
2 Chronicles 1 verses 7–12, 18–19
2 Corinthians 11 verses 13–15, 31
2 Corinthians 9 verses 6–8, 219
2 Corinthians 9 verses 9–15, 223
2 John 1 verses 9–11, 34
2 Peter 3 verse 8, 21
2 Thessalonians 3 verses 10–13, 235
3 John 1 verses 1–2, 47
Acts 4 verses 32–35, 9
Deuteronomy 14 verses 22–23, 213
Deuteronomy 8 verses 17–20, 48
Ecclesiastes 11 verse 2, 109
Ecclesiastes 2 verse 26, 35
Ecclesiastes 5 verse 5, 79
Galatians 3 verse 10, 221
Galatians 5 verse 18, 223
Genesis 14 verses 18–20, 211
Genesis 2 verses 10–15, 201
Genesis 28 verse 22, 212
Genesis 3 verses 1–13, 27–28
James 1 verse 12, 26
James 1 verse 22, 253

James 1 verses 13–16, 29
James 1 verses 2–4, 25
James 1 verses 3–4, 91
James 1 verses 5–7, 14
James 4 verses 1–3, 15
John 15 verses 1–2, 236
John 5 verses 2–9, 249
Leviticus 27 verses 30–33, 213
Luke 12 verse 48, 209
Luke 12 verses 15–21, 41
Luke 8 verses 43–48, 207
Malachi 3 verses 8–1-, 216
Matthew 16 verse 26, 45
Matthew 19 verses 16–24, 11
Matthew 23 verse 23, 218
Matthew 25 verses 14–30, 67
Matthew 5 verse 17, 222
Matthew 5 verses 1–12, 3
Matthew 6 verses 19–34, 42–43
Micah 6 verses 1–8, 252
Nehemiah 13 verses 10–11, 216
Numbers 18 verses 20–32, 213
Philippians 2 verse 13, 32
Philippians 4 verses 11–12, 13
Proverbs 1 verse 7, 20, 242
Proverbs 11 verse 14, 241
Proverbs 13 verse 11, 204
Proverbs 13 verse 20, 241
Proverbs 14 verse 15, 242
Proverbs 15 verse 22, 241
Proverbs 16 verse 18, 93
Proverbs 18 verse 9, 204
Proverbs 21 verse 5, 59
Proverbs 22 verse 7, 80
Proverbs 27 verse 12, 92
Proverbs 3 verse 26, 17
Proverbs 8 verses 32–35, 37
Psalms 112 verses 1–10, 35–36
Psalms 118 verse 8, 16
Psalms 37 verse 21, 79
Psalms 73 verses 2–3, 99
Romans 10 verse 4, 222
Romans 15 verse 4, v

Romans 5 verses 1–2, 222
Romans 8 verse 10, 46
Romans 8 verse 13, 46
Titus 1 verse 11, 33
Titus 1 verse 7, 33
Titus 3 verse 9, 223
shamar, 201
Simplified Employee Pension. *See*
    Individual Retirement Account,
    SEP IRA
Social Security Act of 1935, 146
Solomon
    essence of his writings, 20
    goes to Gibeon, 18
    who he was, 18
spiritual tail-chaser, 32
standard deduction, 169
stewardship
    parable of the talents, 67
style grid
    equities, 61
    fixed income, 62
sub-advisor, 124

T

time value of money, 70
tithe, 210
tsalach, 37
tsaleach, 37

U

U.S. Department of Housing and
Urban Development, 182
U.S. Savings Bonds, 138
UGMA. See Uniform Gifts to
Minors   Act
Uniform Gifts to Minors Act, 139
Uniform Transfers to Minors Act,
139
UTMA. See Uniform Transfers to
Minors   Act

V

value investing, 60
volatility, 102

W

Wealth
money as a store of, 3
spiritual definition, 7
standard definition, 3
wisdom and, 15
Worldcom, 228
WOW Factor, the, 204
www.idanetwork.org, 188

✂✂✂

For more information
on
Scripture and personal finance,
be sure to visit us at
www.truewealthbuilding.com

✂✂✂